TRADE *for* GOOD:
The Essential Guide to Business and Finance in UK and International Trade

30% of the book proceeds will be donated
to causes for good,
including Fairtrade Foundation
and innocent foundation

TRADE *for* GOOD

The **Essential Guide** to **Business** and **Finance** in UK and **International Trade**

KEVIN SHAKESPEARE

TRADE *for* GOOD:
The Essential Guide to Business and Finance in UK and International Trade

First published in 2011 by
Ecademy Press
48 St Vincent Drive, St Albans, Herts, AL1 5SJ
info@ecademy-press.com
www.ecademy-press.com

Printed and bound by Lightning Source in the UK and USA
Design by Michael Inns
Typesetting by Karen Gladwell
Cover photograph: Sundari tea plucker by Simon Rawles

Printed on acid-free paper from managed forests. This book is printed on demand,
so no copies will be remaindered or pulped.

ISBN 978-1-905823-97-0

Contents

TRADE *for* GOOD

Contents (cont'd)

INTRODUCTION

For some years now I have wanted to write a book which captures all current information on business and finance, as it impacts the world of trade. At the same time I wanted to recognise that trade is a force for good, providing employment and development opportunities.

I would like this book to be remembered for several reasons:

1. *For providing students, employees and the business world with essential reading, which will support what they do in business, from managing working capital to getting paid.*

2. *For offering the reader the opportunity to gain something positive:*

    ▽ *For students, the opportunity to pass a qualification, but also to use the information from this book to develop their careers.*

    ▽ *For employees, the means of doing their job more efficiently and managing their careers.*

    ▽ *For businesses, the means to manage what they do effectively – applicable for both small and large business, covering business across all sectors from retail to manufacturing, to service sector companies.*

3. *Being a key source of reference. In addition to the reading material, the book contains details of key intermediaries in the world of trade.*

4. *For being an enjoyable read in its own right with details of several successful businesses across different business sectors.*

5. *By providing the reader with the opportunity to join me in giving something back from the world of trade. This starts with 30% of the book proceeds being donated to essential causes, and a commitment to start a lasting legacy of education and support. Further details of what is provided are covered shortly under the heading 'Supporting A Better Future Through Trade.' The essential causes this book will support are The Fairtrade Foundation, the innocent foundation and UK manufacturing.*

TRADE *for* GOOD

BOOK ENDORSEMENTS

"This book will be vital reading for anyone involved in trade, at all levels of business. It is a key source of reference to students undertaking the qualifications provided by the Institute of Export and International Trade."

Lesley Batchelor, *Director General, Institute of Export and International Trade*

"This book extremely helpful to both new and experienced exporters has covered all the topics required to be a top exporter. The author deserves praise for his understanding of the subject and the capability of putting it into writing."

Bryan Treherne, *MBE, UK Trade & Investment*

"Having attended workshops, with Kevin as my Tutor, and read his study material, I am pleased to endorse his book and the information that Kevin has produced as a valuable learning resource for students. This will prepare students well, across a range of qualifications and will be a key learning tool for moving forward within their careers."

Marion Murray, *Student*

"ITS has been working with Kevin in a partnership capacity for a number of years. This book provides essential resources for students studying in a variety of different industry qualifications. What has been missing until now is a good book written in a manner that can be easily understood; this book covering current business practice is exactly what is needed."

John Edson, *Senior Partner ITS*

"During my professional studies I have found Kevin Shakespeare to be of great assistance, with his knowledge of business and finance, and how this supports businesses when they trade overseas. The support has helped me increase my knowledge and I would recommend the written material and practical advice provided by Kevin."

Arlene Jones, *Student*

SUPPORTING A BETTER FUTURE THROUGH TRADE

For me this is more than just a book, it is equally about making a difference through trade. For this reason the book will support the following benefits to both the reader and the world of trade.

Essential Causes

30% of the book proceeds will be donated to charity:

➤ 10% to **The Fairtrade Foundation**

➤ 10% to **the innocent foundation**

➤ 10% to **support UK Manufacturing**

Further information about these organisations is contained in this book.

Lasting Legacy of Education and Support

By clicking through into the website which accompanies this book, the reader of each book will have the opportunity to benefit from further education and support by registering their interest in any or all of the following:

➤ *To receive two six monthly updates (extending to June 2012). These updates, provided free of charge, will cover what is new in the world of business and trade.*

➤ *Receive discounts of up to 25% on future books – this book will be the first of several books on the topic of UK and International trade, further books will cover core disciplines of Transport & Logistics, and Sales & Marketing strategies.*

➤ *Request further detailed reports on a subject area of this book, subject to availability. These requests can be made through the website, with reports available for nominal fees from £25 to £100 depending on length and complexity of report.*

➤ *Join the Institute of Export and International Trade as an Affiliate Member with the first year's membership free, this represents a saving on joining fees of £60.*

Improving Standards in Education and Business

Education and career benefits will be available to the reader:

➤ *The reader will qualify for 15 CPD points through reading the book, awarded by the Institute of Export and International Trade. These points can be 'topped-up' further by passing on-line mini-modules with The Institute to gain further points and evidence knowledge.*

Kevin Shakespeare

TRADE *for* **GOOD**

HOW TO USE THIS BOOK

This book has been written in a manner that the reader
will hopefully find easier to understand:

▼ *Some of the more detailed sections will contain a reminder of*
'Key Learning Points' *and a summary of* **'Key Learning
Themes'**, *along with a* **'Topic Refresher'**

▼ *Use of Summary boxes and* **'Hints & Tips'** *are provided to
re-enforce understanding, along with* **'Top Learning Points'**

▼ *A detailed glossary at the end of the book to highlight key terms*

In writing this book there may be some parts of content that are
repeated in different sections. This is intentional to ensure that key
material is covered in the context of the particular section.

If you've enjoyed **Trade for Good**, then please visit
www.tradeforgood.info for updates.

Post a review on **www.amazon.co.uk**

ABOUT THE AUTHOR

Kevin Shakespeare has been involved in the world of trade, from a young man of 17 working in a small business, to joining National Westminster Bank, The Bank of Scotland and today Lloyds Bank, carrying out a variety of roles in senior positions covering the world of trade and dealing with businesses of all sizes. In the last 10 years Kevin has also worked with The Institute of Export and International Trade as an Examiner and member of their Professional Qualifications Education Board – more recently working with the Institute to update examination material and a move towards new learning styles which is encouraging individuals and businesses back into the world of trade.

Kevin runs his own business, Shakespeare Business Management, and sits on several committees and boards involved in directing the world of business, trade and education. Professional and industry qualifications have been achieved with a number of organisations including The Association of Corporate Treasurers, The Institute of Financial Services and British International Freight Association.

Kevin provides training to students covering trade, business and finance and recently appeared on the BBC programme 'Working Lunch' to discuss the impact of a declining pound on British exports.

This experience and role as a key influencer provides the content you see in this book – content which is both current and true to the reader.

SUPPORT AND THANKS

In writing this book I have been fortunate to draw on the support and expertise of a number of individuals, businesses and organizations that are experts in their own field. In particular I would like to thank the following for their assistance as key reference sources:

> *-Anne Gillan*
>
> *-Asset Based Finance Association*
>
> *-Bryan Treherne*
>
> *-Cotecna Inspection*
>
> *-John Edson*
>
> *-Liz Devine*
>
> *-Sarah Aldridge*
>
> *-Sandra Strong*
>
> *-Wendy Whewell*

TRADE *for* GOOD

CHAPTER ONE

BUSINESS FINANCE

Chapter 1 is divided into three sections with illustrations provided by way of hints, summary boxes and key learning topics

*The Essential Guide to Business and Finance
in UK and International Trade*

SECTION ONE

BUSINESS ORGANIZATIONS

Contents

1 | BUSINESS FINANCE

About This Section

Before setting up in business it is necessary to consider what type of organizational structure is appropriate. This may vary depending on:

- *The type of activity being engaged in*
- *The size of business being undertaken*
- *Key factors such as liability, tax status and financial reporting*

This section shall look at the different types of organisational structure, with their associated advantages and disadvantages.

When setting up a business it can be easy to overlook some of the key liability and tax implications involved; time must be invested to ensure that the correct legal status and procedures are established at the outset.

Type of Business

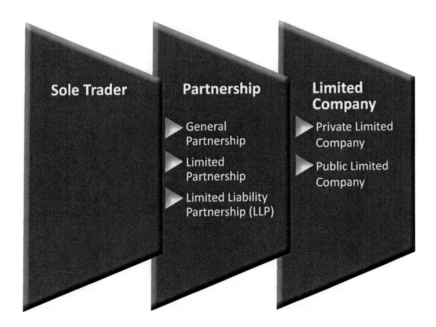

Franchising is another form of business and a means of buying into the success of an established business e.g. national hotel chain, national food outlet. The 'franchisee' buys a licence to use the name, the producer's services and management systems of the 'franchisor' company. The licence usually covers a particular geographic area and runs for a limited time, after which it should be renewable as long as the terms of the franchise agreement are met.

BUSINESS FINANCE

1

Sole Trader

A sole trader is where an individual is the sole owner of a business. The business is often quite small in terms of size and the number of staff employed. Examples of a sole trader include plumbers, decorators and newsagents.

A sole trader business is easy to set up. No formal procedures are required and operations can usually commence immediately. The owner can decide the way in which the business is conducted.

Although the sole trader must produce accounting information to satisfy the taxation authorities, there is no legal requirement to produce accounting information relating to the business.

The sole trader will have unlimited liability, with no distinction between the business wealth and the sole trader's personal wealth if debts have to be paid. The owner is personally liable for the debts of the business.

Advantages and Disadvantages of being a Sole Trader

Advantages	Disadvantages
Easy to set up	**Unlimited liability**
Flexibility to change quickly	**Limit to the amount of capital that can be raised, capital may be hard to find**
Ease of decision making – only one person needed to take the decision	**Finance/loans can be expensive in comparison with loans for limited companies**
Requires little capital to set up	**If the owner becomes ill the business is at risk**
Owner takes all the profits, they are able to use the money as they think fit	**Large organizations may be able to change prices without feeling the impact in the way a sole trader would**
Sole trader status works well for certain types of business	

Partnerships

A partnership arises when two or more people own a business, and share in the profits or losses of the business. Each person contributes something to the business – such as ideas, money or property. Common forms of partnerships are solicitors, accountants, estate agents and doctor's surgeries.

Management rights and personal liability will vary depending on which form the business takes:

- ▽ **General partnership** *(Partnership Act 1890)*
- ▽ **Limited partnership** *(Limited Partnership Act 1907)*
- ▽ **Limited liability partnership (LLP)** *(Limited Liability Partnership Act 2000)*

Section 1 - Business Organizations

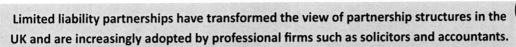

Limited liability partnerships have transformed the view of partnership structures in the UK and are increasingly adopted by professional firms such as solicitors and accountants.

General Partnerships

- Involves two or more owners carrying out a business purpose.
- General partners share equal rights and responsibilities in connection with the management of a business – and any individual partner can bind the entire group to a legal obligation.
- Each individual partner assumes full responsibility for all of the business debts and obligations. A creditor may choose to pursue any of the partners for the full debt owed, in the case of insolvency.
- Partnership profits are **not** taxed to the business but pass through to the partner who will include any gains on their individual tax returns.
- Partnerships are allowed to have between 2 and 20 members, although there are exceptions, notably accountancy firms and solicitors who can have more than 20 partners.

Limited Partnerships

- Allows each partner to restrict their liability to their business investment.
- Not every partner can benefit from this limitation – at least one partner must accept general partnership status, exposing themselves to full personal liability.
- The general partner retains the right to control the business, while the limited partner/s do not participate in management decisions.
- Both general and limited partners benefit from business profits.
- Arrangements may apply for single or limited duration projects, for example a property purchase or in the film industry.

Limited Liability Partnerships (LLP)

LLPs offer some personal liability protection.

- The LLP itself is responsible for any debts that it runs up, not the individual partners.
- In an LLP a partner is not responsible or liable for another partner's misconduct or negligence.
- The LLP pays no UK tax, but its members do in relation to the income or gains they receive through the LLP.
- LLPs must produce and publish financial accounts with a similar level of detail to a similar sized limited company; in essence the reporting requirements and administrative duties are more demanding than required for normal partnerships.
- The rights and responsibilities of all members would usually be laid out in a 'Deed of Partnership.'
- There are no limits on the number of members.

Advantages and Disadvantages of Partnerships

Advantages	Disadvantages
Ability to raise higher levels of capital	**Unlimited liability, unless an LLP**
Applies well to specialised businesses	**All partners can be liable for debt (unless an LLP)**
Shared knowledge and shared responsibilities	**Limits on access to capital**
Broadly easier to set up	**The risk of relationships breaking down between partners**
In case of illness there exists a better chance of continuity	
Limited liability with an LLP	

Limited Companies

A limited company can take the form of a private or public limited company.

- *It has its own legal identity.*

- *It can own things, and buy and sell in its own right.*

- *It can sue and be sued.*

- *The financial accounts of the business are the accounts of the company, they are not the accounts of the owners (shareholders).*

- *The shareholders have no liability for the debts of the company beyond the value of the shares they hold. The company's finances are separate from the personal finances of their owners.*

- *Control can be organised on the basis of one vote per one share.*

- *The company must be set up and run in the manner laid down by the Companies Act. Companies are governed by Memorandum and Articles of Association – which includes an outline of the nature of business undertaken.*

- *The profits earned by the company may be retained in the business or distributed to the shareholders as dividends.*

- *A balance sheet of accounts has to be produced at business year end.*

Section 1 - Business Organizations

Features of Private and Public Companies

Private Companies

- *Generally, but not exclusively, smaller businesses*
- *Owned by their shareholders Limited by shares*
- *Possible to set up by guarantee, with liability limits set by the company (this is used by charities and social enterprises)*
- *Can have one or more members.*
- *They cannot offer shares to the public*
- *Not obliged to appoint a company secretary*
- *A private company can convert into a public company, it may want to convert in order to raise finance to expand*

Public Companies

- *Generally larger businesses*
- *Can raise money by selling shares on the stock market*
- *Must have share capital of at least £50,000*
- *Must have at least two shareholders, two directors and a qualified company secretary*
- *Allowed to raise capital by offering shares or debentures to the public*
- *This can be done through obtaining a listing on the Stock Exchange*
- *Public companies are subject to stricter legal requirements – in relation to share capital, directors and accounts*

Advantages and Disadvantages of Limited Companies

Advantages	Disadvantages
Private Limited Company	**Private Limited Company**
Can raise large sums of capital	**Can be costly and time consuming to set up**
Limited liability	**More complicated accounts than other forms of business organization**
Flexibility of determining the proportion of salary and dividends taken, compared with a sole trader whose basic accounts are subject to tax at fixed rates and thresholds	
Ownership is transferable	
Public Limited Company	**Public Limited Company**
No limit to the amount that can be raised	*Minimum of £50,000 to set up*
Ability to exploit economies of scale for larger businesses	*Annual accounts will be subject to particularly close scrutiny*
	Expensive to set up and high degree of regulation

BUSINESS FINANCE

1

Factors to Bear in Mind When Setting Up In Business

Set-Up: *how difficult is it to set up?*

Management: *who runs the company?*

Finance: *how easy is it to get access to finance?*

Tax and National Insurance

Financial Information: *how complex is it to produce?*

Profits: *who gets the profit?*

Liability: *how far does this extend in the event of business failure?*

Section 1 - Business Organizations

SECTION TWO

BUSINESS FINANCE

Contents

1 | BUSINESS FINANCE

About This Section

It is likely that finance will be required at sometime during the life of a business – although businesses should do all they can to avoid or at least seek to reduce the level of finance required.

This section will look at the circumstances in which the need for finance may arise. *There will be a specific emphasis on working capital and how the need for finance arises during the working capital cycle.* Ways in which the impact can be minimised shall be discussed, along with effective use of banking and trade instruments to support businesses trading in the UK and Overseas.

In the trade environment in particular there are some useful alternatives that can be used to reduce, or even eliminate the need for finance.

Finance during the Business Lifecycle

Finance may be required during the life of a business

For What Purposes Is Finance Required

To Start a Business

Finance may be required to invest in premises, machinery, recruitment and marketing, all prior to sales contracts being completed. This sort of start-up capital is harder to obtain from a lender, as a business will not have a trading record on which a lending decision can be based.

Consequently, capital is more likely to be invested by the owners or family of a start-up business, **_unless_** the owners have a track record of having previously operated similar businesses successfully. In such cases banks or other investors may be more likely to invest.

Government grants or support schemes may be a possibility here, particularly if the business undertakes a specific purpose such as an environmental, research business.

To Buy Assets Such as Plant and Equipment

Arranging finance to buy assets may not be as difficult because the finance can be provided against the asset itself, subject to the asset valuation.

Purchase or Rent Property

A property purchase may apply more for a business with an established trading history, unless the owners are prepared to invest a large amount of their own capital. The property (factory) may also require refurbishment to suit the business purpose.

Renting a property (factory) is a likely alternative although even then the landlord of the property may want rental payments in advance (e.g. quarterly, annually).

To Arrange Funds to Buy Out a Partner or a Shareholder

During the course of a business there may come an occasion when a partner or shareholder wants to sell their stake in the business. Banks will apply normal lending criteria to such decisions, although they offer the likes of Succession Finance that are available for such circumstances.

A business may also use such an event to review its strategy, which could include the likes of Equity investment from a Business Angel or Venture Capital firm.

Business Expansion

This can take several forms:

- *Large increase in sales, particularly export sales.*
- *Expansion in the UK or Overseas markets, which may require a physical presence overseas.*
- *Acquisition of another company in the UK or Overseas.*

As with lending for working capital banks will be familiar with finance for business expansion. In such circumstances the business strategy will come under particularly close scrutiny – what is termed as due diligence. The business opportunity must be clear and compelling.

Raise Capital to Be Returned To Owners or Shareholders

This is usually applicable for larger established businesses. Lenders will want to see that owners are still committed to the business post lending. They may also seek a larger lending margin to justify the risk of lending in these circumstances.

Finance for Businesses in Financial Trouble

There may be occasions when a business needs finance simply to stay afloat, for example during times of recession or where a competitor has entered a market and taken market share.

Banks do provide Business Support Units that will look at businesses in such a position. If it is a viable business then a bank will work with the owners to establish how it can be run as a going concern. There may be a short-term finance injection to keep the business running, and longer term restructuring to ensure it runs effectively thereafter.

To Cover Working Capital Needs
- *As part of the day to day business needs*
- *To finance growth in the business which in turn puts increased pressure on the working capital cycle*

The working capital cycle in UK and international trade

Introduction

The working capital cycle is the period of time that elapses between the points at which cash is used in the supply/production process, to collection of cash from a customer.

In international trade the impact of the working capital cycle can be greater as a result of:

- *The time involved in receiving and shipping goods from/to more distant suppliers and customers.*
- *The supplier and/or customer are in another country with its own laws, legal systems, regulations and economic circumstances. Chasing slow payers is more difficult.*
- *Settlements through the international banking system can take longer.*

Attention to the working capital cycle is vital for a business, to ensure it can trade profitability and within arrangements financially.

This section shall look at stages of the working capital cycle and how to manage the elements of the cycle effectively, along with the key working capital ratios needed to manage the business.

Stages of the Working Capital Cycle

Supply Side

Contract to Purchase of Stock/Raw Materials

-on immediate payment or credit terms

- lead time may be necessary to produce and ship goods

Stock
(Work in Progress)

Receive imported goods

-refine manufacture

-ready as finished product

Sales Side
(Trade Creditors)

contract to sell

ship goods to customer on credit terms?

BUSINESS FINANCE

1

Ongoing Costs to the Business

- *Employee Wages*
- *Production Costs*
- *Costs of Fixed Assets (e.g. Property, Machinery)*

Supply Side

The working capital cycle begins with the business purchasing stock/raw materials –the basic principle of the working capital cycle being that cash will be paid out to the supplier **before** it is received in from the buyer (customer).

The nature of the relationship with the supplier however may determine the settlement method used. From the perspective of the buyer payment on open account –with credit terms – is preferable, but not always easy to obtain.

Stock Side

Once received, the stock/raw materials will be used in the production process. Some goods may be 'ready made' and can be supplied direct onto the end customer (buyer). In other circumstances work will be carried out on the stock, and it will become part of the firm's work in progress

(WIP). Work will continue on the WIP until it is completed as a finished product.

Whilst a business will incur labour costs and overheads during all parts of the business process, these can be more focused and higher during the 'work in progress' period. Time to completion is vital as the business incurs costs before cash is received in.

The basic principle of the working capital cycle is again that cash will be paid on stock and the production process, before it is received in from the buyer from the sales contract.

When trading overseas it is always important to recognise that lead times are extended, the consequence of which is increased pressure on working capital.

Section 2 - Business Finance

Sales Side

The working capital side ends with sales to the customer. Cash is received in to offset expenditure incurred from the supply and stock sides. Naturally the earlier cash is received the more positive impact this will have on cash flow, reducing the period in which cash is going out of the business without any funds coming in.

From the perspective of the buyer, however they too are going to want to hold onto their cash for as long as is possible to improve their own working capital. Their position may not be dissimilar from the one which your own business has just gone through on the supply side.

Summary

Stages of Cash Movements

Supply Side		*Cash Outflow*
Stock (Work In Progress)		*Cash Outflow*
Ongoing Costs to the Business		*Cash Outflow*
Sales Side		*Cash Inflow*

In most trading businesses cash outflows are more likely to take place before cash is received into a business

BUSINESS FINANCE

1

Challenges and Opportunities in International Trade

In international trade there are additional challenges that arise for the UK business such as culture, distance, currency and banking settlements. These challenges also present opportunities to build lasting and successful relationships, whilst allowing the business to trade profitability.

The chart below provides an example of issues that a business may face when importing and exporting:

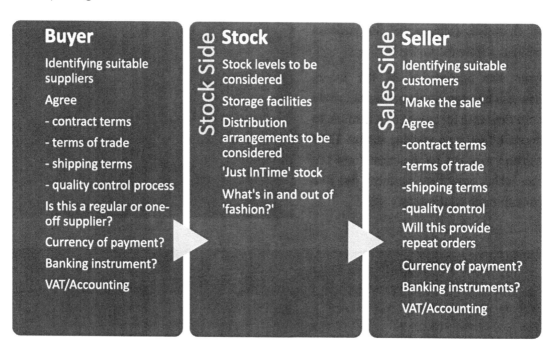

The **opportunity** for the UK business is to build strong and lasting relationships with overseas suppliers and customers, with an understanding from all parties. The importance of relationships in business should never be underestimated; it should be viewed as a partnership with both parties benefiting from the relationship.

Clear processes **can exist** for terms of trade covering payment, shipment, insurance and quality control. Over time these can be modified as trust increases – in this way the initial challenges faced by businesses can be turned into an opportunity which benefits both the working capital cycle and ability of the business to trade profitability.

Managing the Working Capital Cycle

Before we look at efficiency and best practice let us look at what 'good can look like' as outputs from the working capital cycle.

- *On the **supply** side these include good supplier relationships, good payment terms and an efficient quality control process. The business will maintain a good credit rating and payment history.*

- *On the **stock** side, stock is of the required quality that sells (turns over quickly, with ready sources of supply for urgent orders and large contracts).*

- *On the **sales** side, good customer relationships apply with good payment terms. Sales orders are fulfilled quickly and efficiently, with a strong internal credit control process. There are low levels or no history of bad debt.*

Best Practice

The cheapest and best sources of working capital exist within the business itself – where as far as possible the cash is 'self-funded.' This is preferable than having to raise finance externally OR by damaging relationships through 'reigning' in credit terms to customers and delaying settlements to suppliers.

> *Good management of working capital will generate cash*
>
> *Businesses can fail for lack of cash, rather than lack of profit*

Each element of working capital has impacts in terms of time and money. If a business can get money to move faster around the cycle the business will generate more cash and need to borrow less money to fund working capital. For example:

- *Collect monies due from debtors more quickly*
- *Reduce stock levels relative to sales*
- *Negotiate improved terms with suppliers*

A further factor to consider is whether cash available in the business should be used to purchase assets such as property, cars and computers.

To conserve cash and reduce dependency on borrowing money, a business may want to consider leasing or hire purchase of such assets, so as avoid using cash needed for the working capital cycle.

BUSINESS FINANCE

1

Receivables Management (Debtors)

Profits only come from customers who pay

Negotiating Payment Date:

Businesses must always be clear about the DATE of payment and deal in specific terms that have meaning. Avoid terms that are not specific and open to interpretation. Positive examples include:

- *Payment is due immediately after the contract has been agreed.*
- *Payment is due on the 16th July.*
- *Payment is due 30 days after shipment from the UK port.*
- *Payment is due 30 days after the exporter sends the shipping documents.*
- *Payment is due 30 days after acceptance of the Bill of Exchange.*

Credit Control Policy:

- *Ensure the credit control policy receives priority in the business.*
- *Ensure the policy is understood clearly by staff and customers. This includes sales staff, production and accounts.*
- *Review additional risks of trading internationally; language, culture, legal systems, government intervention etc.*
- *Check out customers thoroughly before trading with them. Information can be obtained from Credit Reference Agencies and Industry sources. Maintain a discipline of continuing to check out customers e.g. on an annual basis. These credit checks should equally apply to customers based overseas, even if this involves using the services of a more local credit reference agency in the country concerned.*
- *Check with other companies in the business sector (market intelligence) to establish if they are aware of any positives/negatives on prospective customers.*
- *Establish credit limits for each customer – and stick to them. Ensure principles are maintained for larger orders.*

Customer Management:

- *Keep very close to your larger customers.*
- *Establish customer profitability modelling, starting with the largest customers. Ensure the costs analysis incorporates additional costs associated with international trade, for example shipping, insurance and higher bank costs.*

Section 2 - Business Finance

- *Look out for early warning signs, for example a debtor starts to delay payment. Debtors due over 90 days (unless within agreed credit terms) should generally demand immediate attention.*
- *Monitor debtor balances and ageing schedules, do not let debts get too large or too old.*

Invoicing Controls:

- *Invoice promptly and clearly – ensure invoice has the correct bank details.*
- *Consider charging penalties on overdue accounts.*
- *Depending on the nature of the product sold consider accepting credit/debit cards as a payment option.*

A business may want to consider discounts for early payments. The need to do this may depend on particular circumstances, but could be beneficial if the cost of discount is less than the cost of borrowing from outside the business.

HINTS and TIPS

Stock (Inventory Management)

Know how quickly items of stock are turning over

- *Determine average stock holding times for all items of stock. Do stock holding times match demand from customers?*
- *Establish if any parts of stock purchases can operate on a 'just in time' basis to reduce stock holdings and obsolete items. It may depend on the degree of customisation necessary to complete as finished goods.*
- *Establish stock (product) profitability to determine the value of certain stock ranges, modelling to include breakeven points, gross and net profit.*
- *Apply tight stock controls with access to stock closely controlled, with a stock management system in place. Review security procedures.*
- *Consider selling off outdated or slow moving stock, the longer it is kept the harder it is for a business to sell.*
- *There may be circumstances where there is merit in considering part of the product being outsourced to another manufacturer rather than the business making it itself. In recent years this trend has become more common place with manufacturing outsourced overseas.*

1 | BUSINESS FINANCE

Payables Management (Creditors)

Purchase Control:

- Purchasing in the company should be tightly managed, avoid spreading it around a number of people.

- Purchase quantities should be geared towards demand forecasts. If possible taking accounts of stock holding and purchasing costs.

- Establish a system that determines the cost to the company of carrying stock.

Choice of Supplier:

- Where applicable shop around potential suppliers:

  - obtain quotes.

  - use a competitive tendering process if necessary.

  - note 'headline price' is not the only factor, discounts and credit terms will be factors.

  - ensure comparable costs of importing are factored into cost comparisons.

- Ensure alternative suppliers are available, in case of need to reduce dependency on a single supplier.

- Establish if the supplier has a returns policy.

Supplier Control:

- Establish a tight supply contract, for example if a supplier does not consistently deliver in accordance with specifications can you charge back the cost of delays.

- Can suppliers be' staggered' when necessary, or if required can they deliver goods on a just in time basis.

- Agree lead times for suppliers, particularly important where goods are imported from overseas.

Business Management:

- For smaller value suppliers consider the likes of procurement cards, online ordering, bulk purchasing.

- Ensure your business is in a position to pass on cost increases.

Summary

Business Practice	Consequence
Collect receivables faster	*Release cash to meet purchases and production*
Collect receivables slower	*Delays cash receipts putting a strain on the business*
Obtain improved payment terms from suppliers	*Increase cash reserve through not having to pay out cash so early*
Turn around stock faster	*Frees up cash*
Stock moves more slowly	*Consumes more cash*

In most trading businesses cash outflows are more likely to take place before cash is received into a business

Use of Banking and Trade Instruments to Improve Working Capital

Introduction

In some instances it is possible to improve business cash flow by negotiating on contract terms, and linking settlement to a trade (bank) instrument, whilst also retaining the confidence of the customer or supplier that payment will be made. This may result in use of bank guarantees, or negotiating periods of credit through term bills of exchange that incorporate periods of credit.

The options available can be summarised as follows:

Advanced Payment Guarantees	UK Exporter receives payment or part payment EARLIER in the cycle
Standby Letters of Credit	UK Importer does not have to pay for the goods until later in the cycle
Letters of Credit for Importers and Exporters	UK Importer can make payment LATER in the cycle UK Exporter can receive payment EARLIER
Term Bills of Exchange	UK Importer can gain a period of credit Payment made LATER in the cycle UK Exporter can receive payment EARLIER
Transferable Letters of Credit	For the UK importer / exporter responsibility for paying the supplier is TRANSFERRED to the buyer
Online Trade Solutions	EARLIER settlement of trade transactions
Credit Card Acquiring	UK Exporter offering payment option resulting in EARLIER settlement
SEPA Direct Debit	UK Exporter to Europe can increase certainty and timing of payment by direct debit

1 | BUSINESS FINANCE

Note: Where the Bank is issuing a guarantee they are undertaking that their customer will meet an obligation. The bank in turn will mark this as part of a credit facility and may require security to cover their liability.

The Bank will levy a fee for issuing guarantees which is likely to be based at the same level as any borrowing facilities, for example 2% to 3%.

Advanced Payment Guarantee

> *An advanced payment guarantee provides protection for buyers who are asked to provide payment before goods or services are supplied.*

To complete a contract on behalf of the buyer (importer) a UK business (exporter) who is supplying the goods may require an advance of monies from the importer – who in turn may be reluctant to do so whilst the contract is unfulfilled. For the UK business payment may be essential if the contract is to be completed and can also apply as an alternative to other forms of finance.

Use of an Advance Payment Guarantee issued by the supplier's bank should provide the buyer with the comfort that they can advance monies – knowing that the guarantee can be called upon if the supplier does not perform in accordance with the contract terms.

Such guarantees can be issued for between 10%-30% of the contract value, although negotiations can take place for advances up to 100%. The guarantee will have an expiry date.

Guarantees of this nature are more commonly used in project-based work, such as construction projects and supply of machinery where there are longer lead times and the exporter will have longer working capital periods to cover, consequently the need for an advanced payment to support the production process. There are, however, opportunities to use Advanced Payment Guarantees more across the range of exported goods as they provide a strong way of supporting an exporter's cash flow.

The bank issuing the guarantee will take a counter guarantee from the exporter indemnifying the bank in the event that the guarantee is called upon. The bank is also likely to seek security covering them against the guarantee liability. A fee will be levied by the bank usually at the same level as any existing borrowing facilities e.g. 2%/3% as appropriate.

From the perspective of the importer overseas they have a bank guarantee of payment. Whilst they will have parted with their money earlier the timing of payment is one that should in any case be part of the contract negotiations.

Section 2 - Business Finance

Standby Letters of Credit

A Standby Letter of Credit serves a different purpose from the better known commercial (documentary letter of credit). It operates more as a secondary payment mechanism – issued by a bank on behalf of a UK importer providing a guarantee to the exporter of their ability to perform under the terms of the contract agreed between buyer and seller.

The beneficiary of the Standby Letter of Credit, the overseas exporter, is able to draw on the Credit if they provide documentary evidence, as outlined in the Credit, for example a statement of default, copies of unpaid invoices. The Credit will have an expiry date.

Through issuing the Credit the UK importer can 'avoid' having to make payment up-front gaining a period of credit that would not have been possible previously, effectively allowing the importer to operate on open account terms.

> **Whilst the exporter will not have received the money as early as previously they still have a bank guarantee of payment, which will be preferable to trading on account terms providing improved certainty of receiving money on time.**

If the Credit is called upon the issuing bank will have recourse to their customer (the UK importer). They may also wish to take security to cover their liability. The bank will levy a fee for issuing the Credit, usually at the same level as any borrowing facilities.

Further details on Standby Letters of Credit are provided in a feature item in the Letter of Credit section.

Letters of Credit for Importers and Exporters

A Documentary Letter of Credit in itself can still operate as a means of improving working capital for a business, and can apply for both UK importers and exporters, especially for international trade outside of Europe and North America.

- *For an importer it may help to avoid having to make payment up-front, with settlement due after documents have been produced, checked and accepted under the Letter of Credit.*

   If a term Letter of Credit applies it introduces a period of credit whereby payment would take place say 90 days after acceptance of the documents, and accompanying bill of exchange. The importer's liability under the Letter of Credit will remain for the additional term.

- *From the perspective of the exporter they have the security of a Letter of Credit. They may also be able to discount the accepted bill of exchange in order to receive cash immediately without having to wait to the end of the 90 day period.*

   When bills of exchange are discounted by the exporter's bank they are taking a credit risk on the issuing bank of the Letter of Credit that they will make payment after 90 days. The charge levied will reflect this risk and the relevant country risk.

1 BUSINESS FINANCE

⬜ *In some cases, more applicable in the Far East the exporter's bank may advance monies immediately on receipt of the Letter of Credit **and** before documents are submitted and checked. When this arises the bank is accepting additional **performance risk**, namely that the exporter will perform their obligations under the export contract in order that the contract is fulfilled.*

Term Bills of Exchange

Bills of Exchange can be used in several ways in international trade:

▽ *As part of more formal banking instruments such as a Letter of Credit.*

▽ *Separately as a standalone instrument used as the sole payment mechanism OR*

▽ *As part of a Documentary Collection where documents of title - the bill of lading - accompanies the Collection and is not released until the Bill of Exchange is paid.*

In essence the Bill of Exchange serves the same purpose – unconditional and issued by a business (exporter) that directs the recipient (importer) to pay a sum of money. In the event of non-payment it is possible to take legal action, with in some countries the act of protesting a bill being similar to an act of bankruptcy.

Bills of Exchange can be drawn payable at:

▽ **Sight** – *payment at presentation, must be paid as soon as it is presented to the importer.*

▽ **Term** – *payable at a future date e.g. 90 days after acceptance. The term acceptance refers to the importer accepting the bill by which they agree to undertake/pay on the future date specified.*

It is the period between payment and acceptance when the drawee (exporter) is without funds. This period representing what has already been agreed in the contract negotiations will result in an additional working capital requirement until payment is received.

The working capital gap can be bridged by a third party (usually a bank) agreeing to discount the bill of exchange, by which the funds are advanced to the exporter until the bill is paid. In so doing the bank is taking a credit risk against either the importer, or more likely the importer's bank who will guarantee payment on behalf of the importer (a process known as avalisation). An exporter's bank will normally only discount against the credit risk of the importer when they are a large and well known corporate business.

The discounting bank will levy a charge based on their perception of the risk involved through the importer, their bank and the country concerned.

For Term Bills of Exchange to operate outside of a Letter of Credit or Documentary Collection this suggests a higher level of trust between buyer and seller. They can also be used in certain industry sectors such as land purchases, staged payments under construction projects.

Transferable Letters of Credit

Transferable Letters of Credit can apply for businesses with limited borrowing capability of their own. It is a 'regular' Letter of Credit with an additional term – Transferable – that allows a transfer of the Credit to another supplier, often the original supplier of the goods, or at least the primary component of the goods.

| Letter of Credit issued by the end customer – the final buyer of the goods, for example a UK high street store | → | Issued to first beneficiary, for example a UK importer, who purchases goods from the Far East and sells to UK high street stores | → | Letter of Credit is transferred to a second beneficiary -the supplier of goods in the Far East |

Aside from trade transactions involving a middleman Transferable Letters of Credit are not commonly used in international trade, it is possible for example that the end customer may look to bypass the UK importer and deal direct with the end buyer.

> **To apply the UK importer must be able to demonstrate they can add value for the end buyer:**
> - *Either by adding to the product design prior to turning them into finished goods OR*
> - *Demonstrating an expertise in dealing with foreign suppliers and the product being imported.*
> - *The end customer must also be willing to issue a Letter of Credit themselves. To do so they must receive something tangible in return, for example favourable contract terms.*

For the UK business in the example quoted use of Transferable Letters of Credit removes some funding requirements inherent in the working capital cycle. It does not, however, remove them from responsibility for performing their obligations under the contract.

Online Trade Solutions

Most banks have developed their online banking services to include an ability to instruct and monitor trade services online – for example electronic ordering of Letters of Credit, Bills of

1 | BUSINESS FINANCE

Exchange and Bonds/Guarantees. Moving on from this there are more advanced services still that allow for document imaging which enable businesses to manage both domestic and international trade transactions from purchase to payment.

In some respects these services are a variation on the concept of electronic invoicing which is increasingly a theme in the business and banking world.

The more advanced trade solutions, including what is termed SWIFT Trade Services Utility (TSU) provide for:

- *Raising of a purchase order online visible by buyer and supplier, and their respective banks (through a secure Web Link).*
- *An online view of all trade documents, such as Bills of Lading, Packing Lists and Insurance Certificates. Accessible by buyer, supplier and their respective banks this can facilitate 'acceptance' of these documents by the UK importer, with payment made on the basis of this acceptance.*

Banks offering these services will seek an indemnity from their customers, as exchange is online and not in physical format.

From a working capital perspective the benefit of online trade solutions lay in the linking of the physical supply chain with the financial supply chain.

- *Enhanced visibility can result in earlier payment, and improved trust between buyer and seller*
- *Banks can more easily provide Trade Finance solutions based on visibility of documents*

Although online trade solutions have tended to be used more by large UK importers and exporters, for example high street stores they are now starting to apply lower down the corporate scale, as the benefits provided can apply equally for smaller businesses.

For the UK exporter online visibility and acceptance of the purchase order increasingly makes Purchase Order finance more accessible, as all parties to the transactions including banks can view acceptance of the purchase order and provide finance based on acceptance by the importer and their bank.

Collecting Payment by Credit Card

Whilst many businesses may associate credit card payments as applicable for consumer purchasers, they can equally apply for business to business transactions of a lower value, for both the UK and overseas.

For the business invoicing sales the following considerations apply:

- *Can the offering of settlement by credit card encourage their customer to pay?*
    - *a) With the buyer receiving the benefit of not having to pay for their credit card for up to six weeks?*
    - *b) As a result of the convenience factor, which could include credit card acceptance online and/or by telephone?*
- *Most banks provide a good range of online information which link to a business accounting system and sales ledger.*
- *Credit is normally within three working days.*
- *Charges usually apply by means of what is termed an interchange fee, shared between the acquiring merchant (e.g. bank) and the card issuer; for smaller businesses this can equate to 2%-3%+ making charges particularly expensive for higher value sales. Accordingly credit card settlements may apply more for sales of spare parts than large sales orders.*
- *A per transaction or service fee may also be levied, and/or a set up and terminal charge. If these escalate it may be worth negotiating charges with the acquiring merchant.*
- *To offer credit cards as a method of payment, businesses will need to make arrangements with a merchant acquirer/their bank, who can discuss:*
    - ▼ *Options for accepting payment (online, telephone, card terminal)*
    - ▼ *Charges and interchange fees applicable*
    - ▼ *The level of information available online to the business*
    - ▼ *Whether non-UK credit cards are accepted.*

SEPA Direct Debit

The concept of the Single European Payments Area (SEPA) is the creation of a 'zone' for the Euro in which all electronic payments are considered domestic and where a difference between national and cross-border payments does not exist.

In November 2009 the SEPA Direct Debit was launched, all branches of banks in the euro area must be reachable for SEPA Direct Debit. It applies to transactions in Euro – the debtor and creditor must each hold an account with a bank located within SEPA zone. It may be used for single (one-off) or recurrent direct debit collections; the amounts are not limited.

The SEPA Business to Business Direct Debit Scheme (B2B)

This allows business customers, as debtors, to make payment by direct debit, as part of their business transactions. Specific rules apply:

- *In the B2B Scheme the debtor is __not__ entitled to obtain a refund of an authorised transaction.*
- *Debtor banks must ensure that the collection is authorised by checking the collection against mandate information.*
- *In responding to the needs of the business the B2B Scheme offers a significantly shorter timeline for presenting direct debits and reduces the return period.*

Use of Escrow Accounts

The use of Escrow accounts is as much about improving the element of trust in UK and International trade and to improve the chances of the exporter (seller) being paid, and paid on time. Escrow accounts can work for the benefit of both buyer and seller.

The term 'Escrow' refers to monies deposited by a buyer to a trusted third party (the 'escrow agent') –for example a bank or legal firm – that is released to the seller (exporter) once they have met their obligations.

The process operates in the following circumstances:

- *When the seller (exporter) has a concern that a buyer does not have the means to pay for goods and services, they may be unwilling to accept the associated credit risk.*
- *The buyer as a means of allaying these concerns can place an agreed sum of money in an escrow account with the escrow agent, who undertakes not to release the money until the seller has fulfilled their obligations under the sales contract.*
- *The buyer in turn may have a concern that, if they hand over money directly to a seller, they may not receive the contracted goods or services.*
- *An agreement document will usually be completed between buyer and seller, governing what constitutes release of funds.*

When considering use of an Escrow account it is worth noting that fees will have to be paid to the escrow agent and that time will be needed to negotiate the terms of the escrow agreement. Consequently in some cases escrow will be used for large purchases and for specific events such as the sale of a large asset.

Key Working Capital Ratios

To end this section on the working capital cycle we shall look at some key ratios/formulas that can be used to measure elements of the working cycle and hence used to review, manage and change business performance.

Whilst these high level ratios are important in themselves to manage business performance, it may be necessary to obtain a more detailed review by calculating each – or the key/individual components – of stock, debtors and creditors. In essence these ratios provide a top-level summary to show directionally where the business is.

Of equal importance to a business will be the trends in these ratios and what messages these trends are showing. The outcomes will vary according to the nature of business involved, with good practice being to compare outcomes with averages for the industry.

Some of the key working capital ratios are highlighted below. Any business should take time to calculate and assess these ratios – if not as a minimum banks and credit reference agencies will be assessing these and forming an opinion of the business.

Debtor Days (Receivables Ratio)
Formula: *Debtors : Turnover x 365 =* _____ *days*
Meaning: The business can take on average _____ days to collect monies due.
Compare this with the official credit policy of the business.
Note: UK businesses have an industry average of 70 debtor days, higher than companies in Europe. For example, in Germany the average is 48 debtor days. less than 45 days is good; more than 45 days is poor

Creditor Days (Payables Ratio)
Formula: *Creditors Purchases x 365 =* _____ *days*
Meaning: *On average your business pays suppliers every* _____ *days*
How does this compare with the credit periods being negotiated. If it is longer are supplier relationships and the company's credit rating being damaged by late payment?

Stock Turnover
Formula: *Cost of goods sold Stock x 365 =* _____ *days*
Meaning: *On average the business turns over the value of its stock every* _____ *days.*
Compare this with what you would expect from the industry sector. Is there a cost to the business of carrying extra stock?

Current Ratio
Formula: *Current Assets ÷ Current Liabilities*
Meaning: *Current assets are assets that can readily be turned into cash or will do so within 12 months. Liabilities are amounts due to pay within 12 months.*
For example 2x means a business should be able to receive £2 for every £1 owed. An output less than 1 times could present problems.

BUSINESS FINANCE

1

Other ratios can be used in the business as part of management accounting, for example:

- *Bad debts as a % of sales*
- *Cost of bank finance*
- *Debt concentration*

SECTION THREE

SOURCES OF BUSINESS FINANCE

Contents

1 | BUSINESS FINANCE

About This Section

This section will look at the sources of business finance available. For a business, the objective is not just to obtain finance, it should also include _obtaining the correct type of finance on competitive terms._

Reference shall be made to circumstances in which a particular finance can be identified and the means by which it can be successfully applied – helping choose from the range of finance options available.

Whilst the finance needs of a business may be met from a combination of sources it is important that a meaningful proportion of the money is provided by the owners of a business. The existence of permanent capital invested will increase the confidence of potential lenders and investors.

When deciding which forms of finance to use, business owners need to decide on some key initial principles:

- _The level of personal savings they are prepared to commit to the business_
- _How much ownership, and how much control, they are prepared to give up_
- _The level of debt they are prepared to take on_

When considering the amount of finance required to support working capital, exporters must also bear in mind that transportation and insurance costs may also need to be included in the amount sought.

BUSINESS FINANCE

1

Section 3 - **Sources of Business Finance**

Sources of Finance

Finance Options Available to Businesses

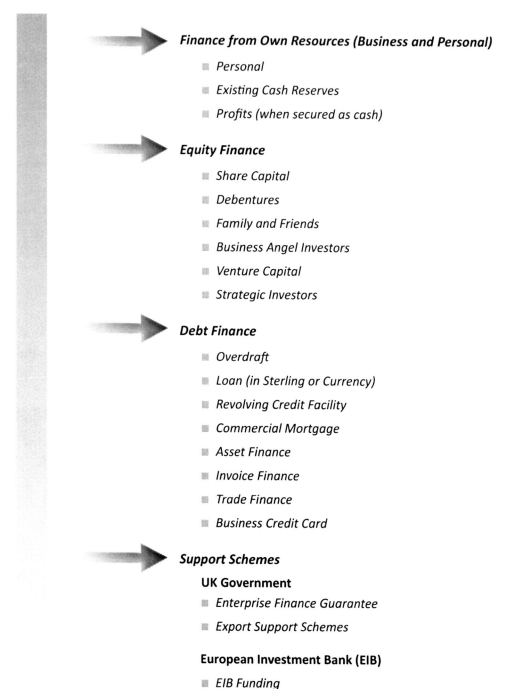

Finance from Own Resources (Business and Personal)

- _Personal_
- _Existing Cash Reserves_
- _Profits (when secured as cash)_

Equity Finance

- _Share Capital_
- _Debentures_
- _Family and Friends_
- _Business Angel Investors_
- _Venture Capital_
- _Strategic Investors_

Debt Finance

- _Overdraft_
- _Loan (in Sterling or Currency)_
- _Revolving Credit Facility_
- _Commercial Mortgage_
- _Asset Finance_
- _Invoice Finance_
- _Trade Finance_
- _Business Credit Card_

Support Schemes

UK Government

- _Enterprise Finance Guarantee_
- _Export Support Schemes_

European Investment Bank (EIB)

- _EIB Funding_

Section 3 - Sources of Business Finance

Finance from Own Resources

Personal Resources

If available, personal resources can be one of the most cost effective and easiest means to inject funds into a business. It will also demonstrate a commitment to the business which investors and banks are likely to want to see as a requirement of their involvement. They will view use of personal savings as an indication that individuals are motivated to succeed.

From a personal perspective the individual must be committed to the business and confident of success before committing. They must also consider what percentage of their personal savings they should use; for example, there may be circumstances when they wish to retain savings for their personal needs. The business may additionally require further cash during the early years after formation.

Aside from the amount of savings put in, it will cost the individual the interest they would have earned on the sum were it invested.

Personal savings are the most common source of funds for a new business.

Existing Cash Reserves (Retained Profit)

Cash reserves can be built up from finance initially introduced into a business, or through retained profits – as opposed to taking profits out of the business through Dividends or Directors' salaries.

A cash reserve may be used for large asset purchases or to support short-term cash flow needs, in anticipation of a large cash receipt from a sales contract.

Businesses may be impacted by economic cycles and should seek to retain profits in the business during good times, in case the reserve needed to be called on in a harder economic climate.

Lenders or investors will assess closely the level of retained profit that is being put back into the business as a measure of continued commitment on behalf of the owners/directors.

Trading Profits in the Business Year

In a similar vein profits made in the business financial year can be used to meet ongoing working capital needs, once they are realised as cash. As a means of 'avoiding' equity finance or debt finance and if possible, business owners can review the amount of money they are withdrawing for their own salaries/personal needs.

1 | BUSINESS FINANCE

Equity Finance

Equity finance is the act of raising money for company activities by selling a share (equity) of the business to individuals/investors, who in return are likely to be shareholders with ownership interests.

Equity financing does not usually involve a direct obligation to repay the funds; instead the equity investor becomes a part owner and thus able to exercise some degree of control over how it is run. Equity investors generally accept more risk than debt financing.

Advantages and Disadvantages of Equity Finance for Businesses

Advantages ✓	Disadvantages ✗
No obligation to repay the money	*The founders of the business must give up some control of their company*
May be more likely to be available to new businesses than debt financing	*Investors may have different ideas about the strategic direction or day to day operation of a business*
Investors can be good sources of advice and contacts for businesses	*Equity financing may require detailed legal and accounting work*

Share Capital

Applicable to Limited Companies, share capital represents **ownership** of a company. Shareholders choose who runs a company and are involved in making key decisions.

Whilst for larger businesses shares are more obviously associated with the stock market, private limited companies are equally likely to issue shares in their company in return for a lump sum investment. This can be from family and friends, or through equity finance from the likes of business angels and venture capital firms.

Shares may also apply as part of an employee share scheme.

The advantage of raising money in this manner is that a business does not have to pay the money back plus interest – instead shareholders are entitled to a share of the profits of the company known as **dividends**.

The main types of shares are

  ▽ *Ordinary shares*
  ▽ *Preference shares*

Ordinary Shares

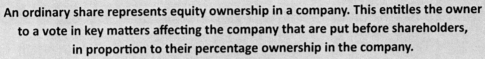

An ordinary share represents equity ownership in a company. This entitles the owner to a vote in key matters affecting the company that are put before shareholders, in proportion to their percentage ownership in the company.

- *In addition to voting shareholders can take a more active role in the management of a company by taking a seat on the board or an Executive position. In the cases of Angel Investors or Venture Capital firms this is more likely to happen.*

- *Ordinary shares are standard shares with **no** specific rights or restrictions. They have the potential to provide the highest financial gain but also carry the highest risk. Ordinary shareholders are the last to be paid if the company is wound up (accordingly they are considered unsecured creditors).*

- *Ordinary shareholders have the opportunity to share in any profits that have been made by the business, after tax has been deducted and after dividends have been made to any preference shareholders.*

Preference Shares

Preference shares carry some distinctive features:

- *They have preference over ordinary shares with respect to:*

  - *Dividend payments.*

  - *In the event of liquidation, payments are made to preference shareholders before any payments are made to holders of ordinary shares.*

- *Preference shares usually carry a fixed percentage dividend. They are callable at the option of the issuing company and generally they have **no** voting rights.*

- *They may also have an option for conversion to ordinary shares.*

For preference shares to be attractive to investors, the level of payment needs to be higher than interest on debt, to compensate the investor for additional risks.

For the investor preference shares are less attractive as they cannot be secured on the company's assets.

BUSINESS FINANCE

1

Section 3 – Sources of Business Finance

Advantages and Disadvantages of Preference Shares for a Business:

Advantages	Disadvantages
Dividends do not have to be paid in a year in which profits are low, this would not be the case with other forms of finance such as loans or debentures	*Permanent burden on the company to pay a fixed rate of dividend before paying anything to the other shareholders*
As preference shares do not carry voting rights, they avoid reducing the control of existing shareholders	*The cost of raising the preference share capital can be higher through having to pay a high dividend*
Redeemable preference shares have the advantage of repayment of capital whenever there is surplus cash in the company	*For an investor preference shares do not carry voting rights and are less attractive*

Debentures

A debenture is a loan issued by a business. It takes the form of a document containing an acknowledgement of the debt:

▽ *Issued by the company.*

▽ *Undertaking to repay the debt at a specified date, or at the option of the company.*

▽ *To pay the interest at a fixed rate, and at the intervals stated.*

Features

▨ *The debenture will usually specify a fixed interest rate, and fixed repayment date.*

▨ *The company is effectively borrowing money from the holder of the debenture.*

▨ *Debentures are generally secured e.g. by the company offering some assets as security.*

▨ *Interest is paid on the debenture even if the company does not earn profits. If interest is not paid then debenture holders can take action against the company to force repayment.*

Unlike an ordinary shareholder, debenture holders:

▨ *Do not have voting rights.*

▨ *Do not have an ownership stake.*

▨ *Do not have a say in running the business.*

Debentures are usually issued by larger companies seeking to raise long-term finance, sometimes for specific projects, e.g. the building of a new factory.

A convertible debenture arises when at the end of a certain time frame a debenture is converted into ordinary shares.

Points to Note with Debentures

1. The company accepts certain conditions (risks) when issuing a debenture:

   - Interest has to be paid at the agreed rate and at the agreed period.

   - Repayment of the principal amount must be paid at the agreed time.

   If the company is not generating sufficient earnings debentures can be a risky form of raising finance.

2. As debentures are usually secured by a fixed asset of the company they tend to be more appropriate for businesses that are having to invest in assets, such as factory or machinery as a means of developing the business.

Advantages of such an investment are

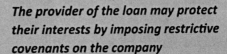

Advantages	Disadvantages
Interest payments under loan stock/ debenture are tax allowable	The provider of the loan may protect their interests by imposing restrictive covenants on the company
Such loans do not usually carry any voting rights	Interest rates payable may need to be attractive to attract take up of loan stock/debenture
The control of the company does not change	Secured assets may not be disposed of without the loan stock holders permission

Family and Friends

If this source of financing applies it is important to remain professional and be clear on what the financing will be used for; create a business plan to evidence these aspects. From the point of view of the individual investing, they should be clear on purpose and what benefit they will receive from the investment; it should operate as a standard business arrangement. If, for example, the investment is in the form of a loan (with or without recourse), a loan agreement should be established.

BUSINESS FINANCE

1

Advantages of such an investment:

Advantages	Disadvantages
Convenient to set up *Available quickly* *Could be few contractual requirements*	*Can be a limited, one-time source of funding* *It may be common for family and friends to need their money back quickly if they have an urgent need*

Business Angel Investors

Business Angels are private investors who provide capital for new and expanding businesses – by investing their own funds. In addition to their financial contributions they provide business expertise and contacts. Many business angels will have had success in business in their own right, they will seek to use their expertise to help make and manage day-to-day business decisions.

Angels may specialise in particular business sectors and the contacts they can provide may prove invaluable, as well as the mentoring they can offer to the business owners.

Business Angel networks exist to help businesses identify Angels who may provide investment, by chosen business sector.

Advantages of such an investment are

Advantages	Disadvantages
Businesses receive more than money, they receive business expertise and industry contacts *Business angels can be patient about their investment – they want to see it succeed and will do what they can to achieve success*	*Angels may require a very high return for their investment* *They can be difficult to find* *If more than one business angel there may be divergent interests of the different investors*

Venture Capital

This can be associated with high growth companies, with investment generally made as cash in exchange for shares in the invested company. Venture capital typically comes from institutional investors (e.g. banks, pension funds) and high net worth individuals who invest in a **fund** pooled together by venture capital firms.

Section 3 - Sources of Business Finance

At the time of putting their money in a fund the investor should have an awareness of the business sector that the fund will invest in. The venture capital firm will normally comprise small teams with strong industry experience in certain business sectors, such as technology.

Venture capital can be attractive for new companies with limited operating history that are too small to raise capital publicly and not yet able to secure a bank loan. In exchange for the high risk that venture capitalists assume by investing in smaller and less mature companies, they usually get significant control over company decisions and a significant portion of ownership. They may also in certain circumstances put their own management into the company to run the business.

Advantages of such an investment are

Advantages	Disadvantages
In addition to the investment the business receives industry expertise and contacts The venture capital firm may have more money to invest if successful	Must be a 'fast growth' business To realise their investment the venture capital firm may want to sell the business, or become a public quoted company, within 3 to 5 years – in order to get a return on their investment A business must be prepared to give up a controlling interest in the company

Strategic Investor

A strategic investor is an individual or company that adds value to the money it invests with its contacts, experience and knowledge of the market.

The aim for the investor may be to gain access to a particular product or technology that a company is developing, or to support companies that could become customers for the larger company's products. The strategic investor will have a strong knowledge of the sales and marketing processes applicable to the specific product.

Advantages of such an investment are:

Advantages	Disadvantages
Enhances the credibility of the business within the industry Investment can come with access to benefits such as manufacturing, distribution and marketing	It may force a business to alter its strategy to serve the investor As a consequence such dependency may have its risks It can prohibit a business from selling to competitors of the investor

BUSINESS FINANCE

1

Summary

When Equity Finance Can Be Most Appropriate

- *When business expertise and contacts are sought in addition to the finance*

- *When debt finance is not available or the company has no assets to support lending*

- *When the business does not want to be constrained by lending covenants or through having debt on the balance sheet*

Debt Finance

Traditional debt finance such a bank overdraft remains a common source of additional finance for a business especially to meet working capital needs but also in some cases to support longer term growth in the business and to finance asset and property purchases.

Nowadays the types of finance available have extended beyond the more common sources of overdraft and loan; indeed, the alternative sources of finance may be more appropriate to specific circumstances, as this section will outline.

From the perspective of the lender, too, there are benefits in providing the more structured lending, in terms of cost of capital and more direct security. To assist explanation of these potentially lesser-known areas of finance the content shall provide additional focus to these areas.

HINTS and TIPS

With all forms of bank finance a business should ensure they understand the terms on which finance is provided. These include:

- *The cost of borrowing – this comprises the lending margin and the banks cost of borrowing*

- *Any arrangement or renewal fees for providing the finance*

- *Any unauthorised overdraft fees –what they represent, when they apply and what they cost*

- *Any security requirements the bank is seeking*

- *Any lending covenants*

- *Any non-utilisation fees, for finance approved but not used*

- *Businesses should only seek to borrow the amount they need and avoid paying additional fees for finance that is not required*

Overdrafts

Whilst overdrafts may no longer be a favoured source of borrowing, they do still have a time and a place for businesses, for example, to cover low value and short term working capital needs.

Overdraft Features:

- *They are generally easier to arrange or increase.*
- *They are subject to a pre-agreed limit.*
- *Interest is paid on the amount of the overdraft.*
- *Overdrafts are usually reviewed annually and a renewal fee taken.*
- *Businesses must be careful concerning non-authorised overdrafts, which can carry heavy fees.*
- *In small and start-up businesses banks invariably prefer to provide an overdraft, rather than establish a formal loan.*

Advantages	Disadvantages
Overdrafts are a flexible way of funding the day to day finance requirements of the business (meeting working capital needs)	*Interest rates can be higher than more structured loan arrangements*
Interest is only payable on the amount the business is overdrawn	*A business may be left with no contingency funds if they are regularly overdrawn*
Banks may not ask for security for 'small overdrafts'	*Banks can ask for repayment at any time*
	Banks are increasingly charging non-utilisation fees on the amount of an approved overdraft which is not drawn

Loans

Term loans can be used for a variety of business purposes but are usually associated with a specific event, for example, acquiring an asset such as a property or machinery, or expanding into a new market. They are not as suitable for meeting the working capital needs of a business.

Loan Features:

- *A loan is an amount of money borrowed for a set period.*
- *There is an agreed repayment schedule.*

1 | BUSINESS FINANCE

- *The amount repaid will depend on the amount and term of the loan, and rate of interest.*

- *The terms and cost of loans can vary by provider.*

- *A bank will usually seek security for a loan, unless the business is in a strong credit position.*

- *Loan conditions and financial covenants are likely to be a condition of borrowing.*

- *Loans can be subject to **payment holidays** usually at the beginning and sometimes during the life of a loan. These involve the payment of interest only for a defined period – with no capital payments*

Loans can be taken out in sterling or currency. For an exporter a loan in currency may have particular benefits in managing against exchange rate exposure and using the source of repayment to directly repay the borrowing.

Advantages	Disadvantages
A business is guaranteed finance for a specific period, for example three to ten years – unless the loan conditions are breached	**Loans can carry strict terms and conditions, and banking covenants**
Payment holidays can be useful for managing cash flow, and for cyclical business needs	**They can lack flexibility whereby a business is paying interest on the full loan amount, irrespective of whether the full funds are required**
Whilst interest is paid on the loan –unlike equity finance – you do not have to give the lender a percentage of your profits, or a share of the business	**Where security is a requirement, business assets or personal assets (for example the house) could be at risk if repayments are not met**
If interest rates are fixed you will know the level of repayments throughout the life of the loan	**There is likely to be a charge if the business wants to repay the loan early, especially for fixed rate loans**
Businesses may be more comfortable with a business loan as they have a greater understanding of how such loans operate	**Regular payments could cause cash flow difficulties if a business is not generating enough cash to meet the loan repayments**

Commercial Mortgages

Features:

- A popular form of finance used to buy buildings and land for business purposes.
- Available to most types of business: start-ups, small to medium sized businesses and large businesses.
- The lender usually holds the legal rights over the business property, until the loan is repaid.
- Can be used by businesses to expand, take on more storage space or buy their own office premises.

Advantages	Disadvantages
The business owns a large asset, which can increase in value. Unlike other forms of finance the business in this case retains ownership.	An asset can go down as well as up in value.
If the loan repayments are similar in value to current rental costs, a business will not need to adjust their budget.	When a business signs up to a commercial mortgage it is committed for a long period of time e.g. 10 to 30 years.
Mortgage interest payments are tax deductable, with payments made with pre-tax money.	If a business fails to meet repayments they may have to pay additional interest, and this could lead to the property being repossessed.
If the lender agrees a business might be able to sub-let some of the business space.	
It may be possible to design a repayment plan that meets the needs of the business.	
Limits the need to incur capital expenditure.	
Mortgage schedules are pre-set improving cash flow predictions.	

BUSINESS FINANCE

1

Revolving Credit Facility

Features:

- An agreement between a bank and a business to provide a certain amount in loans.

- The business is under no obligation to actually take out the loan, but may take part of the funds at any time, over the agreed facility period.

- Can be used to provide liquidity for a company's day-to-day business operations (working capital needs) – and can apply where the business income is seasonal, or dependant on single large contracts.

- Revolving credit facilities are usually set for fixed periods e.g. weekly, monthly, and quarterly. Only at the end of the drawdown period can repayments be made to reduce the borrowing.

- The frequency of the drawdown is likely to depend on the level of business activity and how frequently cash is available to reduce the level of the revolving credit.

- The business may be required to pay a fee to the lender for any money that is undrawn from the amount approved on the revolving credit facility (termed a non-utilisation fee).

Advantages	Disadvantages
Approved finance is available when it is needed.	Because of its flexibility a business may be tempted to set the limit at a higher level than is actually required.
A business can use as much or little of the facility as is required – provides for flexibility in working capital arrangements.	Interest rates will vary and are set at the time each revolving credit is redrawn.
Can reduce borrowing costs PROVIDING close attention is paid to the working capital elements of debtors, creditors and stock. Careful budgeting and close control of the business can reduce borrowing costs.	Budgeting is harder due to the variable nature of the lending amount.

Asset Finance

In its simplest form, asset finance is any kind of lending secured by an asset. If the loan is not repaid the asset is taken

Along with specialist lenders, most banks provide asset finance covering Hire Purchase, Leasing and Stock Finance. For both the lender and a business there can be advantages to this form of finance.

For the lender, they are able to provide finance attached to a specific asset that should provide improved credit weighting of its lending book. As a result this type of lending will be more profitable for the bank than say lending by way of overdraft that is not so specific.

For the business, it allows them to utilise an asset and replace it as technology develops and/or business circumstances change, such as company expansion.

Examples of asset based lending include machinery, cars and computers used in a business.

Hire Purchase

The lender funds the purchase of the asset and the business repays over a period – usually between one and seven years. At the end of the period, the business owns the asset.

Other features can comprise:

- *Repayments by fixed or variable interest rates.*
- *Option to lower or defer repayment to suit income or cash flow cycles.*
- *A hire purchase agreement allows the business to select their own supplier and negotiate the best deal **and** claim capital allowances for some types of capital expenditure such as plant and machinery, and agricultural buildings. Capital allowances can be a significant tax incentive for businesses to invest in new plant and machinery or the upgrade of information systems.*
- *Repayment holidays whereby interest only payments apply for a given period, for example, at the beginning at the facility, with capital payments weighted more heavily towards the end of the facility, when the asset is fully operational in the production process.*

Leasing

The lender pays for the asset and leases it to the business in return for rental payments. At the end of the agreement – between one to seven years – the business has two primary options:

- ▽ *Extend the rental period, paying a nominal rent.*
- ▽ *Sell the asset and retain a portion of the proceeds.*

Although the business is unable to claim capital allowances on the asset it can offset the rental payments against taxable profits.

An **Operating Lease** is a lease with a short term, compared to the useful life of the asset or piece of equipment. It is commonly used to acquire equipment on a relatively short-term basis. By way of example in the case of cars the lender leases the vehicles to the business for a fixed monthly amount, with the lender assuming the residual value risk of the vehicles. For a business this

1 BUSINESS FINANCE

provides a means of leasing the cars that the cost is known in advance. Operating leases as a consequence of their benefits can be an expensive option, with the risk premium priced into the monthly payments.

A Finance (or Capital) Lease operates as follows:

- *The business will select an asset (e.g. equipment, vehicle, software).*
- *The lender will purchase that asset.*
- *The business has use of the asset during the lease, paying a series of rental payments for use of the asset.*
- *The lender will recover a large part or all of the cost as the asset **plus** earn interest from the rental payments received from the business.*
- *The business has the option to take ownership of the asset.*

The Finance Lease differs from the Operating Lease in that the business has use of the asset over most of its economic life, and beyond.

Advantages	Disadvantages
Financing is at a fixed rate with fixed repayments	**Can be an expensive form of borrowing**
Allows access to an asset without owning it	**Can be inflexible; settlements may still be required, even if the asset is no longer required**
Allows a business to rent new or used assets directly	**Hire purchase can attract high deposits**
Saves on start-up capital costs, improving cash flow	**Although the business is not the owner, they are still usually responsible for maintaining the equipment as specified by the terms of the lease**
Can offer tax advantages	
The borrowing is linked to a specific purpose, reducing the tendency to 'over estimate' borrowing requirements	
An asset is funded over its working life	
Leasing is 'inflation friendly', even if the costs go up over a period the business still pays the rate at when the lease began	
Under leasing there can be option to buy equipment at the end of the lease term	
Frees up other forms of security which are not required for asset based lending	

Of the two forms of lending *Hire Purchase* is far more popular for businesses who buy plant and machinery. This is as a result of the capital allowances that Hire Purchase can offer and the fact that businesses can own goods outright.

Stock Finance

Another form of asset based lending, although not as commonly used, is finance that is secured against stock, which can be in the form of raw materials, work in progress and finished goods. A lender is more likely to lend a higher percentage against stock value for finished goods that are immediately ready for sale, and have a trading pattern of regular sales and ready buyers.

Stock finance provides a funding solution for businesses that require maintaining a high level of stock as part of their business, releasing capital that would otherwise be tied up. In some cases, however, lenders will **only** provide stock finance if it is a 'bolt on' to another form of finance, notably invoice finance – as stock by itself may not be sufficiently strong security to lend against.

From a lender perspective there will be several key factors to consider as part of the lending decision:

- *The nature of the stock; can it easily be sold on in a distress situation?*
- *To what extent are these finished goods ready for sale?*
- *The stock trading history, does it regularly 'turn over',* **with** *a regular repayment history from debtors?*
- *The percentage of loan to stock value sought.*
- *Are there any retention of title clauses imposed by the supplier in the purchase contract – which may trigger in the event of non-payment by the business?*
- *Are there any deferred payment clauses in the sales contract if the product does not perform as expected?*
- *The level of stock control a business maintains, including weekly and monthly stock takings.*

Advantages	Disadvantages
Releases capital that would otherwise be tied up in raw materials, work in progress and finished goods	**Stock finance is not always readily available, especially for raw materials or goods undergoing work in progress**
Is flexible, can be used as a 'revolving facility' with flexibility to drawdown as when and needed	**Finance can be expensive**
Can be particularly useful for businesses in the retail, wholesale and international trade – allows for seasonal stock requirements	**The amount advanced – loan to stock value – may not meet the valuation expected by the business**

BUSINESS FINANCE

1

Invoice Finance

Invoice Finance is a means of optimising cash flow, sometimes known as cash flow or debtor finance. It can be over-looked, notwithstanding, it is one of the most flexible assets in a business. Its increased popularity is reflected in this form of finance increasing during a period of UK recession, making it a strong growth product amongst UK businesses.

The basic principle is that finance is provided against the value of the business sales ledger, and ultimately the credit of the customer being invoiced – namely is the customer being invoiced a good credit risk, are they financially sound enough to make payment and will they make payment.

There are two elements to invoice financing:

▼ *Factoring: where the lender collects the money due and controls the sales ledger*

▼ *Invoice Discounting: control over invoices and the sales ledger is retained by the business*

In the past factoring has suffered from a perception of lender of last resort to be used when no other forms of lending were available. Nowadays, the benefits of invoice financing enjoy a better understanding, providing funding that a business needs to trade, based on actual sales rather than the balance sheet itself as with other forms of finance. The business receives the majority of the value from its invoices immediately, without having to wait for the customer to pay, either on time OR after the due date.

Lenders can also provide invoice finance for overseas debtors (exports) and in doing so they will assess the strength of the debtor and country risk. It would be more common to finance invoices for exports to Europe and covering invoices issued to large well-known companies. A lender may also be more likely to provide finance for overseas debtors if this is combined with a majority share of UK debtors, in order in their view to balance the risk.

In general terms, lenders are more reluctant to provide invoice finance on overseas debtors unless the contract is a 'clean export' to a large known business in a country with a strong credit rating. There are, however, some businesses whose exports meet these criteria and in these cases it is important that such financing is seriously considered. Invoice finance remains popular for exports to Europe.

The Growth of Invoice Finance

There are several reasons why invoice finance has increased in popularity:

1. *Due to the fact that finance can be provided on an undisclosed basis. The purchaser of the goods and services does not know that finance is being provided against the invoice.*

   This is known as Confidential Finance, whilst traditionally this is associated with confidential invoice discounting (CID), confidential factoring is a recent concept that is new to the market.

2. *Finance being flexible, debt can grow or decrease in line with sales turnover.*

3. *Lenders especially banks prefer to lend on invoice finance as it is a more efficient form of lending than the likes of overdraft. Banks have to set aside less capital for invoice*

finance, as lending is linked to the sales ledger **and** security is more enforceable.

These principles have been tested in law through the Spectrum case in the UK, which upheld the earlier Brumark case ruling:

That a lender could *not* claim a fixed charge over book debts if the borrower was free to use the proceeds at they wished

In the case of an overdraft the borrower (business) IS free to use the proceeds as they wish

In the case of an invoice finance facility, the borrower IS NOT free to use the proceeds. The funds, as will be described below, are paid into a Trust account maintained by the lender

Accordingly an overdraft only ranks as a floating charge, a less secure form of security for the lender that will rank them BELOW other creditors in the event of company failure

Factoring

Factoring involves a factoring company (many are owned by Banks) taking over the credit management function and sales ledger of a business and collecting funds from the customer. The factoring company buys the trade debts and will advance around 85%-90% as soon as they receive a valid invoice. The balance, less charges, is paid to the business when the customer pays the invoice.

In practice, factoring tends to apply more readily for finance of less than £1million, where the cost of an invoice discounting facility cannot always be justified by the lender. In essence, factoring will be the product more applicable to smaller companies.

Traditionally the process of factoring described above is on disclosed terms, whereby the customer being invoiced knows that a factoring company is involved and finance is being provided. Recently, however, **Confidential Factoring** has been offered by lenders.

Under Confidential Factoring, the factor will help the business chase outstanding invoices but in the name of the business itself, in order that the customer being invoiced does not know the debts are factored.

Confidential Factoring can work as follows:

- *The business receives up to 85% of the value of customer invoices as they are raised*
- *A dedicated telephone line is established by the factor, for all incoming calls from the customer*
- *The telephone line is answered in the name of the business, preserving confidentiality*
- *All correspondence from the factor reflects the name and branding of the business, such as collections, letters, statements etc*
- *The factor continues to provide credit control and credit management with the customer unaware that the business is using this service*

BUSINESS FINANCE

1

Invoice Discounting

A business maintains control of its sales ledger, while still benefitting from increasing working capital. Normally discounting takes place on a **Confidential** basis, without disclosure to the customer being invoiced.

Before providing finance, the lender will evaluate the business, its customers, its contracts, business processes (credit control) and accounting systems.

If approved lending will be provided to a set percentage of the sales ledger, for example 85%-90% - this may be the whole of the sales ledger, or that part which the lender is prepared to provide finance against. The lender may only agree to advance against a part of the sales ledger if they are unhappy about the creditworthiness of some customers.

Under this arrangement the business still undertakes the credit control and manages the outstanding debt. The business will be subject to regular checks from the lender to ensure that credit control systems and procedures are effective.

In broad terms the following steps can normally apply (although with some lenders procedures will differ):

Step 1
A business (supplier) provides the goods/services to their customers and invoices them.

Step 2
The lender is advised the value of the invoices raised.

Step 3
The lender advances an agreed percentage (e.g. 85-90%) of the invoice value, usually by the next working day, sometimes same day.

Step 4
The business collects the debt in the usual manner, with payment made to a 'Trust account' that is held and administered by the lender. As far as the buyer (customer) is concerned they are making payment to the supplier and are unaware that this is a Trust account – hence it is undisclosed to them.

Step 5
When the customer pays the invoice, the business receives the remaining invoice balance (less any charges*). Payment is made out of the Trust account into the actual account of the business. It can be common for the same bank to be both lender and holder of the main business account, which effectively keeps the transfer from Trust to main account intra-bank, which is both quicker and cheaper.

*Charges can be based on:
a) A service fee (a percentage of sales turnover)
b) An interest charge, based on the funds advanced

Invoice Discounting and Asset Based Lending

It may also be possible for funds advanced under invoice discounting to be increased when a number of assets are taken into consideration. Some lenders and invoice discounting brokers offer an Asset Based Lending service that provides finance against:

- ▽ *Invoices*
- ▽ *Stock values*
- ▽ *Plant and machinery*

Factors to Consider with Invoice Finance (Suitability for Finance)

1. **Clean Invoices**

   Lenders generally seek 'clean invoices' before agreeing to finance. This is where there is clear evidence of delivery of the goods or services, and a low level of disputes or credit notes. It may, therefore, not be available for some industries where there is a high level of retentions and variation orders, for example construction.

2. **Collectable Debt**

   A lender will want to ensure that the sales invoice give rise to 'collectable debt'. They will seek to ensure that the following applies:

   - *Signed proof of delivery of goods and services*
   - *Strong contract terms and conditions (which the lender will require to see as part of the contract)*
   - *Financially sound customers*
   - *A product the lender understands*

   Lenders are unlikely to fund invoices that relate to staged payments, or interim payments.

   Some lenders may also require a wide spread of customers, or indeed may prefer to fund invoices only to the top customers of a business.

3. **Unpaid Invoices – With/Without Recourse Facilities**

   When agreeing a finance facility it will be important to consider the basis on which unpaid invoices are debited back to the business – after how many days will this happen; clearly the longer the period the better.

   Non-recourse finance *can be available, but invariably this is linked to 'Bad Debt Protection' under trade credit insurance. In the event of the customer going out of business the customer's debt is insured.*

4. **Security**

   In addition to taking security over book debts a lender may require a higher level of security, preferably by taking a Debenture over all the assets of the company:

1 | BUSINESS FINANCE

- *Land and buildings*
- *Stock*
- *Book debts*

By taking a Debenture it ranks the lender as 'first in line' for payment in the event of a company running into financial difficulties. It allows the lender to appoint a Receiver to run the company.

5. Terminating an Invoice Finance Facility

When signing-up for an invoice finance facility a business should be clear on the clauses applicable to terminating the facility. Some lenders may apply 'tie-in' periods of at least a year's financing with high termination costs. This should be clear at the outset in order for a business to aware of its options and outcomes.

6. Committed Facilities

A lender may also consider committed facility especially in competitive situations where they want to provide the invoice finance facility.

Under a committed facility it binds the lender:

- *To provide finance*
- *Up to the stated amount*
- *For a stated period (sometimes up to 3 to 5 years)*

Advantages	Disadvantages
As invoice financing is popular amongst lenders this can reflect in competitive lending terms, especially where a business has 'blue chip' customers and what are termed 'clean invoices,' where the buyer has no or limited rights of recourse.	It may reduce scope for other borrowings, as book debts (debtors) will not be available as security.
In the case of factoring it can be a cost effective means of outsourcing the sales ledger, whilst freeing up time to manage the business.	In the case of factoring, it will be important that the factoring company deals with your customers in a professional and courteous manner, and does not negatively affect the business relationship
Cash is released into the business as soon as sales orders are invoiced.	Minimum invoice turnover may be a requirement, for example £100,000 for factoring to apply, and £500,000 to £1,000,000 for invoice discounting to apply.
In the case of confidential invoicing discounting, which is the most popular form of lending, the customer is unaware that finance is being provided (confidential factoring which is relatively new to the market may have the same effect).	Invoice finance may only be available for the higher credit rated debtors, or higher costs may apply for debtors with a lower credit rating. A lender may be less prepared to provide finance against overseas debtors, especially for sales to smaller businesses overseas.
A business knows exactly when they are going to be paid which assists cash flow and financial planning .	Invoice finance may not apply for invoices with retention or variation clauses.
Lenders generally price invoice finance more competitively than overdrafts and commercial loans.	Invoice finance may not be available for part shipments where there is no 'complete' delivery of goods or services.
Non-recourse finance (with credit insurance) offers protection from bad debts.	Exiting arrangements can be difficult and incur penalty/termination fees.
	Disputed invoices must be dealt with quickly to avoid them being debited, under recourse.

1 | BUSINESS FINANCE

HINTS and TIPS

When considering what a lender can offer by way of invoice finance a business needs to consider several factors, both to ensure they are receiving competitive terms – but also in order that they are able to maximise the benefits that this form of finance can provide.

1. *The basis on which interest is charged should be clear, including the total interest rate and how this is calculated, namely the interest margin and bank's borrowing rate. The general principle should be that lending by invoice finance should be more competitive than other forms of lending, as banks require less capital put aside for what is considered a more secure and identifiable form of lending.*

2. *Any further fees/charges should be clearly stated at the outset, for example some banks may charge for transferring the monies from the Trust to the main business account.*

3. *Online access to the Trust account should be available, which allows the business to view the status of their invoices. Online access may also be able to provide functionality to assign invoices and drawdown funds.*

4. *The time period in which it takes funds to move from the Trust account should be clear at the outset, be this same day or next day.*

5. *Review the level of the sales ledger that the lender is prepared to advance – does this include overseas debtors. Clearly more, or even all the sales ledger is preferable, with the higher the percentage per invoice the better.*

6. *Be aware of any restrictive clauses in the lenders documentation, for example, relative to the title to the goods. This may be covered under security requirements. Ideally bank security should be limited to a charge over the debtor book/sales ledger it is advancing against. If a debenture is required this should be reflected in the overall terms on which finance is provided.*

7. *Be aware of any restrictive 'tie-in' periods, which could be linked to provision of finance. Some lenders may insist on notice periods being applied before exit, with a one year notice period not uncommon. Exit fees could also apply.*

8. *The lenders policy on disputed invoices should be clear at the outset, with respect to what constitutes a disputed invoice and how quickly a lender will debit the business by way of recourse.*

9. Lenders may also provide Trade Credit protection of the part of the finance package. If they do, or offer it separately be clear on whether this is being offered as an added value benefit or whether there are terms/charges applicable.

10. Is the Invoice Finance supplier you are considering a member of the Asset Based Finance Association (ABFA*)?

*As a trade body the ABFA have membership criteria that members have to meet to be in order to be a member. This provides businesses with an element of security, that the organization they are dealing with is a recognised, industry-accepted provider. The ABFA represent 95% of the market of Invoice Discounter providers. ABFA provide information on their website, including a facility for helping businesses find a member who might want to fund them. The website is **www.abfa.org.uk** with the Member Search Facility accessed from the 'Public Enquiries' part of the website at - **http://www.abfa.org.uk/public/membersCriteria.asp** along with product information and case studies.

Trade Finance

In comparison with other forms of lending Trade Finance is not as well understood by many businesses, especially not amongst small and medium sized businesses. It does however provide clear benefits to enhance working capital through borrowing short term and directly linking this borrowing to the supply chain itself. It can also be combined with Asset Finance and Invoice Finance to provide an end-to-end working capital solution.

The popularity of Trade Finance varies amongst lenders that are invariably Banks. The larger UK Banks will be more established and experienced in this type of finance, and accordingly will promote this form to their customers. From a profitability perspective, however, the position is currently being determined relative to the capital that a bank has to set aside for Trade Finance:

▽ *If it is rated in the same way as Invoice Finance, it is likely that its popularity will increase further.*

▽ *A move, however, to rate it in the same way as overdrafts will impact the extent to which banks promote this form of finance.*

Further updates will be provided once this becomes clearer. In the meantime this should not diminish from the benefits that can be provided.

Trade Finance can mean different things to different people and businesses. For the purposes of this section we shall record the types of finance as follows, some fulfil a similar function and in general are variations on a theme:

BUSINESS FINANCE

1

> **Discounting Bills of Exchange**
> **Import Loans**
> **Supplier Finance**
> **Export Loans**
> **Purchase Order Finance**
> **Forfaiting**
> **Commodity Finance**

Discounting Bills of Exchange

Discounting can be provided on a stand- alone basis – on a bill of exchange presented on its own – or where the bill is part of a Letter of Credit or Documentary Collection. In discounting the lender (usually a bank) is taking a risk on the party who has accepted the bill of exchange, which can be:

> ▼ *The issuer of the Bill of Exchange - the buyer of the goods and services. Usually this will be a company for whom the lender may not be prepared to provide a discount, unless they are a large business, or*

> ▼ *A buyer's bank that can add their acceptance to that of the buyer (known as an 'Aval'), which is more likely to provide the comfort by which the UK lender can discount.*

Discount costs should reflect the creditworthiness of the accepting party and country risk, if the accepting party is based overseas.

One of the benefits of a bank discounting a bill of exchange is that it is usually without recourse to the customer, and treated as an 'off-balance sheet' form of finance.

Import Loans

In the case of a pre-import loan this provides the borrower with financing to pay for the goods being imported, at an early stage in the working capital cycle. A post-import loan is naturally later in the cycle.

This is perhaps one of the more popular forms of trade finance that lenders provide, providing a loan against a specific import contract. Although it can apply irrespective of the type of import settlement (Open Account, Documentary Collection or Letter of Credit), some lenders may have stricter rules around only applying it to Letters of Credit where the structure around settlement is more assured. Should this be the case, the business has the option of 'shopping around' for an alternative lender who will provide what is termed a Clean Import Loan based on open account settlement.

Section 3 - Sources of Business Finance

Security will usually be required by the bank. This may vary from bank to bank but is likely to include a 'Letter of Pledge' over the goods being imported. Some banks may also require wider forms of security such as a Debenture over all the assets of the company. In determining the level of security, and the amount advanced against the contract value, the bank will review:

▼ *Trading history.*

▼ *The type of goods involved (e.g. perishable/non-perishable), and how saleable they are in the UK or overseas market.*

▼ *Transport and insurance terms, as to the level of 'control' the importer has over these factors. In some circumstances they could also request that the Bill of Lading is made out in favour of the bank, in order to increase the control held by the bank.*

In addition to providing the importer with finance needed in the working capital cycle an import loan can also facilitate prompt payment that allows for good supplier relationships, AND enhances the importers credit rating.

Supplier Finance

From the perspective of a UK business this involves their bank providing finance to the supplier of the goods. This assists the UK buyer in that it is supporting a known and trusted supplier on whom they are reliant. Supplier finance does arise but has tended to be more limited to large UK retailers and high street companies who, as part of 'being their bankers,' want the bank to be able to lend directly to their supplier, without recourse to the UK Company. It can also arise where a UK bank has an overseas presence in the supplier's country; it knows the local customs and effectively lends to the local company as part of a commercial decision in its own right. There are certain banks that are better placed to provide this sort of arrangement.

Outside of the above circumstances, some UK banks may be prepared to lend to a supplier overseas if this is offered with recourse to the UK company; effectively treating this as part of a lending facility.

Export Loans (Finance)

A less common form of finance and in cases where banks provide, they may look for stronger 'assurances' about the ability of the exporter to perform in accordance with the contract terms – performance risk. This will include an active and successful trading history amongst the exporter and their overseas customer. If provided, banks may more likely look at linking export loans to a Letter of Credit or Trade Insurance policy, and may also seek stronger security in the form of a Mortgage or Debenture. They may also consider that Invoice Finance is a more appropriate means of lending.

1 | BUSINESS FINANCE

Export finance as a result may be used more for exports outside of Europe and The USA, perhaps covering regions where invoice finance does not go to as readily. It may also be used:

▽ *In conjunction with an import loan where the UK business is both importing and exporting goods, where the bank can link all sides of the supply chain.*

▽ *For longer term contracts where the UK business has a long manufacturing process and a long time to wait before receiving cash from the export contract.*

Pre-shipment financing involves a bank providing finance against confirmed orders in order to enable the exporter to make and supply ordered goods.

Post shipment finance provides access to finance after shipment but before payment maturity.

Purchase Order Finance

An exception to the rule of export finance being difficult to obtain is purchase order finance. This may grow in popularity as banks increasingly deliver electronic trade and invoicing solutions that provide for the viewing of documents online. This visibility in turn provides the opportunity for a bank to finance immediately based on what they can see has been agreed between buyer and seller. This is most appropriate using the Purchase Order as the key document evidencing contract sale. A development known as SWIFT Trade Services Utility (TSU) is one of the means by which this type of finance can be offered.

In its most 'advanced' and cleanest form, purchase order finance can operate as follows:

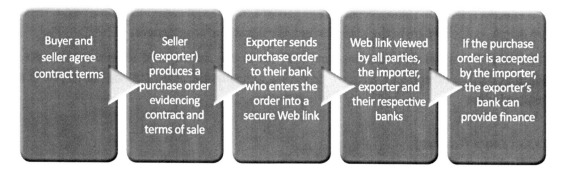

Buyer and seller agree contract terms → Seller (exporter) produces a purchase order evidencing contract and terms of sale → Exporter sends purchase order to their bank who enters the order into a secure Web link → Web link viewed by all parties, the importer, exporter and their respective banks → If the purchase order is accepted by the importer, the exporter's bank can provide finance

* This type of finance works best and quickest when all parties share access to a secure Web link – not all banks however will be able or willing to offer this degree of sophistication. Before offering such a facility, it is also likely that a bank will want to see evidence of regular trade between an importer and exporter of goods, which in turn must be readily saleable in the local market. Monetary sums are also likely to be modest with a short financing period, as banks may not want to lend against large contracts which require longer production cycles.

In some cases the importer's bank may also require the addition of their guarantee of payment.

Forfaiting

Forfaiting involves the purchasing – payment of cash – of an exporter's receivables, purchased at a discount to the value of the receivables. The purchaser of the receivable – the forfaiter – must now be paid by the importer. The receivables themselves, such as a bill of exchange or possibly a promissory note, then becomes the debt instrument. From the perspective of the exporter this provides cash instead of deferred payment.

In view of the risk involved in relying on the importer's credit standing to pay, the receivables are usually guaranteed by the importer's bank.

Forfaiting still applies in international trade and is perhaps more applicable nowadays to export trade with higher risk countries. Consequently costs can be higher, with specialised forfaiting companies playing a key role in the provision of this type of finance. Forfaiting can also apply as a means of raising money on major transactions where a business will be paid in stages over a longer period.

Commodity Finance

Finance will only be available for certain commodities, such as mining, energy and agricultural crops. Finance is provided by isolating assets that have predictable cash flow attached to them. A business in these circumstances borrows against a commodity's expected worth.

If events go to plan, the lender is reimbursed through the sale of the assets. If not the lender will have recourse to some or all of the assets.

Commodity Finance has tended to apply for the larger companies who are dealing with commodities on a 'bulk basis;' that is not to say, however, that smaller companies could benefit **providing** they are in a specific business sector.

Business Credit Cards

Business (Corporate) credit cards are more a form of deferred payment, whereby a business can receive up to 6 weeks free credit before paying for purchases. They are usually applicable for smaller value purchases, as the seller will not be keen on paying the costs of settlement for higher value receipts. This is known as the interchange fee and can incur a 2%-3% charge/deduction on the amount being sold.

Procurement cards can also be used by businesses to separate the cost of procurement from other expenses. Some large suppliers, such as stationery chains, may also offer certain incentives to pay by card as they receive the funds earlier than with a period of credit, for which, they in turn, are prepared to offer a discount on the purchase amount. As a large acceptor of credit cards, their merchant fees are likely to be somewhat less than the 2% charge highlighted above.

Advantages	Disadvantages
Provides a cash flow benefit to the business	*If payment is not made promptly interest costs can be very high*
Cost effective providing monthly bills are settled on time	*If control procedures are not in place employees may overspend (limits can be placed on a per employee card basis)*
A lot of banks provide 'fee free' cards for the first year	*Charges for use abroad can be high, including the exchange rate conversion used*
Quick and easy to use	
Easy to reconcile, with online account reconciliation and VAT management	

Summary

The following are examples of where finance needs can be matched to particular types of debt finance.

Working capital	*Overdraft, Invoice Finance, Trade Finance, Currency Loan*
Machinery, equipment & vehicles	*Loan, Asset based finance, Trade Finance*
Property	*Commercial Mortgage*
Daily Operating Expenses	*Business Credit Card*
Fluctuating Finance Needs	*Revolving Credit Facility*

These are examples only and circumstances will vary by business need.

Section 3 - Sources of Business Finance

Debt vs. Equity – Advantages and Disadvantages

Advantages of debt compared to equity

- *Because the lender does not have a claim to equity in the business, debt does not dilute the owner's ownership interest in the company.*

- *A lender is entitled only to repayment of the agreed-upon principal of the loan plus interest, and has no direct claim on future profits of the business. If the company is successful, the owners reap a larger portion of the rewards than they would if they had sold stock in the company to investors in order to finance the growth.*

- *Except in the case of variable rate loans, principal and interest obligations are known amounts that can be forecasted and planned for.*

- *Interest on the debt can be deducted on the company's tax return, lowering the actual cost of the loan to the company.*

- *The company is not required to send periodic mailings to large numbers of investors, hold periodic meetings of shareholders, and seek the vote of shareholders before taking certain actions.*

Disadvantages of debt compared to equity

- *Unlike equity, debt must at some point be repaid.*

- *Interest is a fixed cost which raises the company's break-even point. High interest costs during difficult financial periods can increase the risk of insolvency. Companies that are too highly leveraged (that have large amounts of debt as compared to equity) often find it difficult to grow because of the high cost of servicing the debt.*

- *Cash flow is required for both principal and interest payments and must be budgeted for.*

- *Debt instruments often contain restrictions on the company's activities, preventing management from pursuing alternative financing options and non-core business opportunities.*

- *The larger a company's debt-equity ratio, the more risky the company is considered by lenders and investors. Accordingly, a business is limited as to the amount of debt it can carry.*

- *The company is usually required to pledge assets of the company to the lender as collateral, and owners of the company are in some cases required to personally guarantee repayment of the loan.*

1 | BUSINESS FINANCE

Factors to Consider When Borrowing from Banks

- For a business there are **several finance options** that extend beyond the more common overdraft or loan. The type of finance required should be influenced by the actual financing need as alternative sources may be more appropriate in reducing lending costs and lending timescales, alternatives such as:

  - borrowing against the assets (asset finance)

  - borrowing against the debtor invoice (confidential invoice discounting)

  - borrowing against the import/export contract (trade finance)

- Whilst it is accepted that overdrafts may arise because of the uncertain nature of business cash flows, alternative forms of finance should be considered for any **core finance requirements.**

- In general, banks **price overdrafts higher**, additionally the amount sought is less certain as a result of which businesses may ask for excess amounts. Banks in turn have to set capital aside irrespective of whether the full overdraft is used, and may charge arrangement fees and non-utilisation fees accordingly.

- In setting lending margins and pricing finance, banks will consider the impact of the finance in terms of risk-weighted assets. Some types of finance such as overdrafts and loans will attract a higher risk weighting than other assets such as invoice finance.

- If Banks have **strong security** this will improve their internal weightings, for example, by achieving a lower rating on probability of default. This in turn can make the borrowing more attractive to the Bank improving the overall lending terms.

- The **margin** over cost of funding will naturally be a key aspect, but the **cost of funding rate** itself can also make a difference. For overdrafts, the margin should be over base rate, for other forms of lending the bank will specify the basis of cost of funds; this may be influenced by how the particular bank is able to raise funds itself, which is usually facilitated at LIBOR (London Inter-Bank Offered Rate). By way of example a **better credit rated bank** may have lower cost of funds that in turn may be reflected in the cost of funding charged to the customer. Consequently there may be benefit in businesses also checking this rate as part of the overall comparison of total lending costs.

- For non-overdraft lending, businesses should consider **fixing the cost of funding rate** they borrow at (known as interest rate hedging). This will provide certainty of borrowing rate, notwithstanding, the decision will also be influenced by underlying and prospective interest rate trends, which influence the cost of the interest rate hedge, which Banks factor into the equation. In these circumstances entering into an interest rate hedge is a means of protecting a business against unfavourable changes in interest rates.

- When businesses have ongoing but fluctuating borrowing needs, consideration can also be given to borrowing on a **revolving credit basis**, such credits allow for drawdown periods when increased borrowings can be drawn down e.g. on a monthly or weekly basis. Drawdown periods can also be used to reduce borrowings, whereby businesses can use cash received to reduce the level of borrowing drawn, and consequently reduce interest costs.

- Borrowings would normally be drawn in sterling, however there are circumstances in which **currency borrowing** can be considered. This especially applies where businesses have a ready stream of currency income during the normal course of their business. This may also have benefits in minimising currency exchange risk that would arise from having to convert currency income streams to sterling.

- Finally the cost of **unauthorised overdrafts** must be considered, and banks should be asked to specify these up-front, comprising the margin and fees that would apply for any unauthorised overdrafts. Additional fees such as returned cheque fees or returned payment fees should also be detailed.

What Banks and Equity Providers Like To See

The following categories represent details of headings and information that Banks and Equity providers like to see included before providing equity or finance. Inclusion of these items will not just help receive approval but may also influence the terms received by way of equity stake or fees and lending margins.

- **A Strong Business Plan**

  Whilst content here shall be high level only it will provide an insight into the requirements of a business plan. The plan should incorporate the following:

  - ▼ Executive Summary

    A short description of the business opportunity and how it will be achieved

  - ▼ Summarise The Business

    Company summary: ownership structure, history or start-up plan for new businesses

    Locations and on-site facilities

    Operations, production and IT facilities

- **Products and Services**

    Description of products and services

    What makes them different (unique?)?

    Why customers would buy them

BUSINESS FINANCE

1

Supply chain and distribution

Whether you hold any patents, trademarks or design rights

Future plans for products and services

- **Market analysis summary**

  Market segmentation and target market strategy

  Target customer base

  Recent and prospective market trends

  Market participants

  Main competitors

  Distribution and buying patterns in the market

- **Strategy and implementation summary**

  Value proposition

  Marketing strategy (including marketing programs)

  Pricing and promotional strategy

  What will the pricing policy be going forward?

  Distribution and sales strategy (including sales programs)

  Milestones

- **Risk analysis**

  With mitigating actions

- **Management summary**

  Organisational structure

  Management team (detail any gaps)

  Personnel plan

- **Financial plan**

  Any key assumptions

  Key financial indicators

  Break-even analysis

  Projected profit and loss

  Cash flow forecast

  Projected balance sheet

  Business ratios (for reference these are quoted below)

  Long-term business plan

Sample business plans by industry sector and business plan templates may be available in the public domain to assist completion. When drafting the business plan it is important to view it not just as a measure of securing finance but also as a means of measuring success within the business:

▼ *You must be clear on what the finance will be used for*

▼ *Forecasts should be provided over a 3 to 5 year period*

▼ *Any detailed information such as balance sheet/financial information and market research can be added as an Appendix*

The business plan should be a living document, which is regularly updated. It is not just produced for specific purposes.

Ways In Which The Banks Risk Can Be Minimised

Tangible Security

Although security will not be the reason a bank lends, the stronger it is from their point of view the more likely the credit application will proceed. From a bank perspective they are likely to rank the value of security in the following order:

Strongest Security

▪ *A mortgage is the best form of security the bank can take – it can dispose of the asset and the transfer of title to the bank prevents the borrower from disposing of the asset. Not all assets, however, are suitable to a mortgage, especially those that are required in the day-to-day operation of the business, such as working capital.*

▪ *Charges are different from mortgages because they do not involve the transfer of legal or equitable interests in the asset to the lender. Under a charge the asset is 'earmarked' or reserved for the lender.*

▪ *A legal mortgage over land or debts must be created by either a deed or by an assignment in writing. An equitable mortgage transfers a beneficial interest in the asset to the lender, but title remains with the borrower.*

▪ *A fixed charge can be created by businesses over specific property, for example, land, buildings and fixed plant and machinery – whereby the business is not free to transfer, assign or sell the asset. A bank will normally capture this under a Debenture, where its standard security will normally also extend to assets acquired after the debenture has been executed e.g. for acquired property.*

▪ *A negative pledge clause is generally included in all bank charge forms. This being an undertaking by the borrower that they will not create any subsequent charges which would rank higher than the bank's charge.*

1 | **BUSINESS FINANCE**

Next Strongest:

- *A bank debenture can also take the form of a floating charge on present and future assets. In this case the owner of the asset is able to deal with transfer, assign or sell the asset in the ordinary course of the business. This is more applicable to charges over stock and debtors. Bank's will not view this security as so strong as they don't have control over the asset and in a distressed situation the value of the stock and debtors may not be realised.*

- *A Guarantee is the most common form of indirect security. A third party makes itself responsible for the debts of a borrower. From a bank perspective they will want this guarantee supported by a tangible asset, for example if the owner of a business provides a personal guarantee then this may be supported by a mortgage over their personal property. This can especially apply where the business has no land or property to offer as security.*

- *Individuals can also use life assurance policies to secure loans. In these circumstances the bank would consider whether there is a ready and liquid market for the sale of such policies.*

- *Quoted stocks and shares can be attractive as security providing they are listed securities, for example on the London Stock Exchange.*

Directors/Management Equity In The Business:

If equity is put into the business by the Directors/Managers, the bank will view this as a commitment from the Directors to put their own equity at risk.

Detailed Financial Analysis:

Further sections of this book will describe the type of analysis required. The more in-depth the analysis, the greater the understanding that a business is able to display convincing potential investors and lenders.

Government/European Support Schemes

Enterprise Finance Guarantee

Introduction

The Enterprise Finance Guarantee provides a guarantee facility for small businesses, intended to improve the availability of working capital. The guarantee will fund:

- *Working Capital*
- *Investment by businesses seeking to grow or develop*

It takes the form of a government guarantee to the lender, covering 75% of the loan amount. It replaces the Small Firms Loan Guarantee Scheme, with expanded eligibility such as higher amounts guaranteed and availability to businesses of a higher sales turnover.

- *Between 1 April 2011 and 31 March 2012 the Enterprise Finance Guarantee will enable up to £600million of additional lending*

Eligibility

- *Small businesses in the UK with an annual turnover of up to £25million*
- *Eligible businesses are able to borrow between £1,000 and £1,000,000 for terms of up to 10 years*
- *Loans for most business purposes are eligible, with some restrictions e.g. buying a business overseas*
- *Any applicable loan will first be assessed by the lender in accordance with their own lending criteria, before consideration of the Enterprise Finance Guarantee criteria*

Use of the Enterprise Finance Guarantee

The decision on whether the Guarantee is appropriate to use with any lending rests with the participating lender. There is no automatic entitlement to receive a guarantee loan, and no pre-qualification process.

Financial institutions such as banks and finance houses will lend to eligible businesses under the Guarantee. The lender is entitled to seek unsupported personal guarantees, but not permitted to take a charge over a private residence.

The Guarantee works in the event of business failure and only becomes available when the Bank makes 'formal demand' against the borrowing that is not met. The borrower remains liable for the full amount of the outstanding debt, including any interest due.

Type of Lending Covered:

- *New term loans (terms between three and ten years).*

- *Refinancing existing term loans, where the loan is at risk due to deteriorating value of security or where for cash flow reasons the borrower is struggling to meet existing loan repayments.*

- *Conversion of an existing overdraft into a term loan to meet working capital requirements.*

- *Guarantee on invoice finance facilities to support an agreed additional advance on an SME's debtor book. This can supplement the invoice finance facility already in place.*

- *Guarantee new or increased overdraft borrowing for SME's experiencing short-term cash flow difficulties.*

Fees Payable:

- *Capital and interest payments as with other forms of borrowing, and possible arrangement fees to the lender.*

- *A premium is payable to the Department for Business, Innovation and Skills (BIS) – equivalent to 2% per annum on the outstanding balance of the loan. This is collected quarterly in advance through the life of the loan.*

Information That Businesses Need To Provide:

Businesses will need to provide all the information normally required by a lender for a loan application, supporting information is likely to include:

- *Current business plan*

- *The purpose for which the loan is required*

- *Details of other investments, and financial commitments of the business*

- *Financial projections*

- *Historic trading figures*

- *Statutory and Management accounts*

- *Details of any other publicly funded support received by the business within the past three years*

Bank Participation in the Scheme:

Banks have launched and promoted schemes backed by the Enterprise Finance Guarantee, each have their own features, such as:

- *Availability by way of variable and/or fixed interest rates*
- *For fixed interest rates there may be a higher minimum amount applicable*
- *Minimum loan periods*
- *Flexibility on drawdown options*
- *Payment holidays – whereby no capital repayments are required, for defined periods (e.g. a year)*

From a Bank perspective, they may view the Guarantee as applying in circumstances where the borrower has insufficient or no security to support finance facilities, for example start-ups and expanding businesses. If security is available for finance then the Bank may NOT choose to progress borrowing under the Guarantee.

In essence The Enterprise Finance Guarantee enables small businesses with a workable business proposal, but lacking sufficient security, to borrow money from Banks.

Export Support Schemes

At the time of going to print there have been a number of government initiatives to support exporters. Summary information is detailed below, with further detail available from this book's Website

- **ECGD Bond Support Scheme** - *designed to increase working capital resources of SME's (small and medium sized businesses), for example by allowing release of monies retained in respect of advance payment guarantees*

- **ECGD Export Working Capital Scheme** - *designed to meet the working capital needs of UK exporters at pre-shipment and post-shipment stages*

- **ECGD Foreign Exchange Credit Support Scheme** - *the scheme aims to share with banks the risk on foreign exchange exposure arising from foreign exchange contracts provided to SME exporters, where there is some other form of ECGD support*

- **Export EFG Scheme** - *a government guarantee to lenders to facilitate the provision of short-term export finance lines to exporting SME's*

- **Short Term Credit Insurance** - *wider eligibility of short term credit insurance for SME's*

1 | BUSINESS FINANCE

European Investment Bank (EIB) Funding for Small and Medium Sized Businesses

Introduction

One of the European Investment Bank's (EIB) top priorities is to support the investments of small and medium sized enterprises (SME's). The support includes what are termed EIB loans for SME's channelled through banks. The banks have to apply for and secure financing from the EIB.

EIB funding can be provided for **permanent** increases to working capital.

The following UK banks have successfully applied for financing: Barclays, Lloyds, HSBC, RBS, and Santander.

Features and Benefits

- Businesses with 250 employees or less are eligible to apply (with certain sectors excluded such as arms, property investment, gambling and tobacco).
- A key benefit of an EIB funded loan is cheaper credit from the participating bank – which is passed onto the business through a reduced loan cost or via cash back.
- The loan must be for a minimum of two years and the loans cannot be used for short-term working capital needs.
- Examples of projects on which finance may be provided include:
  - Research and development expenditure
  - Purchase, renovation or extension of tangible assets, including business premises
  - Projects that enhance certain industries or provide environmental benefits
  - Building up of distribution networks in domestic or other EU markets
  - Permanent increases to working capital
- To apply for an EIB loan a business must contact their bank. Any loan will be subject to each bank's own lending criteria.
- Businesses must agree that upon reasonable notice that they will permit a representative of the EIB to inspect the sites/works that is the subject of the loan.

Bank Participation in the Scheme

Banks have launched and promoted schemes, each have different features, for example:

- Minimum borrowing amounts, in some cases starting from £25,000
- Maximum borrowing amounts can extend to high levels, for example £10m
- Minimum funding of 2 years, terms can extend to 25 years
- Base rate linked or fixed interest rate finance
- Reduced loan cost or cash back, for example 0.6% of the loan amount
- Banks may make some loans available for limited periods

Section 3 – Sources of Business Finance

Topic refresher: **Top learning points**

If Finance is Required:

■ *Consider the most appropriate form of finance to the business event or circumstance. For what purpose is finance required?*

  ▼ *To purchase new machinery?*

  ▼ *To move or expand premises?*

  ▼ *To stock up for increased sales?*

  ▼ *To take on new stock and/or suppliers for increased sales?*

  ▼ *To offer customers increased credit terms?*

  ▼ *To buy out an existing shareholder?*

Different forms of finance will be available, at different terms, to meet these needs.

■ *The following factors can influence the ability to obtain finance:*

  ▼ *A solid business plan*

  ▼ *Regular and robust financial reporting*

  ▼ *A good credit rating*

  ▼ *Strong security*

  ▼ *A good working relationship with the bank or equity provider*

  ▼ *Realistic expectations*

  ▼ *Being open to advice from banks and outside investors*

■ *Always use forms of finance that you understand and can control.*

BUSINESS FINANCE

1

CHAPTER TWO

FINANCIAL INFORMATION
AND BUSINESS PROFITABILITY

Chapter 2 is divided into two sections with illustrations provided by way of hints,
summary boxes and key learning topics

*The Essential Guide to Business and Finance
in UK and International Trade*

SECTION ONE

FINANCIAL AND MANAGEMENT REPORTING

Contents

Financial Information and Business Profitability

2

About This Section

It is possible to view financial and management information as time consuming that adds complexity, time and money. Understandably some companies may not have the time to produce reporting, with the likes of accounting and bookkeeping being outsourced to specialist providers.

Irrespective of who produces the financial information there are tangible benefits that can be derived from giving this area the attention it deserves:

▼ *It can help provide information that allows Directors and Owners to get closer to what is actually happening in the business, providing for a concise overview.*

▼ *It can improve what the external view of the business looks like, which in turn may improve how banks view a credit proposal and how customers and suppliers view dealing with a business.*

▼ *It provides an historic, current and future view of the business.*

This section shall look at the types of information available, covering items that a business has to produce *AND* those it should produce.

Types of Business Information

Financial accounts describe the performance of a business over a specific period and the position at the end of the period (this can be known as the Trading period, with a maximum period of one year in length).

Companies are required by law to prepare and publish financial accounts. The level of detail required in these accounts reflects the size of the business with smaller companies being required to prepare only brief accounts.

Financial reporting is subject to International Financial Reporting Standards (IFRS), previously known as International Accounting Standards. IFRS applies in over 100 countries around the world, including the European Union. All listed EU companies (public limited companies) have been required to use IFRS since 2005. IFRS are considered a 'principles based' set of standards in that they establish broad rules as well as dictating how certain items should be treated, for example:

▼ *A financial statement should reflect true and fair view of the business affairs.*

▼ *Assets based at either historical or current cost.*

▼ *Concepts of capital.*

Management accounts are used to help record, plan and control the activities key to the decision-making processes such as sales, margins and stock level. They analyse recent historical performance and usually include forward-looking elements. They can be prepared for any period although a good discipline is to produce monthly, unless it is a high turnover business such as in Retail where a higher frequency may be required.

Management accounts are perceived as a time consuming task, they are however fundamental to the operation of a business AND are often required by a bank providing finance, in order to view business performance and evidence good practice.

In broad terms financial accounts are concerned with providing information to shareholders, lenders and creditors. Management accounts provide the essential data with which businesses are run.

In these circumstances there may also be differences between what a bank requires and what a business needs:

- *A bank may only require the higher-level information such as monthly balance sheet and profit & loss account, unless there are conditions (covenants) attached to the borrowing to produce further reporting, or where the business has cash flow difficulties.*

- *A business should look to use management accounts to manage the business against* **pre-set budgets**. *Reports produced should include a cash flow forecast and a breakdown of costs in the business.*

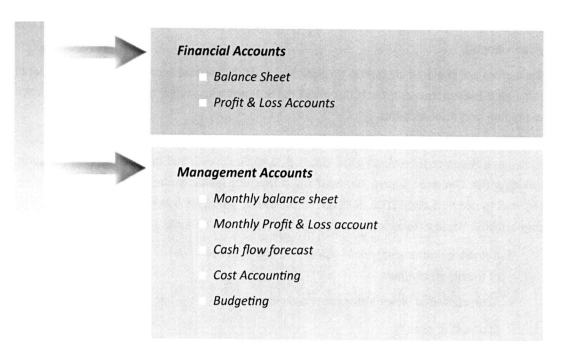

Financial Accounts

- *Balance Sheet*
- *Profit & Loss Accounts*

Management Accounts

- *Monthly balance sheet*
- *Monthly Profit & Loss account*
- *Cash flow forecast*
- *Cost Accounting*
- *Budgeting*

Section 1 – Financial and Management Reporting

Balance Sheet

A balance sheet is a means to 'show off' the success of a company

What a Balance Sheet Looks Like

ASSETS	LIABILITIES
Current Assets	**Current Liabilities**
Cash at Bank	*Creditors*
Petty Cash	*Tax Due*
Debtors (less bad and doubtful debts)	*Accrued Expenses*
Stock	*Bank Overdraft/Short term borrowing*
Prepaid Expenses	
Fixed Assets	**Long Term Liabilities**
Land	*Bank Borrowing*
Buildings	*Other Long Term Debt*
Equipment	*Shareholder Loans*
Less Depreciation	
Intangible Assets	**Capital & Reserves (Shareholders Equity)**
Goodwill	*Share Capital*
	Retained Earnings (Reserves)
Other Assets	
Total Assets	**Total Liabilities and Capital & Reserves**

*Note: For illustration purposes this covers some of the primary elements of the balance sheet.
In practice there may be other categories that can arise during the course of business.*

The balance sheet provides a snapshot of a business, for a given time only. It is essential to produce for purposes of statutory reporting; it provides a useful assessment tool, internally, for the business and externally for banks, credit reference agencies, customers and suppliers.

A standard balance sheet has three parts: assets, liabilities and ownership (stockholders) equity. The main categories of assets are usually listed first, usually in order of liquidity. Assets are followed by liabilities. The difference between assets and liabilities are known as net assets or net worth (capital) of the company.

2 **Financial Information** *and* **Business Profitability**

The key components of a balance sheet are

Current Assets

The assets in a business that can be converted to cash in one year or less, arranged on the balance sheet in order of their expected conversion to cash. They include:

- *Cash at bank*
- *Stock; both raw materials and finished goods*
- *Debtors; representing the amount of money owed to the business by customers who have purchased on credit terms. The amount of bad debts – known and expected – should be deducted from the debtors figure*
- *Prepaid expenses; goods and services already paid but not yet fully used, for example prepaid rent or prepaid insurance premiums*

Fixed Assets

These are the tangible assets of a business, representing what the business owns. Fixed assets are for long term use; they are not for resale and include land, buildings, equipment, machinery, furniture and vehicles.

Many small businesses may not own a large amount of fixed assets as they may only start with a minimum amount of capital.

All fixed assets (except land) are shown on the balance sheet at original (or historic) cost, less any depreciation.

Intangible Assets

These are assets that you can't see or touch but have value. Intangible assets include franchise rights, goodwill and patents.

Current Liabilities

These are the obligations of the business that are due within one year. Liabilities are arranged on the balance sheet in order of how soon they can be repaid. They include:

- *Creditors, representing the amount of money owed by the business to suppliers who have supplied on credit terms*
- *Short term loans (less than a year)*
- *Current maturities of long-term debt*
- *Accrued expenses (such as rent or payroll accrued but not yet paid)*
- *Any taxes due*
- *Any amounts due to stockholders*

Long Term Debt/Loans

Obligations of the business that are not due for at least a year, such as bank debt or shareholder loans

Capital & Reserves (Shareholders Equity)

These represent the funds "owing" to shareholders, being the balance of assets and liabilities. They usually comprise:

- *Share capital*
- *Retained earnings*
- *Capital and Reserves*

Assessing a Balance Sheet

By assessing your balance sheet banks, investors, suppliers and credit reference agencies can assess the ability of the company to:

- *Meet short term obligations and solvency*
- *Pay all current and long term debts as they arise*

Most importantly they will form an opinion of whether THEY want to undertake business with the company.

Financial ratios are a common means of assessing a company. As well as establishing the position of the company at a point in time they are also measured in terms of:

- ▼ *Comparing the trend of the ratio over periods in time (for example the last 3 years), to determine if it is getting better or worse.*
- ▼ *Comparing with other companies in the same industry.*

This sector comparison is important as it can be used by banks, suppliers and customers to compare your business to that of a competitor. Such a selection process may be vital in determining which of the businesses in your industry they will invest in:

- ▼ *Banks for example may only lend to a set number of businesses in a certain industry sector.*
- ▼ *Suppliers will prefer to deal with better performing companies, especially if they have the choice of who to supply to.*

2 | Financial Information and Business Profitability

The key financial ratios:

1. Current Ratio =   Current Assets ÷ Current Liabilities

This is a measure of financial strength. The number of times current assets exceed current liabilities is an expression of how solvent a business is.

A ratio of 2:1 is considered as strong although this will vary by type of business:

▽ *Too low a ratio may mean that the company is not able to meet its debts*
   as they become due.

▽ *Too high a ratio may mean that cash is lying idle and is not being used effectively.*

A ratio can be improved, for example by paying down debt, putting profits back into the business or selling a fixed asset to generate cash.

2. Quick Ratio =   Current Assets – Stock ÷ Liabilities

The quick ratio (also known as the acid test ratio) is a measure of whether a business can meet its obligations if adverse conditions occur. Generally a ratio of near 1 is considered satisfactory depending on the industry sector, whereby a company can use its near cash or quick assets to pay its current liabilities. This applies **as long as** collection of receipts from debtors is not expected to slow.

3. Working Capital =   Current Assets – Current Liabilities

Working capital should always be a positive number. Bank loan agreements may also specify a level of working capital that a business must maintain.

4. Debt/Net Worth Ratio =   Total Liabilities ÷ Net Worth (Capital & Reserves)

This ratio indicates:

▽ *Whether a business is solvent.*

▽ *How dependent a company is on debt financing (or borrowings), as compared to*
   owner's equity.

▽ *How much of a business is owned and how much is owed.*

It measures a company's ability to absorb losses without reducing its ability to service existing debt. The higher the ratio the greater the risk a lender will view the business, making it correspondingly harder to obtain credit.

> ## *Summary: Checklist When Compiling a Balance Sheet*
>
> ### Assets
>
> - [ ] *Are all current assets included?*
> - [ ] *Have accounts receivables been adjusted for any bad debts?*
> - [ ] *Is stock value at replacement cost?*
> - [ ] *Are all appropriate prepaid expenses included?*
>
> ### Liabilities and Net Worth
>
> - [ ] *Are all liabilities, both current and long term included on the balance sheet?*
> - [ ] *Check that assets minus liabilities equal net worth (capital).*
>
> ### Financial Ratio
>
> - [ ] *Have the following ratios been calculated:*
> *current ratio, quick ratio, working capital and debt to net worth ratio?*
> - [ ] *Is the current ratio greater than two? If not are adjustments required?*

Balance Sheet of Exporters

Whilst the balance sheet of a UK business should carry the same categories irrespective of whether it is trading domestically or overseas, for an exporter in particular there are specific factors that will receive closer consideration for credit assessment and business viability purposes.

The degree to which a bank, for example, will examine the undernoted factors, may depend on the level of finance required, and whether security is by way of stock and debtors.

1. Debtors

A detailed breakdown of debtors may be required:

▼ *By country*

▼ *With further segmentation by payment history, debtor terms and product provided.*

A lower credit rating is likely to be applied (unless the debtor is a major corporation) to overseas debtors, especially where the country risk is considered to be higher, for example outside of Europe. This will also take account of the fact that it may be harder for banks to obtain a credit assessment on overseas debtors.

To improve the credit rating a bank will continue to look for a spread of good quality debtors.

2. Stock

The value of stock will be influenced by:

▼ *Where stock is held, a bank would prefer this be stored in the company's premises in the UK.*

Financial Information and Business Profitability

2

▼ Stock in transit 'on the water' will be lower in value.

▼ Whether the stock is pre-sold, which would attract a higher value.

▼ The type of stock, perishable goods will attract less.

3. Fixed Asset Valuations

Fixed assets such as land and buildings can be more easily accessed if they are located in the UK where a more accurate valuation can be placed.

HINTS and TIPS

There may be ways in which a business can improve a credit valuation, which would require to be discussed with the bank, for example:

- **Seeking finance for stock which is pre-sold**
- **Where a business has control over the transportation and insurance through specific Incoterms**
- **Where Bank instruments such as a Letter of Credit are in place providing documentary control and structure to the trade transaction**
- **Where additional measures such as independent inspection certificates are put in place or Bills of Lading are made to the order of a Bank to increase the level of bank control**

Profit and Loss Account

What a Profit and Loss Account Looks Like

Gross Income (Turnover)		_____
Less Discounts & Allowances	_____	
Less Cost of Sales	_____	
= Gross Profit		_____
Less Overheads	_____	
Less Other Expenses	_____	
= Net Profit Before Tax		_____
Less Tax	_____	
= Net Profit (or Net Loss)		_____

The Profit and Loss account (P&L) shows the profit or loss of a business over a given period of time, for example 3 months, 1 year. The P&L will show the **revenues** (income) received by a business and the **costs** involved in generating that income. It is a key piece of information that lenders and investors will want to see – and should be produced regularly by the business to review performance. The information is used to work out tax.

A Limited Company must produce a P&L account by law.

The key components of a P&L account are

Turnover
The value of sales made over a trading period, the total of all money that comes in from sales to customers.

Discounts/Allowances
For example early payment or bulk purchases.

Cost of Sales
The direct costs of manufacturing items, or buying in items to sell them on. These include materials, packaging, delivery and any specific labour hired to produce the product.

Expenses/Overheads
The overhead cost of running a business (sometimes called fixed costs); these include rent, marketing costs, sales, telephone, postage and stationery.

Maintaining Records

Records must be kept to draw up a profit and loss account:

- *A list of all sales and any other income.*
- *A list of all expenditure, including day–to–day expenses and equipment.*
- *A separate list for petty cash expenditure.*
- *A record of goods taken for personal use and payments to the business for these.*

Assessing a Profit and Loss Account

On its own a P&L account may reveal only limited information. It does, however, become much more meaningful when compared with previous periods and with other companies in the business sector.

Financial ratios can also be drawn to review the performance of a company. This would include:

Net Profit Margin =   **Net Profit ÷ Turnover x 100**

This indicates the amount of net profit per £1 of turnover a business has earned.

2 | Financial Information and Business Profitability

The Cash Flow Forecast
What a Cash Flow Forecast Looks Like

	January		February		March	
	Expected	Actual	Expected	Actual	Expected	Actual
RECEIPTS						
Cash Sales						
Cash from Debtors						
Capital Injection						
Total Receipts						
PAYMENTS						
Finance Payments						
Loan Repayments						
Interest Paid						
Total						
Payments to Creditors						
Salaries/Wages						
Rent/Rates/Water						
Insurance						
Repairs to Equipment						
Heating/Lighting/Power						
Postage/Printing/Stationery						
Fuel/Travel						
Telephone						
Professional Fees						
Capital Payments (e.g. Equipment purchase)						
Other Payments/Costs						
Total Payments						
Opening Balance						
Total Receipts						
Total Payments						
Net Cash Flow +/-						
Closing Balance						

> **The benefits of a cash flow forecast is that it can prepare a business for events before they may happen, allowing the business to structure accordingly**

In many respects the Cash Flow forecast is the most important aspect of accounts preparation, as it is a live tracker of projected business performance. The accounts should be prepared by the company for internal management use, and will be required by a lender to evaluate how the business will be able to repay the borrowing.

Cash flow forecasting requires the business to predict how much cash will come into and go out of a business over a period of time. In most cases a business should produce monthly cash flow forecasts highlighting daily movements during the coming month. Estimates can be made based on:

▽ *Previous activity*

▽ *Seasonal peaks*

▽ *Forecasting customer by customer (including how long it takes each customer to pay)*

NB If a business is registered for VAT this VAT must be added to sales, and then paid over to HM Revenue & Customs.

Preparing a regular review of cash flow will enable a business to:

▪ *See when problems are likely to occur and sort them out in advance.*

▪ *Identify any potential cash shortfalls and take appropriate action.*

▪ *Ensure a business has sufficient cash flow before it takes on any major financial commitment.*

▪ *Avoid overtrading, a business can see when it has sufficient assets to take on additional sales.*

Cost Accounting

> **Cost accounting is one of the main principles of management accounting**

▽ *It is used to determine costs and profitability of products or sections of a business.*

▽ *It comprises all elements of cost incurred in carrying out a business activity.*

▽ *The information provided from cost accounting can be used to arrive at a selling price for goods and services, OR to determine where savings are possible.*

Factors Influencing the Cost of a Product (Goods and Services)

Direct Costs	Indirect Costs
Costs which are directly related to production of goods or services – costs that benefit a specific product	**Costs which are not directly accountable to a product – costs that benefit more than one product**
Clearly identifiable costs	**Costs that are incurred across a range of goods and services**
Examples include salaries, suppliers, travel, equipment	**Examples include rent, directors salaries**
Costs incurred by the product in order for it to exist	

The Key Role of Fixed and Variable Costs, and Break-Even Points

The break-even point of a business, or a specific product, is the point at which the revenue (income) received, is equal to the cost of making the product.

Costs are divided into two primary types:

1. **Fixed costs:** *costs that do not vary with sales volume.*
2. **Variable costs:** *costs that do vary with sales, these costs change based on the level of sales or production.*

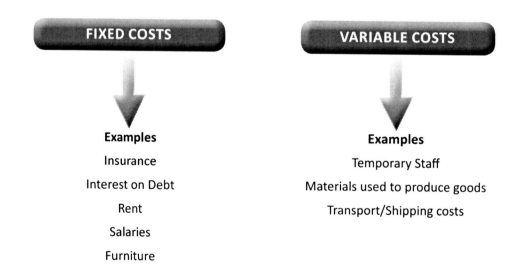

FIXED COSTS	VARIABLE COSTS
Examples	**Examples**
Insurance	Temporary Staff
Interest on Debt	Materials used to produce goods
Rent	Transport/Shipping costs
Salaries	
Furniture	

How to Calculate Fixed and Variable Costs

Direct Costs	Indirect Costs
Gather together all invoices, loan paperwork and bank statements	**Define variable costs e.g. temporary staff**
Make a list of all weekly, monthly or annual expenses that occur regularly and do not change throughout the year	**Determine variable costs per activity**
Add these expenses together to calculate the fixed costs needed to run the business	**Add the variable costs together**

When setting a price it must be higher than the variable costs of producing the product or service. <u>Each sale</u> thereafter will make a contribution towards covering the fixed costs:

AND MAKING PROFITS

Budgeting

A budget is a means of PLANNING and MANAGING the financial performance of a business

The Importance of Budgeting

The following items highlight why budgeting is important:

- *The act of budgeting forces the business to think through all the important events and develop a picture of where the business will be in 1-2 years (or even further forward).*

- *Budgeting is an effective way to control cash flow, allowing businesses to invest in new opportunities at the appropriate time.*

- *It allows performance to be monitored.*

- *It improves decision making.*

- *A budget is a requirement of lenders and demonstrates good management.*

What a Budget Should Include

Projected Cash Flow
- The cash budget projects the future cash position, starting with:

- *an opening balance*
- *cash in*
- *cash out*
- *closing balance*

Costs
- Expenditure should be detailed under four categories:

- *Fixed costs: rent, rates, salaries and financing costs*
- *Variable costs: including raw materials*
- *One-off capital costs: e.g. purchase of computer equipment or premises*
- *Sales & Marketing: costs should be clearly identified*

Revenues
- Sales or revenue forecasts can be based on a combination of sales history and how effective future sales activity will be

Project Activity
- *Ideally a cost-benefit analysis of individual projects to highlight and justify key activity*

It is important to recognise that a budget is not just about numbers, a written plan must be prepared, covering:

- *A Marketing Plan, detailing how sales will be achieved.*
- *An Operating Plan, covering operational strategy around stock, infrastructure and employment.*
- *A Finance Plan, detailing what finances are required and how finance needs will be met.*
- *Risk Management; detailing risks to the plan, and how they will be mitigated.*
- *A summary of where the business will be in 2-3 years time.*

Budgets can vary in format; an example budget is detailed below for reference:

	Year 1		Year 2	
	Expected	Actual	Expected	Actual

Year 1 figures should include projections on a monthly basis

Profit & Loss

Revenue

Cost of Goods Sold

Sales and Marketing Costs

Finance Costs

Capital Equipment Purchases

Other Expenses

Balance Sheet

Cash

Stock

Debtors

Creditors

Fixed Assets

Monitoring Performance against Budget

Once set performance against budget should be measured on a monthly basis. Over the life of a budget adjustments to plan may be necessary and in some cases strategic decisions may be required to help achieve targets, or to change business direction.

Reforecast of budget is a common business occurrence and should be seen as a positive business experience.

SECTION TWO

FACTORS INFLUENCING PROFITABILITY OF A BUSINESS

Contents

2 | Financial Information and Business Profitability

About This Section

This section will concentrate on those factors that influence the profitability of a business. It shall look at the categories of profitability and how they are influenced by approaches to:

▼ *The Business Credit Rating*

▼ *Pricing of goods and services*

▼ *The costs of producing goods and services*

▼ *Measuring business performance*

▼ *Customer profiling and customer relationships*

▼ *Management of cash flow and provision of finance*

▼ *Efficient accounting and reporting processes*

Whilst each business will differ – based on their specific needs – there are some key principles that should be followed and will be addressed in this section.

For a business trading internationally these principles become increasingly important when the additional considerations of distance, language and transport are factored in.

Key Profitability Measures for a Business

Gross Profit

The difference between revenue generated from sales and the cost of goods sold (those costs that go into creating the products that a company sells). It is the profit before the likes of administration costs and selling costs are taken off.

The Gross Profit Margin indicates the profit in percentage terms that a business makes on its cost of sales, calculated as:

$$\text{Gross Profit} \div \text{Turnover} \times 100$$

Net Profit

Sometimes referred to as the 'bottom line', net profit is calculated by subtracting a company's total expenses from total revenue. It represents the profit remaining in a business after all expenses have been taken out, **before tax**. A net loss would arise if this were a negative figure:

$$\text{Net Profit} \div \text{Turnover} \times 100$$

Break-Even Analysis and Contribution

A business has to be sure that it can cover both direct and indirect costs if it is to make a profit. A technique for achieving this is break-even analysis – established by determining the CONTRIBUTION that each product makes to their fixed costs.

The following example may help illustrate the point:

- *Selling price of a product: £9 per unit.*
- *Direct costs: £5 per unit.*
- *Indirect costs: £1,000 in total.*
- *Each time the business sells a product it is making a CONTRIBUTION of £4 to its indirect costs.*
- *Therefore once the business has sold 250 of its products it will have paid all the indirect costs, **and** will start making a profit.*

For certain businesses with high fixed costs, such as in factory, equipment and premises this sort of analysis is very important, and should be a key part of decision making, namely will the business generate more than 250 sales?

Pricing Goods and Services

In many respects pricing is a balance between:

The Internal costs of production

The demands of the particular industry

The strategic goals of the business

There are not necessarily any 'rights and wrongs' on pricing although a business should always bear in mind the following:

Internal Forces

- *A business should be clear at the outset as to what profit margins are acceptable and 'how low' they can go in pricing.*
- *They are in business to make money, and the price should reflect the value of the goods and services.*
- *Prices quoted must be sustainable, for example if further orders are won can the business continue to produce at a level that remains profitable.*
- *Depending on the type of product/service should pricing be based on an hourly rate or product rate?*
- *Will there be discounts for bulk purchases?*

Customer Forces

- Customers may consider low pricing as being linked to low quality.
- What are the circumstances of the customer buying? Are they buying on the basis of quality, price or some other factor such as warranties, after sales service or credit terms?
- Will the pricing quoted reflect credit terms – if sales are being made on a cash up-front basis this could translate into a discount based on immediate payment?
- What credit rating does the potential customer have – are they a good payer?

Market Factors

- Who are the competitors and how do they price?
- How does the price sit with market prices? Too high in comparison with the competition and business will not be gained – too low and customers may become suspicious.
- Is the product being sold as a niche product, or of a particular quality? This could raise the price being charged.

When trading internationally additional factors must be considered:

- The impact of exchange rate movements. If, for example, sterling is weak, this provides increased sales opportunities.

  The challenge for a UK business is to price competitively but at a level which is sustainable and continues to provide profit, were the exchange rate to strengthen.

  A weak exchange rate can be a good means of establishing export sales to a new market as long as the business strategy is clear. Businesses should avoid using the weakness in sterling to try to obtain higher profit margins, but equally they need to have a clear strategy for when the currency strengths, especially if future sales are a core part of the business strategy.

- Whether pricing should be in sterling or local currency.

  Whilst sterling may be more convenient for the UK exporter the foreign customer, who is after all the buyer, is likely to prefer their local currency. They compare costs with local suppliers, and deal in a currency with which they are familiar, avoiding currency exposure.

- The extent to which transportation and insurance terms are factored into the price.

- The terms of trade negotiated could affect the price quoted, especially if credit terms are offered to the foreign customer. If Letters of Credit or Guarantees are used these will incur bank charges and likely use of credit facilities, which in turn may require to be factored into the pricing.

Costs of Producing Goods and Services

Materials Costs

These represent the cost of purchasing raw materials needed to produce goods and services, including packaging and storage.

When businesses look to manage costs they should avoid being detrimental to quality, or delaying delivery to the customer.

Factors to be considered include:

- *Identify what the business is good at in the production process, and own these processes.*
- *Are there more cost effective means of production that a business can use – providing this does not impact quality?*
- *Is stock control being managed tightly in order to ensure that unnecessary stock is not being purchased?*
- *Are there assets in the business being used to their optimum output? If there is ageing equipment is it still cost effective to defer paying for the new equipment, or can hire purchase or leasing be used? What is the cost: benefit equation?*
- *Can improved terms be received from suppliers by way of cost, credit terms or quality? Can the terms be linked to a higher number of orders made by your business?*

Labour Costs

These represent the cost of employing a workforce, including costs of national insurance and employer's insurance.

No matter how good the product and how well the business is run the workforce is often the most important factor in the making of a successful business. Good practices can include:

- *The workforce should be sufficiently incentivised to do a good and professional job. This is not just about pay, it is also about working conditions, fair treatment and providing incentives for measuring strong performance – including share ownership schemes in the business.*
- *Employees should be clear on their roles and responsibilities and what is expected of them. Performance should be measurable to avoid ambiguity.*
- *Employees should be encouraged to present new ideas about how to improve business practices. Usually they are the best-placed people in the business to do this.*
- *Ensure employees are performing tasks most suitable to their skills.*
- *Potential employees should be carefully considered. Often positive word of mouth from people in the industry helps to make the correct choice.*
- *Although dependant on size, the business should have a balanced team.*

Overheads

Overheads comprise a broad range of expenses, not directly related to the making of goods and services.

- *Rent and Rates*
- *Electricity*
- *Insurance*
- *Telephone*
- *Postage*
- *Computer/IT Management*
- *Stationery*
- *Transport Costs, incl. Fuel*
- *Bank charges and interest*
- *Repairs and maintenance*
- *Marketing and advertising*

The approach taken to manage overheads has some similarities with how personal expenses and overheads are managed. There are a number of areas of good practice that a business should consider:

- *The business should always be in a position of paying its 'bills' in order that it can continue to function efficiently. It should attempt to negotiate the best price, without comprising quality. In some cases this could result in using the same supplier for a range of services to gain from 'bulk purchasing.' Be prepared to shop around especially for higher expense items.*

- *For smaller value purchases consider online ordering from 'national suppliers,' and use of procurement cards (business credit cards) that can defer payment for up to 6 weeks. The earlier settlement these cards provide may also result in the supplier providing discounted pricing.*

- *High costs to the business such as fuel may need to be managed carefully, especially in periods where the underlying commodity - e.g. oil - is at a peak. Use of fuel cards can be considered, as well as commodity hedging if there is significant volume.*

- *The merits of owning a property vs. renting should be considered; the comparison of mortgage costs vs. rental costs will be a key factor here. In 'hard times' the business may be able to sell such an asset to generate cash.*

- *Taking out warranty contracts for purchases can be important for the business, subject to cost justification.*

- *Outputs from marketing and advertising activity should be clearly measurable, in order to assess what worked well, what didn't and what can be learnt for future campaigns.*

- *There may be benefit in investing in a professional Website, and in the use of technology in general, to improve business performance and customer communications.*

- *The bank account of a business should be monitored closely, ideally on a daily basis, through Internet banking. Avoid unnecessary overdrafts; in the event of surplus balances credit interest should be sought.*

The bank account should be reviewed in order to record the level of bank fees, transaction charges and interest paid/received.

Measuring Business Performance (Management Information)

Whilst there is always a balance to strike between producing too much information and too little, it will be difficult to manage a business effectively without having the means to measure business performance.

Producing such information is not just about identifying areas of weakness in a business; it is also about providing assurance on what works well and highlighting areas of strength.

A business should look to record information in order that the following reports are available on a regular basis, for example, to be reviewed at monthly management meetings:

- *Sales Proposals*

- *Outstanding Orders*

- *Competitor/Market Summary*

- *Stock Reports*

- *Creditor Reports*

- *Product Profitability*

- *Debtor Lists*

- *Gross Margin, Net Margin and Operating Expenses*

Customer Profitability and Customer Relationships

Customer profitability is the difference between the revenues earned from the customer and the costs associated with the customer relationship.

Revenues Earned (Direct & Indirect)	Associated Costs (Direct & Indirect)
Direct	**Direct**
The value of sales	*Production costs*
	Labour costs
Indirect	*Sales and Marketing*
Positive profile from the customer, for example:	*Servicing costs*
	Indirect
-Word of mouth, supporting other sales opportunities	*Costs of providing credit terms (namely how the business finances the credit)*
-Client references/testimonials	*Overheads (apportioned to the proportional value of the customer and management time taken up in managing the relationship)*
	Travelling costs

Benefits of Customer Profitability

Whilst there are challenges in accurately recording customer profitability there are benefits to be gained:

- *By identifying the key customers and profitable customers this will help the business focus resources on the important customers. It can implement a 'Key Client Management Programme' to ensure close contact is maintained with appropriate customers, and where applicable greater 'value add' and higher levels of customer service are provided.*

- *It allows the business to take a decision with respect to 'unprofitable customers' – does it want to retain them, can it alter pricing or terms of trade?*

- *It supports business profiling and allows for future sales and marketing activity to focus on profitable target customers who match the profile of existing customers.*

Customer relationships apply to all elements of the business:

- ▼ *Most obviously customers buying from the business*

   BUT ALSO

- ▼ *Key Suppliers*
- ▼ *Agents/Distributors*
- ▼ *Banks* and Shareholders*
- ▼ *Introducers and Business Intermediaries*

2 | Financial Information and Business Profitability

To a certain extent business is about relationships, the closer they are the more value both parties will receive. Understanding the position of the other party may be a key factor in reaching a conclusion, which benefits both parties.

When trading overseas there may be additional challenges to ensuring a successful relationship such as language and culture. Trust may also be harder to obtain. In such circumstances a UK business should work hard to gain acceptance and trust

In the case of the bank the relationship should be developed whereby there is mutual understanding and the bank relationship manager is viewed as a 'trusted advisor' – understanding the business and its dynamics. Setting up and running a business can sometimes be lonely so the more people you can rely on the better.

The Business Credit Rating

Credit ratings and credit reference agencies are covered in some detail on other sections. **The key point here is the credit rating of the business itself and how this influences how the business is perceived.**

- **Suppliers** *will be influenced by the credit rating:*

   Will they want to supply?

   And on what credit terms?

- **Customers** *may be concerned that quality may suffer if a business has a lower credit rating.*

- **Banks and other lenders** *may be less likely to lend, or may charge a higher fee.*

A business should consider what it could do to improve its credit rating:

1. *Ensure financial reporting is up to date.*
2. *Seek ways of improving what the Balance Sheet and Profit & Loss account look like.*
3. *Pay its suppliers on time.*

CHAPTER THREE

MANAGING THE RISKS

Chapter 3 is divided into four sections with illustrations
provided by way of hints, summary boxes and key learning topics

*The Essential Guide to Business and Finance
in UK and International Trade*

SECTION ONE

KEY RISKS IN UK AND INTERNATIONAL TRADE

Contents

Currency and Payment Risk are also key risks with each of these covered in forthcoming sections

3 | Managing the Risks

About This Section

Risks will exist in any business, irrespective of its size, business sector or areas in which it trades. What each business must do is identify the areas in which risks exist and what actions it will take to mitigate (reduce) these risks.

This section will look at the risks in UK and International Trade, how they arise and how they can be managed effectively – especially in the environment of international trade where additional risks will arise through differences in:

▽ *Culture*

▽ *Language*

▽ *Distance*

▽ *Less knowledge of overseas markets and fluctuating exchange rates.*

The section will provide specific information relative to Incoterms and the role they play in international trade.

Key Risks in UK and International Trade

Contract Risk

This section is intended to provide the reader with an overview of some of the key elements that require to be discussed in contract negotiations, in order to reduce the impacts of contract risk.

Legal assistance may be required in drafting contracts

Will import/export licences be required to trade?

A contract should reflect what has been agreed between buyer and seller

Contract risk arises from the possibility of loss arising from failure in contract performance.

When negotiating contracts it is important that both buyer and seller are satisfied with the terms of the contract. The following aspects should be considered in both contract negotiations, and when finalising the contract document:

Payment Terms

- *When payment will be made*
- *Ho.v payment will be made*
- *Who will pay bank costs, transport and insurance costs*
- *Any price revision clauses, and if so the terms in which they apply*

Goods and Services

- *What goods and services will be delivered*
- *When the goods and services will be delivered*
- *How the goods and services will be delivered – method of transport and insurance used*
- *How quality control will be evidenced (e.g. use of third party to evidence/inspect the goods or services)*
- *What trading licences are required*

Contract Clauses

- *Will any incentives apply for early delivery, or goods and services being of a specific quality*
- *Detailing any specific requirements, for example use of bank guarantees, warranties or retention of title clauses; where the seller retains title to the goods until the payment has been made in full*
- *Language and legal jurisdiction of the contract (preferably English law)*
- *Steps that would be taken in the event of non-payment*

Legal Risks

As laws and regulations change frequently, it may be important for the seller to draft a contract with the support of a legal firm, as a minimum to create a template on which all future contracts can be based.

Trading Licences

A business should always check if any import or export licences are required before entering into contracts – and if applicable what regulations must be followed. This may impact across several business sectors and requires consideration by the business.

Performance Risk

Quality Control	Operational Risk	Performance Risk
the need to ensure products are of the correct quality	managing ongoing business needs, including employment risk	applies for both buyers and sellers, each are dependent on contract performance

Performance risk will differ depending on whether the business is buying or selling.

Seller (Exporter)	Buyer (Importer)
The seller carries the performance risk that they will not be able to perform; not produce goods or services in accordance with the terms of the contract, such as: -Goods or services are not produced on time, or -Goods or services not being of the correct standard or specification	The risk that their supplier (the seller) will not perform according to the sales contract: -By delivering wrong or inferior goods, or not delivering on time

Quality Control

Ensuring quality control will be vital to mitigating against performance risk. In UK and International trade:

▼ *A seller will need to evidence goods and services as being of a required quality.*

▼ *A buyer will need to ensure that they receive goods and services of the required quality.*

Risk can increase where buyers and sellers do not know each other well, and when there are longer distances between them. Risk can be mitigated by:

1. *Inclusion of contract clauses around warranties if the goods and services do not perform as specified – although the contract has to be enforceable.*

2. *Deferred payment until the goods are in operational use.*

3. *By sending samples of the goods being produced.*

4. *Use of an Independent Inspection Agency, evidencing that the goods and services are of the required quantity and of the required standard.*

3 | Managing the Risks

An Independent Inspection Certificate protects both the buyer and seller.

The costs of the inspection should be negotiated as part of the contract price.

Inspection agencies can provide:

a) **Inspection Services.** *This verifies the quantity, weight and quality of the goods. Inspection takes place at the supplier's premises or at the time of loading, or at destination during discharge.*

b) **Testing Services.** *This tests product quality, and performance against health and safety, and regulatory standards.*

c) **Certification Standards.** *Certifying that goods or services meet the requirements of standards set by government or trading/industry bodies.*

Use of Banking Instruments to Manage Delivery Dates

Depending on the terms of trade used working with banking instruments can help to manage delivery dates from the perspective of both buyer and seller. This can apply in the case of Letters of Credit that indicate latest shipment dates and Documentary Collections where documents should be provided and sent to coincide with delivery of the goods.

Operational Risk

Operational risk centres on some of the key risks in managing the day-to-day needs of a business – such as a robust employment policy ensuring:

▽ **Employees feel committed and contribute to the business**

▽ **That stock is securely managed**

▽ **Equipment and machinery is kept in good working order**

▽ **Health and Safety**

Business continuity planning (also known as 'Disaster Recovery') should be in place in order that contingency is available in the event of disruption to the business, for example in the event of equipment failure or fuel shortages.

ISO (Evidencing Standards)

A good means of a business evidencing quality management systems is an ISO accreditation (International Organisation for Standardisation). An internationally recognised achievement ISO requires:

- *A set of procedures that cover all key processes in the business.*
- *Monitoring procedures to ensure they are effective.*
- *Keeping adequate records.*
- *Checking outputs for defects, with appropriate and corrective actions where necessary.*
- *Regularly reviewing individual processes and the quality system itself for effectiveness.*
- *Facilitating continual improvement.*

Compliance Risk

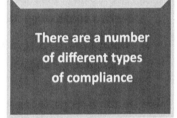

| **Does a business know what rules and regulations it must meet?** | Once it knows what steps does it need to take to ensure compliance | **There are a number of different types of compliance** |

Compliance can take different forms:
- ▼ *Legal compliance*
- ▼ *Import/Export Controls*
- ▼ *Controls specific to the goods and services*
- ▼ *Anti-money laundering*
- ▼ *Bribery and corruption law*
- ▼ *Sanctions Countries*

Compliance risks are associated with the needs to comply with rules and regulations. Some businesses fail to comply because they are not aware of the regulation – indeed concerns over regulation may prevent some businesses from wanting to trade overseas.

Compliance is there for a purpose to protect businesses. In order to identify compliance risks the business should review the nature of the goods or services it trades in:

- *Are there any rules relative to how they are prepared or transported e.g. in the case of food produce or dangerous goods?*
- *Are there any environmental factors to be complied with?*

- *Is any specific documentation required, such as a Certificate of Origin?*

- *Are import/export licences required?*

- *Are there any restrictions around the types of materials that can or cannot be used?*

- *Does the business have to complete any documentation relative to anti-money laundering, anti-bribery or corruption, for example, in the case of large foreign contracts?*

There are a number of reference sources that a business can turn to in order to establish compliance. In the UK, assistance is available from the likes of UK Trade and Investment.

Money Laundering

Several definitions can be applied to money laundering:

- *Concealing the source of illegally gotten money*

- *The process of creating the appearance that large amounts of money, obtained from serious crime, originated from legitimate sources*

- *The act of engaging in transactions designed to obscure the origin of money that has been obtained illegally*

There are three stages to the money laundering process:

1. **Placement** – *moving illegal funds into the financial system, the aim is to move the cash away from its original source and transform it into other forms – large volume of physical cash are broken down into small manageable amounts in order that it can be filtered through the banking system (sometimes through businesses that operate with a lot of cash).*

2. **Layering** – *the purpose of layering is to make it more difficult to detect and uncover a laundering activity. Loans are created by moving monies in and out of bank accounts, sometimes involving offshore bank accounts.*

3. **Integration** – *it is at this stage in which the money is integrated into the legitimate economy. By this stage it is difficult to follow the trail.*

Four Acts of primary legislation govern money-laundering legislation in the UK:

▼ **The Terrorism Act 2000**

▼ **The Anti-Terrorist Crime & Security Act 2001**

▼ **The Proceeds of Crime Act 2002**

▼ **Serious Organised Crime and Police Act 2005**

There are five main offences, some of which can arise unwittingly:

- *Assisting*
- *Acquisition*
- *Concealing*
- *Failure to Disclose - can even arise if suspicions are not reported to the authorities*
- *Tipping Off – telling someone they are under suspicion*

Sanctions

Sanctions can prevent trade with certain countries, and are impacted by the likes of the United Nations, the US Treasury's Office of Foreign Assets Control (OFAC) and European Union governments. Most UK banks will be subject to such sanctions that prevent trade taking place on behalf of their customers.

Specific examples include:

- *A customer buying or selling goods to certain countries*
- *Making or receiving payments to or from certain countries*
- *Selling weapons to certain countries*

Transport and Logistics Risk

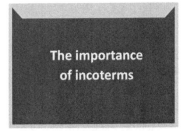

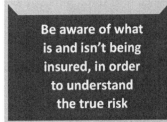

The importance of incoterms	Ensure the business uses a logistics/transport company that can meet their needs	Be aware of what is and isn't being insured, in order to understand the true risk

This is the risk of goods being lost or damaged in transit. The exporter must understand all aspects of transport and logistics especially the different means by which goods can be carried.

Cargo insurance is an insurance against physical damage or loss of goods during transportation. It covers goods transported by sea, land or air and is an essential requirement of international trade. Some UK businesses may take the view that cargo insurance is not required, as their Freight Forwarder will insure against loss – in practice this may not be the case as the Freight Forwarder may apply restrictions on payout. **As a consequence cargo insurance becomes a vital part of minimising the risk in international trade.**

UK businesses should also consider taking more control over the insurance to ensure that their requirements are met. UK insurance rates are also competitive in recognition of the UK having an established insurance market recognised worldwide.

3 | Managing the Risks

International Commercial Terms (INCOTERMS)

New Incoterms rules were launched in mid-September 2010 and have come into effect on 1 January 2011.

The Incoterms rules are an internally recognised standard and are used worldwide in international and domestic contracts for the sale of goods. First published in 1936 Incoterms rules provide internationally accepted definitions and rules of interpretation for most common commercial terms.

They help traders avoid costly misunderstandings by clarifying the tasks, costs and risks involved in the delivery of goods from sellers to buyer.

Delivery Options

Factors determining terms of delivery include:

- *The transportation route*
- *The nature of the goods*
- *The buyer, and their country*
- *The terms of payment*

Whilst first and foremost transport terms (Incoterms) will represent which party pays for which aspects of transportation, and where liability rests, they should also act as part of a risk reduction strategy for exporters.

Exporters should be careful about choosing Incoterms such as FOB (Free on Board) that on the face of it reduces their transportation costs. In all likelihood the costs saved may in any case reflect elsewhere in the contract terms. The importer would have the possibility of delaying sending a vessel to collect the goods, leaving the exporter with extra costs or delayed payment.

> To manage risk effectively, exporters should consider putting themselves
> in a position to control it. For exporters this may mean retaining
> control of the transport chain and the cargo insurance arrangements
> and selling on CIF terms (Cost, Insurance and Freight).

Insurance

From the perspective of a **UK exporter** there are benefits to arranging the insurance themselves:

- *Insurance rates in the UK are competitive.*
- *The exporter will have greater control over the risk as the UK insurance industry is highly regulated.*
- *The exporter could win business from competitors who do not offer insurance.*
- *Risks are avoided which may arise if the buyer is not adequately insured.*

From a UK importer perspective risks are minimised if they arrange insurance themselves. The importer will know how much they are paying and what is included.

The main types of cover available comprise:

- *Open cover for all journeys.*
- *Specific (voyage) policy, for one-off shipments.*
- *Seller's Interest Contingency Insurance – this provides back-up for physical loss or damage where the exporter has not arranged the cargo insurance.*

Standard marine/transport cover applies for general cargo, however, some goods will have special requirements such as Fine Arts and Precious Stones.

Risk Assessment and Ongoing Risk Management

To identify and mitigate against the risks in UK and International Trade, a risk assessment process should be established, reviewing all elements of the business from purchase to sales, ongoing operations and use of reliable third party suppliers.

All risks should be recorded, along with the mitigating actions that the business will take to manage these risks. A monetary value range should be marked against each risk in order to ensure that key risks are identified, and are subject to more frequent review by the business.

Key risks should be discussed at monthly board meetings of the business, with all risks subject to a quarterly or six monthly reviews.

Businesses should also adopt risk management practices through the likes of ISO 31000.

3 Managing the Risks

Summary

Processes Which Reduce Risk in International Trade

- *Use of legal firms to shape contracts*
- *Payment risk:*

  Use of banking instruments such as Bonds/Guarantees, Letters of Credit and Documentary Collections
- *Use of forward foreign exchange contracts to reduce currency risk*
- *Credit insurance*
- *Invoice Finance*
- *Certificate of Inspection to evidence quality and quantity*
- *Speak to specialists, such as UK Trade and Investment and your Freight Forwarder to understand what is required by way of import/export licences, and VAT/Duties*
- *Use of correct Incoterms which afford the seller control, for example CIF (Cost, Insurance and Freight)*
- *Ensure a strong Cargo Insurance policy is in place, covering risks to the business*

SECTION TWO

GETTING PAID

Contents

Documentary Collections and Letters of Credit are also key means of getting paid, with each of these covered in forthcoming sections

Managing the Risks

3

About This Section

Getting paid, and paid on time, is critical for any business to avoid:

▽ *Bad debts, impacting profitability and possibly the very viability of the business*

▽ *Effect on cash flow of late payment*

▽ *Costs to the business in chasing payment*

Getting paid for international transactions has additional complexities with an increasing range of factors that can influence the process, not least language, culture and distance.

This section shall review the methods of payment applicable to UK and International Trade. In addition to looking at the features of each settlement method, it shall also review how a business can mitigate against the risk of non-payment.

The aim of this section is to review the different methods of getting paid at a strategic business level. A lot of the topics detailed, such as Documentary Collections and Letters of Credit are explored in greater detail in separate sections.

Assessing the payment method will be a key aspect (if not the key aspect) of contract negotiations, and should be agreed at the same time as discussing price, currency of payment and transport terms.

Methods of Payment in UK and International Trade

Sometimes referred to as the Payment Risk Ladder, the following diagram illustrates the different methods of payment in UK and International Trade, and the levels of risk applicable for an importer and exporter (buyer and seller). In the case of Documentary Collections and Letters of Credit these apply particularly to international trade.

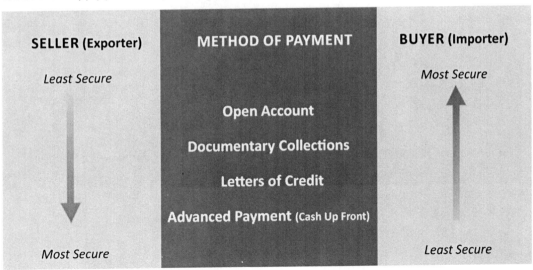

SELLER (Exporter)	METHOD OF PAYMENT	BUYER (Importer)
Least Secure		Most Secure
	Open Account	
	Documentary Collections	
	Letters of Credit	
	Advanced Payment (Cash Up Front)	
Most Secure		Least Secure

3 | Managing the Risks

Mitigating the Risk Impact

It is important to note that there are variations to the core payment methods described above, seeking to provide an alternative means of trading to buyer and seller. Whilst some represent compromise solutions they help to build trust, and from the perspective of the seller (exporter) provide them with the "security" they need to trade.

These are important and frequently applied methods of trading which businesses should consider using to protect their business. They provide an element of cover against the risk of non-payment, and also provide cash flow for the business

SELLER *(Exporter)*		BUYER *(Importer)*
Compromise Position	**Part Payment (Staged Payments)**	Compromise Position
Cash Up-Front	**Advanced Payment Guarantee**	Increased Security
Insuring against non-payment	**Credit Insurance**	Open account trade
Advancing Payment	**Invoice Finance**	Open account trade
Bank guarantee of payment	**Standby Letter of Credit**	Open account trade
Compromise Position	**Escrow Account**	Compromise Position

Section 2 - Getting Paid

Open Account

> **Goods sent (shipped) to the buyer – who takes the possession of the goods - often with a period before they have to pay**

> **Invoice is sent to the buyer requesting payment, often on agreed credit terms e.g. 30 to 90 days**

From the perspective of the seller (exporter), they have little or no control over this process and no guarantee of payment. They will have to part with the goods before they get paid and may have to arrange finance to fund supply and production, prior to receiving payment.

In addition to the risk of the buyer not paying, for some countries there may be the additional factor of country risk, whereby for political or economic reasons the country will block payment out of the country.

For the buyer (importer) this payment method is particularly advantageous in terms of both:

▼ *Security – they know the goods are in transit and quite often they will be able to view the goods before having to pay for them.*

▼ *Cash flow – they will not have to part with their money until a later stage. When credit terms apply this will further enhance the cash flow benefit.*

▼ *Costs – which will generally be lower than other payment methods, including a lower level of bank charges.*

Open account trading should only be considered when the seller is sufficiently confident that payment will be received. This confidence can be built on several factors

▪ *Having carried out detailed credit checks on the buyer, the business is satisfied as to their ability to pay, and pay on time*

▪ *Having verified the standing of the buyer with other companies who supply them*

▪ *When an established trading history is in place, including payments made on time*

▪ *Where credit insurance and/or invoice finance is in place through factoring or invoice discounting*

Buyers in the UK and Europe will expect open account, often with credit terms. If these are offered it is important that the confidence factors highlighted above apply; the seller should avoid simply 'giving in' when there is pressure to sell.

3 | Managing the Risks

Advantages and Disadvantages of Open Account Trading to the Seller

Advantages ✔	Disadvantages ✘
Boost competitiveness in UK and Export markets	**Exposed to the risk of non-payment**
Helps establish and maintain a successful trade relationship	**Further costs will be associated with chasing non-payment**
	Businesses will have to fund working capital

Advanced Payment (Cash Up-Front)

Payment is received from the buyer – prior to the goods being sent (shipped)

Goods are sent (shipped) to the buyer

This is the most secure method of trading for the seller (exporter), and consequently the least attractive for the buyer. Payment is received in full, prior to the goods being shipped.

This method of payment may be considered when:

- *The seller has limited confidence in the ability of the buyer to pay.*
- *The political or economic situation in a country may increase the risk of non-payment.*
- *The seller has a unique market leading product, effectively creating a 'seller's market.'*
- *The goods are being made to the buyer's particular specifications, resulting in a higher cost of manufacture.*
- *There are irregular customers who order goods and services from time to time.*

Advantages and Disadvantages of Cash Up-Front to the Seller

Advantages	Disadvantages
Payment is received before goods are shipped (sold)	**May lose customers to competitors through uncompetitive payment terms**
Eliminates risk of non-payment	**Potential customers may not consider your business if they are aware of the need for cash up-front payments**
Supports working capital through earlier receipt of funds	**In some instances, cash with order could make a business complacent relative, for example, to the need to compete on quality**
Preferable where 'customer specific' products are being produced – namely products that cannot be easily reassigned to another sales contract	

Open account and Advanced Payment are two extremes on the Payment Risk Ladder. In practice, neither may be suitable if buyer or seller feel they are giving over too much control. For businesses, however, there are other options to be considered:

PART PAYMENT (Staged Payments)

Escrow Accounts

Open account with Credit Insurance

Open account with Standby Letter of Credit

Open account with Invoice Finance

Advanced Payment Guarantees

Documentary Collections

Letters of Credit

Part Payment (Staged Payment)

An agreed percentage is paid by the buyer (e.g. 50%) up-front	The remainder (50%) is paid by the buyer after they have the received goods

3 | Managing the Risks

Part payment can take the form of an agreed percentage being paid in advance, in order:

- *To share the payment risk between buyer and seller*

- *To enable the seller to have access to some of the funds in order for them to commence and complete the sales order*

- *In preference to the more expensive and time consuming payment methods, such as Documentary Collections and Letters of Credit in particular, which also require use of banking facilities*

Part payment can, for example take the form of an agreed 50/50 payment, or staged payments during the life of the sales contract. The latter may arise if the contract involves staged deliveries, for example a construction project or manufacture of an asset.

Part payment will not remove payment risk, it will simply reduce the level of risk in monetary terms. For it to take place there needs to be some trust between buyer and seller, and a willingness to negotiate on trading terms.

Escrow Accounts

Monies are deposited by a buyer to an Escrow account with a third party (e.g. bank or legal firm). Buyer and seller complete an agreement document, determining what constitutes release of funds

Funds are released to the seller once they have met their obligations in accordance with the terms of the agreement document

Escrow accounts can apply where the seller has a concern that a buyer does not have the means to pay for goods and services, and the buyer in turn has concerns that a seller may not fulfil their obligations under the sales contract. Can apply for large purchases and for sale of a large asset.

Further details concerning Escrow accounts are provided in the section on **Business Finance.**

Open Account with Credit Insurance

Credit insurance is arranged with a credit insurer - **allowing for sales on open account terms** - **covers against the buyer not paying on time, or not paying at all**	**Open account trading terms apply with the overseas buyer, with the 'security' of insurance cover**

Trade credit insurance applies for short-term trade, generally of less than one year. Customer non-payment is referred to as commercial risk; an exporter can also protect themselves for political risks that may prevent or delay payment (e.g. government regulation, war).

Open Account with Invoice Finance

Open account terms are provided with a period of credit **Invoice issued to buyer**	**Seller receives finance for the invoice immediately, providing security of payment and cash to support working capital**

Invoice finance is an increasingly popular form of lending for banks and finance companies, representing a more efficient use of capital whereby lending is provided for a specific and 'ring-fenced' purpose.

For the seller, it provides both security of payment and cash flow, and can be undisclosed to the buyer through Confidential Invoice Discounting.

Further details concerning Invoice Finance can be found in the section on
Sources of Business Finance.

3 | Managing the Risks

Open Account with Standby Letter of Credit

Standby Letters of Credit issued by a bank (the buyer's bank) guaranteeing that a buyer's payment to a seller will be received on time and for the correct amount	Allows the buyer to trade on open account terms The seller has a bank guarantee that payment will be received

Standby Letters of Credit are increasing in popularity as buyer and seller recognise that this is an alternative **for both parties.**

Advanced Payment Guarantee

Guarantees issued by the seller's bank to the buyer enabling them to advance monies under the sales contract	Seller receives money from the buyer. Provides for security of payment and cash flow for the seller

Whilst Advanced Payment Guarantees may be more associated with longer term trade – where an advance may be an agreed percentage of the contract value – they can also be applied to all types of trade. From the sellers perspective they will require a strong product proposition to persuade the buyer to advance monies.

Further details on Advanced Payment Guarantees can be found in the section on **Business Finance.**

Feature: Negotiating Payment Terms

For businesses with a high quality and valuable product a key principle of trade is not to overcomplicate the settlement process. This applies equally to different business sectors for the sale of goods and services, and also where service contracts apply post sales.

The stronger the product offering, potentially, the stronger the negotiating position; businesses should not be afraid to negotiate from a start position of cash up-front – not just because of the increased security and improved cash flow it provides but also because it makes good commercial sense.

> **Cash-up front supports a principle used widely in the consumer market, namely that an individual (buyer) should pay for goods and services prior to purchasing them.**

Cash up-front need not always mean the buyer having to pay 100% of the value of the sale contract on order. There are variables, for example, 50% on order and 50% on goods dispatch, or alternatively staged payments depending on the delivery cycle.

These principles should certainly apply for new customers and also, in some cases, for existing customers, especially as the customer will already have a positive experience of having received a quality product and quality service.

For export sales, especially outside of Europe, there may be occasions when Export Letters of Credit need to apply, as the foreign buyer will understandably have less knowledge of the seller and may want the security of a Letter of Credit before parting with their money.

3 | Managing the Risks

SECTION THREE

CURRENCY RISK MANAGEMENT

Contents

3 | Managing the Risks

About This Section

This section will look at one of the key risks that businesses face when trading overseas –

Currency Risk

Currency Risk <u>always</u> arises in international trade, even for exports that are invoiced in sterling, where the risk is transferred to the overseas customer who may adjust their purchasing terms accordingly.

The price of essential commodities, such as oil and raw materials used in the business are also impacted by foreign currency exchange movements.

To help provide background, this section outlines some of the history and thinking behind exchange rates and how these factors now impact in today's world.

Most importantly, the means of identifying and minimising the risks of foreign currency exchange movements are highlighted and discussed.

Foreign currencies: the history, theory and practice

The history of how foreign currencies have developed is one of regular change - the 20th century for example has seen periods of fixed and floating exchange rates ending with the introduction of the Euro and rise of growth economies, such as China and India.

17th-19th Century
UK Pound, French Franc and Dutch Guilder used for international trade, along with US Dollar, Russian Ruble and German Reichmark. Money in these times consisted of precious metals and was not printed on notes.

Late 19th and early 20th Century
In 1873 the USA passed the Gold Standard Act. The international value of a currency was linked to a weight of gold; its rate was fixed, reducing the risk of trading with other currencies.

Bretton Woods, 1944
Each country from the 44 Allied nations were to maintain the exchange rate of their country within a fixed value – plus or minus 1% - in terms of gold and the ability of a new International Monetary Fund (IMF) to bridge temporary imbalances of payments. It was so named Bretton Woods after the location where nations met – near Mt Washington in New Hampshire, America.

The US Dollar was at the anchor of the system, with the US guaranteeing other central banks that they could sell their US Dollar reserves at a fixed rate for gold. The IMF and the International Bank for Reconstruction and Development – now the World Bank – were also established at this time.

3 | Managing the Risks

The IMF aims to preserve economic stability and to tackle – or ideally prevent – financial crisis. Over time its focus has switched to the developing world. The IMF is funded by a charge, known as a "quota" paid by member nations. The quota is based on a country's wealth and determines its voting power within the organisation. Those making higher contributions have greater voting rights. The IMF acts as a lender of last resort, allocating its foreign exchange reserves for short periods to any member in difficulties.

The World Bank was set up to drive post-war recovery. Now it is the world's leading development organisation, working for growth and poverty reduction. Owned by the governments of its member states the Bank channels loans and grants and advises low and middle-income countries.

The IMF and World Bank established the Poverty Reduction and Growth Facility in 1999 – aimed at making poverty reduction efforts a key and more explicit element of a renewed growth-orientated economic strategy.

Early to mid 1970's

Following strains within the fixed exchange rate system - which over the years had resulted in currency devaluations – a general revaluation of major currencies took place allowing 2.25% devaluations from the agreed exchange rate.

By 1976, however, all the major currencies were floating.

This has led to decades of deregulation of currency markets; instability has arisen, for example, in the Asian financial crisis of 1997-98.

The Euro

In some respects the breakdown of Bretton Woods led to European countries considering closer monetary co-operation, which ultimately led to the creation of the Euro in 1999.

The Euro (€) is the official currency of the European Union, currently in use in 17 of the member states. The states known as the Eurozone are:

Austria	*Belgium*	*Cyprus*	*Estonia*	*Finland*
France	*Germany*	*Greece*	*Ireland*	*Italy*
Luxembourg	*Malta*	*The Netherlands*	*Portugal*	*Slovakia*
Slovenia	*Spain*			

Section 3 - Currency Risk Management

The Euro is managed by the independent based European Central Bank (ECB) which has sole authority to set monetary policy. A key element that European Union member states should adhere to relates to:

- *an annual budget deficit no higher than 3% of Gross Domestic Product – GDP (comprising the total of all public budgets)*
- *a national debt lower than 60% of GDP or approaching that value*

Outside the Eurozone, other countries, which do not belong to the EU, have currencies that are directly pegged to the Euro, including countries with close trading links in mainland Africa.

Benefits of the Euro include:

- ▼ **Transaction Costs.** *There is no longer a cost involved in changing currencies, benefitting tourists and firms who trade in the Euro area.*

- ▼ **Price Transparency.** *It is easier to compare price in the different European countries, as they are all in Euros. This should increase competition and boost trade.*

- ▼ **Eliminating Exchange Rate uncertainty** *– where movements in exchange rate can destroy the profitability of exports.*

- ▼ **Inward Investment.** *May increase from outside the European Union (EU) as firms take advantage of lower transaction costs within the EU area.*

Today - 2010

The US Dollar remains the world's primary reserve currency, accounting for 64% of the reserve currency held by governments and central banks (as at 2008). The Euro is, however, increasing as a reserve currency accounting for 26%.

Some nations such as Russia and China, the Gulf Co-operation Council have called for a new reserve currency, or a basket of currencies, to replace the Dollar as the reserve currency.

The UK Pound Sterling operates as a floating exchange rate.

In recent times, the closest the UK came to a fixed exchange rate environment was in 1990-1992 during its membership of the European Exchange Rate Mechanism (in place prior to the Euro). In a period of recession, and to try to support the pound, interest rates rose from 10% up to 15%. Billions of pounds were spent by the Bank of England in buying up the falling pound. These measures, however, failed to prevent the pound falling lower than its minimum level and the UK subsequently withdrew from the Exchange Rate mechanism.

3 | Managing the Risks

The foreign exchange 'market'

The foreign exchange market – sometimes known as forex, FX or currency market – operates worldwide between two counterparties, for the trading of currencies. Traders include banks, brokers, corporations, governments and other financial institutions. Notwithstanding that trading is sometimes speculative, the true purpose of the foreign exchange market is to assist international trade and investment, allowing businesses to convert from one currency to another.

There is no centralised exchange – London is the largest trading centre for foreign exchange, representing 34% of total, New York and Tokyo are the next largest accounting for 16% and 6% respectively. London is well positioned in the centre of the world's time zones, trade can take place with Europe during the day, and also with Asia and the USA at the beginning and end of each day. The foreign exchange markets trade 24 hours a day, except weekends. Most markets operate between the hours of 8am and 4pm daily.

Settlements between the parties will be two-way, as this involves the exchange of one currency to another. The parties are likely to mark internal trading limits with which they can trade with one another. Settlement systems have become more sophisticated over time; settlements can take place almost immediately following trade. More recently since 2002 an increasing number of settlements are taking place through a system called **Continuous Link Settlement (CLS)**.

CLS is a process by which the world's largest banks manage settlement of foreign exchange themselves. As of February 2009 there are 62 settlement members, as well as 4,576 Third Party participants (comprising 41 banks). Settling in 17 major currencies, settlement risk is eliminated with finality, using a combination of central bank funds and payment netting between members. The CLS settlement bank is regulated by the Federal Board of New York.

The Foreign Exchange Spot Market

The Spot market trades one currency against another within two days of agreeing the trade. The price is based on the current exchange rate – the value of one currency relative to the other.

One party (for example a Bank) will provide the other party with either a:

- **Bid price** – price to buy
- **Ask or Offer price** – price to sell

There will be a spread (difference) between the bid/offer prices being the price at which the bank is quoting for the trade.

The sell price is displayed on the left side of the exchange rate and is the price at which you can sell the base currency. For example if the £/€ exchange rate quotes 1.1500/03 you can sell 1 Pound at a price of €1.15

The buy price is displayed on the right side of an exchange rate and is the price at which you can buy the base currency. For example if the £/€ rate quotes 1.1500.03 you can buy 1 Pound at a price of €1.1503

Additionally Banks when providing quotes to customers may apply an additional spread.

Forward Foreign Exchange Market

Currencies can be bought or sold on a forward basis, for settlement at a specific future date. The terms of the transaction are agreed up front, with the exchange rate fixed.

The forward rate is calculated by adjusting the current market rate (the spot rate) with "forward points." These forward points take into account the difference in interest rates between the two currencies and the time to maturity.

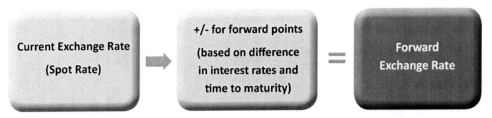

Factors influencing exchange rate movements

Exchange rates play a vital role in a country's level of trade.

▽ *A strong exchange rate results in a country's exports becoming more expensive, and imports cheaper.*

▽ *A weak exchange rate makes exports cheaper, and imports more expensive.*
A weak currency corresponds to a falling exchange rate.

Factors Affecting Exchange Rates

Economic Factors

▽ **Differentials in Interest Rates**
If interest rates are higher than other countries this will tend to attract money into a country, with the value of the currency rising. The opposite will be the case for lower interest rates, which tend to make the exchange rate weaker.

▽ **Differentials in Inflation Rates**
A currency is likely to lose value (weaken) if there is a high level of inflation, or if inflation levels are perceived to be rising. Inflation erodes purchasing power – the number of goods and services that can be purchased with a unit of currency – reducing demand for the currency.

▽ **Balance of Trade Levels** *(also known as current account deficits and surpluses)*
The current account is the balance of trade between a country and its trading partners, reflecting demand for goods and services. Surpluses and deficits in trade of goods and services reflect the competitiveness of a nation's economy – trade deficits for example may have a negative impact, weakening a nation's currency.

▽ **Government Debt** *(to pay for public services and government funding)*
The foreign exchange market usually reacts negatively to increasing government debt, weakening the currency. When debt levels reduce the currency will usually strengthen.

3 — Managing the Risks

Economic Growth

Economic reports will play a factor in the value of a currency. Positive reports boost the value of a currency, as foreign investors seek to invest their money in stable countries with strong economic performance. Reports include:

- *Gross Domestic Product (GDP). GDP is a measure of a country's overall economic output, representing the market value of all final goods and services made within the country*
- *Employment levels*
- *The level and trend in retail sales*

Political Factors

- *Exchange rates will be influenced by political factors. Political instability can cause a loss of confidence in a currency and a movement of funds to more stable political environments.*
- *Central bank intervention and/or introduction of exchange control will have an impact on an exchange rate.*

Market Psychology

- *Unsettling international events can lead to what is termed a 'flight to quality' with investors seeking a safe haven, for example the Swiss Franc.*
- *Speculation can play an important part in exchange rate movements. Speculators anticipate the events before the actual event and position themselves accordingly in order to take advantage.*

The exchange rate world today

Currencies of the World

Currencies can be distinguished by what are termed a hard currency or soft currency.

A hard currency refers to a globally traded currency that can serve as a reliable and stable store of value, in which investors have confidence. Factors contributing to a hard currency can include political stability, consistent monetary policies and backing of reserves.

A soft currency indicates a type of currency whose value may depreciate rapidly or that is difficult to convert into other currencies. It is generally less desirable than a hard currency. Businesses in countries with soft currencies often prefer to take hard currency in exchange for goods and services.

There is no definitive list of hard currencies, although it can be said to include:

US Dollar	*Euro*	*Swiss Franc*
UK Pound Sterling	*Norwegian Kroner*	*Swedish Krona*
Canadian Dollar	*Japanese Yen*	*Australian Dollar*

Dealing with currencies in the business world

How businesses should approach the world of foreign exchange

The impact of foreign exchange rates in international trade can frequently be underestimated. Exchange rate risk is clearer where businesses invoice sales or settle purchases in a foreign currency. It does, however, still impact for imports and exports settled in sterling and directly and indirectly affects all businesses in the price of commodities and materials used in the course of business.

HINTS and TIPS

Although, in theory no direct exchange risk is incurred for imports and exports settled in sterling, the impact of transferring this risk to the foreign supplier or customer must be considered carefully. The business counterparty may want to ensure they are 'recompensed' from both a business perspective and they will want to ensure that exchange rate fluctuations are factored into contract pricing, plus an additional margin to cover uncertainty.

Just as importantly the UK business will not have such a clear visibility of what the exchange rate impact is – for example, if a UK exporter selling into Europe in sterling receives the same price for their goods as two years before, it will be the EUROPEAN CUSTOMER benefitting from the 25% decline in the value of sterling. In relative terms they will be paying 25% less than before!

Invoicing in foreign currency

For a business, there are factors to be considered when invoicing in foreign currency. These can be summarised by looking at the advantages and disadvantages that arise:

Advantages	Disadvantages
It is likely to make the goods and services more attractive to the foreign customer and hence increase the chances of securing the sale	**A business will have to manage the foreign currency exchange risk**
the foreign customer will be able to compare the price against local competitors, and in the case of the Euro: European competitors	**If the payment is not made on time this increases the uncertainty around exchange rate movements, especially if a fixed forward exchange contract has been taken out**
the foreign customer will not have to carry the exchange risk	**When planning and forecasting, fluctuating exchange rates make accurate forecasting more difficult**
If a business also has payments in the same currency it may be possible to cover exchange rate movements by matching currency receipts against currency payments	
If a business has a need to borrow, it may be possible to take out a loan in the foreign currency, in order for the currency receivables to repay the borrowing	
For some countries it avoids potential difficulties which may arise when transferring sterling from the country to the UK	

Identifying the risks from foreign exchange movements

The risk of foreign exchange exposure is the possibility that a firm will gain or lose because of changes in exchange rates. In every international transaction, at least one of the parties (buyer or seller) is exposed to the risk of loss due to fluctuations in exchange rates. A bad experience for either party may impact future relations, and the willingness to undertake future business.

There are three types of exchange exposures:

1. **Transaction Risk.** *A risk that exchange rates will change after a business has agreed a transaction,* **but** *before it is completed and paid.* **Exchange rate movements here will affect actual cash flows and the profitability of the business.**

For example, if a UK exporter was selling $300,000 of goods to the United States:

- An exchange rate of US$1.50/£1 may apply at the time of sale, resulting in the exporter anticipating a receipt equivalent to £200,000
- Should the exchange rate move to US$1.70/£1 at the time of actual payment, this will reduce to £176,470
- Leaving the exporter receiving **£23,530** less than expected

2. **Translation Risk.** More of an accounting risk, but important nonetheless. This risk is proportional to the amount of **assets** held in foreign currencies.

   A UK business may, for example, own a property in the United States to manufacture goods for the US market. If the property is valued at $500,000 then they record the equivalent sterling figure in their balance sheet:

   - At an exchange rate of US$1.40/£1 this would equate to £357,142
   - At an exchange rate of US$1.60/£1 this would equate to £312,500
   - Leaving the UK business with a translation loss of **£44,642** in the value on their balance sheet

3. **Economic Exposure.** The impact of changes in exchange rate on the value of cash expected from a foreign investment project.

Summary

How Exposed Is Your Business?

▼ Estimate the total value of your business that is exposed to foreign exchange risk, for example:

- **Imports**
- **Exports**
- **Assets overseas or assets valued in a foreign currency**
- **Overseas dividends**
- **Settlements to overseas agents or distributors**

▼ Calculate what would happen to profitability when there are changes in respective exchange rates

▼ Also, consider the timing of payables and receivables, and estimate the potential impact of exchange rate fluctuations on the profitability of your business, over specific periods, such as 30 to 90 day periods

▼ Remember that the exchange risk can arise from the period your business calculates a sterling equivalent as part of contract pricing. This may, for example, be prior to agreeing a contract with your supplier or customer

3 | Managing the Risks

Minimising risks from foreign exchange movements

All businesses should seek to minimise risk from foreign exchange movements.

They are in business to make – and protect – a profit from their products and services, and should avoid carrying unnecessary risk from foreign exchange.

A business should aim to keep it simple with respect to how it minimises risk, and not overcomplicate the solution. A useful way of viewing this is to consider what you would do if it were your own personal money.

In order to minimise the exchange risk there are a number of options available, illustrated as follows:

Invoice in your local currency

Matching currency payments and receipts

Settling the currency exposure early

Buying or selling the currency forward

Borrowing in foreign currency

Undertaking a currency option (option to buy to sell)

Sharing the exchange risk with your supplier/customer

Section 3 - Currency Risk Management

Invoice/Settle in Your Local Currency

From the point of view of the UK business, this transfers the exchange risk to the foreign counterparty. In terms of simplicity, it may have its attractions; the counterparty, however, may not be happy with such an arrangement and in the long run the UK business may lose control over pricing, as they lose visibility over exchange rates.

The advantages and disadvantages of currency invoicing are discussed earlier in this section.

Matching Currency Payables and Receivables

This is only possible if a business has both payments and receipts in the same currency. Even then, this may not result in an equal match and there may be residue sums of foreign exchange that require to be managed. Transactions will be settled over an account denominated in the particular foreign currency, for example, Euros or US Dollars. Such accounts can be domiciled with either a bank in the UK or a bank abroad in the particular country.

Most UK banks will provide foreign currency accounts in all the world's major currencies; it may become an issue for 'soft currencies' – although certain banks with a more global presence may be able to provide.

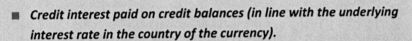

A UK company should expect to receive a similar service on their foreign currency account as they would from their main UK sterling account, including:

- *Credit interest paid on credit balances (in line with the underlying interest rate in the country of the currency).*

- *No fees for operating the account. Charges applied based on the underlying transaction.*

- *On-line access preferably real-time balance and transaction information.*

- *Available in a wide range of currencies.*

- *Transactions credited/debited on day of value, with no loss of float or interest for the customer.*

If these are not standard features of a foreign currency account, do challenge the bank to establish if they are available.

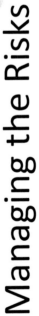

3 | Managing the Risks

A foreign currency account with a bank abroad can arise where a business has a physical presence overseas to sell, distribute or manufacture. It can also apply if there are large volumes of transactions in a particular country, although difficulties may arise as local legislation makes it more difficult to open an account without a presence in the country (what is termed a non-resident account).

The choice of bank abroad may depend on the nature of business. The first step can be to approach your UK bank to establish if they have offices in the country concerned and if so, the nature of business they undertake.

-If the business undertaken abroad is to settle lower volume and low value, regular expense items then it may be possible to use the foreign branch of a UK bank, or a local 'partner' of the UK bank.

-If the business is higher volume and needs more of a local presence, for example, to pay in or draw cash, it will be necessary to explore more closely what the UK bank and/its local foreign partner bank can provide. It may be appropriate for the business needs, or there may be a need to look at another local bank with a specific presence in the locality.

Whilst there may be advantages to using the UK bank or its partner – such as in receiving account information and transferring/receiving funds - these will need to be measured against the ease of doing business locally.

Settling the Currency Exposure Early

From a cash flow perspective, for the exporter it will be advantageous if the buyer of the goods and services settles early, or better still up-front. This will add benefit in that it reduces or removes the period in which the business is exposed to currency movements.

The customer or supplier may not be prepared to settle early, unless the overall contract terms are structured in such a way that it is beneficial for them to do so. The topic of contract pricing and varying the terms of trade is discussed in further detail in other sections.

Buying or Settling the Foreign Currency Forward

One of the most common methods of minimising, hedging against foreign exchange risk, is through what is termed a forward foreign exchange contract, with a bank or provider of foreign exchange services.

A forward contract is where a business agrees to purchase or sell a fixed amount of foreign currency, at a **fixed exchange rate** on an **agreed future date**. Ideally, the date will align with a scheduled payment the business is due to make to a supplier OR due to receive from a customer.

Features and benefits of a forward contract are

- A business is protected against adverse movements in the exchange rate.

- A business will know how much sterling they are due to pay, or due to receive. This provides some certainty of cash flow around future foreign currency payables or receivables.

- The amount and term are set by the business.

- No monies change hands with the bank until the forward contract matures.

- The forward exchange rate is calculated by the bank – calculated by adjusting the current market rate (the spot rate) for "forward points", which takes into account the difference in interest rates between the two currencies and the time to maturity.

- Forward contracts can be extended in certain circumstances. If there is a delay in settlement, the forward contract can be extended avoiding the need to close out. From a bank perspective this involves:

  -calculating if the old contract has a positive or negative value, compared to the prevailing market rate.

  -adjusting the contract exchange rate up or down to reflect the changed value.

  -also adjusting the contract rate up or down to reflect the new forward margin, from the current delivery date to the new delivery date.

- There should be no fees for setting up a forward contract.

- Forward contracts are not available for speculative purposes; they are used for genuine trading transactions.

- The bank may only agree the forward contract if the business has a positive credit rating, or is able to provide security.

From a business perspective, once the forward contact is agreed a business has to go through with completion, regardless of whether the trade transaction completes. Because the rate is fixed, a business cannot benefit from any favourable movement in the exchange rate.

Fixed and Option Forward Contracts

A fixed forward contract is where the maturity date is set for a specific future date e.g. 90 days forward.

Option forward contracts are a useful alternative whereby the maturity date is set between a range of dates, to cover against the eventuality of early or late payment. The rate received from the bank will be slightly less competitive, reflecting the date options set.

3 **Managing the Risks**

Borrowing in Foreign Currency

This method of mitigating foreign exchange risk works well when the currency the exporter is due to receive **are the funds that are used to repay a currency loan**. The currency received then in itself becomes a natural hedge against currency exposure – with the receipts effectively repaying the borrowing.

Most UK banks will offer currency loans in much the same way as is available for sterling loans. They will discourage currency loans if the exporter does not have receipts in currency to repay the borrowing.

Undertaking a Currency Option (Option to Buy or Sell)

A currency option DIFFERS from a forward contract in that the customer does NOT need to take up the option at maturity. It is effectively an option to purchase, which, in exchange, the customer has to pay an up-front premium for the option.

Currency options work well in situations where the customer is not sure whether the currency exposure will arise, for example, in circumstances where they are tendering for a sales contract. It can also apply where there is a lot of uncertainty about the amount and dates when currency will be received e.g. in the case of high value and longer term contracts.

It is in these instances that a currency option is most appropriate, not as a means of speculation, or in circumstances when more conventional means of managing currency exposure are available.

A key point concerning currency options is that it may only be cost effective for banks to provide currency options for higher value amounts, for example, in excess of £200,000 currency equivalent. Hence availability may, in some cases, be impacted.

Sharing the Exchange Risk with the Customer/Supplier

This can arise, although in some instances it may be difficult to manage and requires a good degree of trust between both parties – in order to agree the exchange rate at the time of contract, to date of payment. Any exchange gain should be shared, in much the same way as a loss is shared.

Reducing foreign exchange risk: specific options for specific circumstances

Customer Circumstance	Options for Reducing Foreign Exchange Risk
An importer and exporter of goods and services from Europe – all European business settled in Euros	*Matching of Euro payables and receivables to the optimum level possible. Euros are settled over a Euro account with a bank in the UK*
An exporter whose main sales are in Europe – invoiced in Euros – who also requires a borrowing facility with a Bank	*If the income from the sales is used to repay the borrowing, then a loan can be taken out in Euros. Foreign exchange exposure is reduced as Euro sales proceeds are used to repay the principal and interest*
An importer or exporter entering into a contract in US Dollars, where there is 'certainty' around date of settlement	*A fixed forward foreign exchange contract with maturity at a specific future date e.g. 90 days from now*
An exporter invoicing in US Dollars with uncertainty as to when they receive payment	*An option forward contract which still has to be settled, but with flexibility as to the date of 'take up,' for example with a date option between 70-110 days*
A regular importer bringing goods in from the Far East, settling in US Dollars. Regular suppliers used, with monthly order volumes dependent on UK sales	*To 'lock into' profit margins for the year, the importer may wish to set an annual budget rate, covering the one whole year, with monthly settlements based on an estimate of Dollar purchases* *This is achieved by forward contracts covering a 12 month period, with monthly settlements*
A UK company is tendering for a large contract overseas. It has to base its contract pricing on the prevailing exchange rate	*In the event of winning the tender the UK business may want to protect the current exchange rate. This can be done through a currency option, which the business will not be obliged to take up on maturity, if it does not win the contract*

Managing the Risks

3

Topic refresher: **top learning points**

▽ *Never take risks when dealing with currencies, manage the risk*

▽ *Understand when exchange risk arises and understand the impact on your customer or supplier when it is you that are dealing in sterling (in these circumstances they have the risk).*

▽ *Deal in hard currencies*

▽ *Do not complicate currency risk management*

▽ *Seek feedback and information from your bank or foreign exchange provider; they are there to help.*

Section 3 – Currency Risk Management

SECTION FOUR

CREDIT TERMS

Contents

3 | Managing the Risks

About This Section

This section shall review processes that a business should consider:

▼ *Prior to offering credit terms to a customer*

▼ *After credit terms have been provided*

▼ *Managing on-going customer relationships*

Specific focus shall be provided on credit referencing and credit insurance – two key tools available to businesses that help reduce payment risk and EQUALLY provide a business with the confidence and opportunity to generate sales.

A customer relationship, like any relationship, needs to be managed, none more so that when credit is provided. If a business is parting with goods and services prior to payment, they have even more of a reason to ensure they get paid on the due date.

The principles contained in this section apply equally to UK and International trade, and indeed none more so when the customer is based overseas – distance and language should not be barriers to implementing good business practice. It is also important to note that in some countries overseas governments may prioritise whom they pay first in terms of how critical the supplier is to the process/operation of the country itself. Payment for essential commodities and services may as a result get paid first.

Considering Credit Terms

The provision of credit is something that a customer must earn, **not** be given.

▪ *It can be built up in trust after a good payment history.*

▪ *It should be part of the price and sales negotiation; does credit come at a higher price? (The reverse of early payment discount).*

▪ *If the new business is secured through proactive activity from the sales team and has been a targeted account, then a credit limit is more likely to be offered.*

Before providing credit terms there are a number of stages that a business must consider:

▪ *Know the customer you are dealing with. Before doing anything else get to know the customer yourself: visit their premises, meet their people.*

▪ *Be clear on who in the business can offer credit terms – with agreed processes prior to credit being granted. Care must be taken to ensure it is tightly controlled*

▪ *The means that can be employed to credit check the customer:*
   Checking with other suppliers in the same business sector
   Bank status enquiries
   Using a Credit Reference Agency

3 | Managing the Risks

1. *Other suppliers in your sector can be a good source of information; 'word of mouth' is often based on practical experience, not theory. Working with other companies in the sector can have wider benefits in terms of ongoing co-operation. If required, do not be afraid to ask the customer for details of their other suppliers, in order that you can contact these suppliers.*

   Such references can also focus on the buyer's ability to trade fairly and honestly and not just their payment history.

2. *Bank status enquiries are a means of obtaining a view from the customer's bank. The question is very specific but can serve a purpose e.g. 'is the customer good for £xxxx?'*

   A charge of £30-£50 will be payable through the banking system, with the bank likely to respond in several ways, for example:

The customer is considered good for your enquiry
The customer has a satisfactory record with us of meeting commitments, and should be good for your enquiry
While the proposed commitment appears high we do not consider that it would be undertaken if the customer could not foresee the obligation being met
The proposed commitment appears to be onerous in the context of the customer's known obligations
The customer is not considered good for your enquiry at this time
Unable to reply – insufficient information held

   Where the bank response is not definitive, it may be necessary for a business to exercise an element of caution.

3. *Credit referencing should be considered for a variety of reasons, not least if the business is looking to maintain long term customer relationships, and managing customer payment performance.*

Managing Credit Terms

A business must have a strong credit control policy for existing, as well as new customers

Once credit is provided the emphasis moves to managing credit terms.

Best Practice in Invoicing

- Credit levels should be maintained at the agreed terms. If any extension is made to amount or debtor days granted, this should be part of the same rigorous checks that would take place when credit is originally granted.

- Ask the customer what **they want** included in the invoice. Inclusion of sales/procurement references may, for example, make it easier for larger companies (with many invoices) to identify the sale and allocate payment.

- Issue invoices promptly – if all parts of a business are operating closely together, an invoice can be issued quickly after an order has been placed/work has been completed.

Overdue Debtors

- Any delay in payment, or rejected payment (e.g. unpaid cheque) should immediately be referred to management.

- Management should review all overdue debtors e.g. on a weekly basis:

    The employee in the business who knows the customer best should contact the customer to establish what the issues are, which are resulting in payment delays.

    The credit limit applied to the customer should be reviewed at the same time, to avoid any possible build-up of further outstanding sums.

- Debtor due lists should be an agenda item at board meetings, along with a view of the overall debtor profile (including quality of ledger, aged debtors etc).

- Debtor figures must include **all** sums due from the customer, **not** just sales where an invoice has been raised – otherwise a misleading figure could be quoted for amounts due.

Customer Management

A business gets paid better when building customer relationships

- All parts of a business can be part of an on-going customer management programme – from Director to Sales, to the Credit Controller, to Purchasing. All may be in a position to use their relationship positively.

- A business should clearly identify its key customers by profitability and, if applicable, by volume. A key client management programme should be considered identifying ways in which value can be added to the relationship. Customer contact should take place on a regular basis.

- Try to avoid being over reliant on a couple of customers or one or two export markets.

3 | Managing the Risks

- A business may in certain circumstances want to request Management Accounts from their customer to establish an updated financial position. These Accounts can also be sent to the Credit Reference Agency for them to include in their ratings analysis.

- Customer satisfaction surveys should be carried out to ensure that the customer is happy with the goods and services. If the customer is happy this may make it harder for them to argue that late payment is a result of dissatisfaction.

Setting Credit Limits

- Businesses should **not** operate an 'across the board' credit policy, as not all their customers will be the same.

- Set individual credit limits for each customer, and stick to these limits.

- Grade new customers in new markets and countries, by risk level.

- The terms of trade **must** be agreed when the order is first placed.

Use of Credit References in Business

The use of credit referencing by businesses is becoming an increasing feature. At its most basic but vital level, credit references are used to check out new customers prior to extending periods of credit.

There are, however, additional features that can be used to support businesses, to ENSURE that the scale of information available becomes a key means of managing new and existing customers.

The Scope of Credit Referencing Services

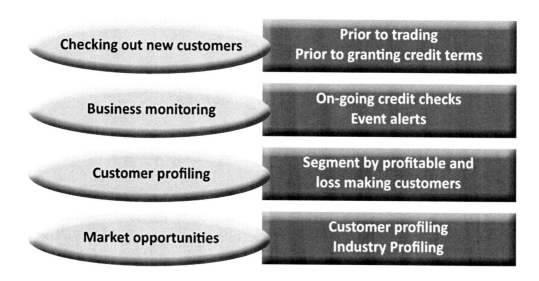

Checking out new customers	Prior to trading / Prior to granting credit terms
Business monitoring	On-going credit checks / Event alerts
Customer profiling	Segment by profitable and loss making customers
Market opportunities	Customer profiling / Industry Profiling

Section 4 - Credit Terms

The Process of Credit Checking

A single bad debt is likely to considerably outweigh the cost of credit checking

Not to mention the cost of chasing late payment, and impact on cash flow

At a very minimum, credit checks should be undertaken on all new customers, especially:

- *When no previous trading history exists.*
- *When credit terms are provided.*

There may be some exceptions to this rule, such as when selling to a multi-national business whose ability to pay will not be in doubt.

Credit checks can still be important when cash-up front is received; difficulties in a customer's credit position will, for example, provide caution in future business dealings.

Whilst cost can be a factor for a business in determining the level of customer data, good practice should prevail and ideally the following information should be obtained to a greater or lesser degree for both new customers and existing customers at regular intervals, and most certainly if order values increase.

Data outputs from a credit reference agency can include

▼ *Company identification*

 -confirm they exist

▼ *Credit status rating; based on factors such as*

 -how new or old the business is

 -the financial strength of the company (including financial ratios)

 -whether any adverse data is recorded, for example, winding up orders

 The outputs of these factors should be provided as well as the rating

▼ *The credit limit that can be applied e.g. the amount of open credit that can be offered*

▼ *Corporate 'Trees, 'including where business is linked by common ownership*

▼ *Payment history**

 - Whether the business has paid on time

 - What the payment trend is

 -How it compares with the average for the industry sector

Managing the Risks

3

▽ **Company officer information: this would detail any adverse information on the likes of Directors and Company Secretary**

▽ **Event alerts, whereby advices are received as business circumstances change**

  -A winding up order is made

  -Increase or decrease in credit lines

  - Change in company director

The extent to which information is available can vary. Details of payment history, for example, may not always be available as this relies on a business providing the information to data companies. Should the information not be available this may in itself inform potential suppliers carrying out the credit check to exercise caution before offering credit.

Where Data Is Drawn From

Data is primarily drawn from public records, such as Companies House, where statutory financial accounts are filed.

Additional data, such as payment history, is collected by data companies, whose purpose is to collect data of this type, working in co-operation with the Credit Reference Agencies. Businesses may be keen to provide additional information, highlighting that there are a good payer will, for example, present them in a good light with customers, suppliers and banks.

Based on this information it will be possible for businesses to:

  ▪ *Prioritise management time on the most important customers*

  ▪ *Improve customer relationships*

  ▪ *Improve cash flow and mitigate against bad debts*

  ▪ *Ultimately to reduce days sales outstanding*

Customer Profiling

Credit referencing can also be used to profile and manage the customer base of a business. This can be achieved by the business providing an electronic file (in different formats) to the credit reference agency, containing details of the accounts receivable, sales ledger and payment history.

The agency will integrate this data with their database to provide monitoring outputs such as:

  ▪ *Identifying the most important customers and how quickly they pay*

  ▪ *Profile the 'best' and 'worst' payers*

  ▪ *How fast customers pay other businesses compared to your business*

  ▪ *Identify customers who pose a risk*

  ▪ *Highlight payment patterns across specific industries*

Marketing and Sales Opportunities

Some credit reference agencies will also maintain consumer and business 'preference' databases e.g. buying habits – either through direct ownership or partnerships with market intelligence companies.

By utilising these databases, and linking them to the business accounts receivables it will be possible for agencies to identify creditworthy businesses and consumers most likely to respond to marketing campaigns and new offers - from within and outwith the customer base of the business, and applicable to the UK and overseas markets

This could improve business focus and maximise marketing efforts by only targeting 'creditworthy' customers likely to use goods and services.

Information on Overseas Customers

The principle and use of information should apply equally for customers based overseas as much, if not more so, than for UK customers. On occasions, the level of information available may be variable.

- *For large public companies based overseas, it should be readily available.*
- *For private customers it may be obtained through links the UK credit reference agency have with overseas agencies, or their own offices in for example the USA or some European countries.*

* In some cases, however, it may be necessary to use the services of an overseas agency directly to obtain key local information. This may arise for example for a large order to an overseas customer who is not known to your business.

Reducing the Risk of Non-Payment

Other sections have concentrated on the payment available, and ways of reducing risk when credit terms are offered. These include managing credit terms by use of:

- *Staged Payments*
- *Bonds and Guarantees*
- *Letters of Credit*
- *Documentary Collections (use of Avalised Bills of Exchange)*
- *Invoice Finance*
- *Escrow Accounts*
- *Retention of Title Clauses*

A further popular means of reducing risk is through **Credit Insurance**.

3 | Managing the Risks

Summary: consequences of not getting paid

To emphasise why it is so important to invest time and research into getting paid, the following illustrates the consequences to a business of not getting paid - and paid on time.

- **Problems in cash flow**

  A business may find it difficult to pay their debts, purchase essential materials and even pay staff wages

- **Self-financing**

  A business may have to finance the loss or late payment of a debt from greatly increased turnover.

- **Reduced competiveness**

  A business suffering from bad debts may have no choice but to reduce the amount of credit they offer, making them less competitive.

- **Impact on supplier relationships**

  If a business in turn takes longer to pay suppliers, this impacts their own credit standing with existing and future suppliers, damaging relationships.

- **Collection and legal costs**

  If a business decides to take action to recover debts, this can often result in collection fees or solicitor fees.

Credit insurance - in the UK and abroad

Credit insurance can apply equally to UK businesses selling domestically and abroad (known as export credit insurance).

Both are important in their own right, as a business looks to trade with minimum credit risk.

1. **UK** – *also known as home trade/domestic insurance. Whilst UK sales are perhaps more of a known quantity, they still may require credit risk cover - the risk of not getting paid. Cover may also be more widely available as it is easier for UK insurers to gain access to accurate company information.*

2. **Export Credit Insurance** – *covering export markets. Availability of cover may depend on the country involved, where access to accurate company information may be harder to obtain and be subject to additional considerations, such as political risk.*

Credit insurance is usually divided into two types:

▼ **Short term** *(less than two years in length) and frequently less than one year. Most export sales will meet the short-term category.*

▼ **Medium/long term** *(in excess of two years). Applicable for capital goods and construction/infrastructure projects which take longer to complete. In practice this is more applicable for larger UK businesses engaged in such activity.*

Short term credit insurance is provided by private insurance companies in the UK. Medium/ longer term credit insurance is provided through the government owned Export Credit Guarantee Department (ECGD) – details of which are provided in the Trade Finance section. Recently ECGD have also announced some support for short term export credit insurance, further details of which can be found on the Website linked to this book.

This section shall concentrate on short-term credit insurance where similar principles will apply for UK and export sales.

Risks Covered

At its core credit insurance protects UK business against the commercial risk of non-payment from:

▨ *Protracted default: a claim can be submitted on expiry of a default period, for example, six months after the due date of payment.*

▨ *Insolvency.*

▨ *Political risk, * for example due to currency issues and political unrest.*

Insurance can be available for up to 90% of sales, although this will vary depending on circumstances. As a consequence, the business will still retain some of the credit (payment) risk – in this way the business retains an interest in the debt.

When Is Credit Insurance Used

> **Political risk can result in payment not being made, or delayed as a result of:**
> ▨ *Cancellation of a contract by the government of the buyer's country.*
> ▨ *When the government introduces regulations preventing import or export of goods – or prevents the payment of currency out of a country.*

If a UK business is not receiving funds on a cash up-front basis, they are assuming payment risk for which they may seek insurance. Whilst businesses may consider this more applicable to customers and countries where there is uncertainty over payment, the principle of payment risk exists for any business whether it is trading on credit terms (open account), or other forms of settlement in international trade such as Letters of Credit.

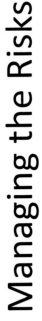

3 | Managing the Risks

Credit insurance should not just be considered as an alternative means of guaranteeing payment. It can be considered as a complimentary means of trading, by providing cover against the risk of non-payment it allows businesses to trade on open account terms to increase sales and improve customer relationships.

Credit insurance premiums will vary depending on the perceived credit risk of the counterparty, and country risk. **The spread of risk amongst a range of debtors may also influence premiums applied and the willingness of an insurer to provide cover – by offering the whole sales ledger to the insurer, this should produce more favourable rates than selecting high risk buyers.**

Types of Credit Insurance

▽ **Whole Turnover Cover**

A policy covering the full debtor book. Credit limits are agreed by the insurer, allowing the business to offer credit up to the agreed amount. The premium paid is calculated against the turnover of the business.

▽ **Critical Customer Cover**

Allows a business to have insurance cover against a number of named customers (e.g. up to 10), usually defined as key customers. The business will be fully responsible for the remaining customers not covered by the insurance. The premium paid is based on the total outstanding debts of the named customers.

▽ **Specific Risk Cover**

Allows a business to have insurance against a single customer or a large contract. The premium paid is based on the contract value or turnover of the customer over the policy period.

Settlements for claims will usually be paid out within 30 days of supported claims documentation.

Ways to Purchase Credit Insurance

There are several ways to buy credit insurance.

1. *Broker. For a lot of businesses this will be the primary way to purchase a policy; brokers will offer tailored advice and provide administrative support on the policy throughout the policy period. Brokers receive commission from the insurer.*

2. *Direct from Insurance Companies. It may be possible to approach some credit insurers direct (but not all insurers will accept clients direct without broker involvement).*

3. *Internet, increasing in use amongst small businesses.*

Section 4 – Credit Terms

Advantages of Credit Insurance	Disadvantages
When available it provides increased security for businesses trading in the UK and abroad, and may help them to trade competitively (on open account terms), which previously they would not have been able to do.	In some cases, credit insurance may be difficult to obtain, especially where the buyer and credit risk is outside of established parameters (lower credit rating, higher risk countries). These may be the same risks that a business needs to insure in order to progress sales.
Consequently, it provides a means by which a business can expand in a controlled and secure manner:	The UK may be at a competitive disadvantage to other countries where government backed insurers may take a less commercial view of risk.
Expanding sales to existing customers.	The cost: benefit equation must be considered. Would it, for example, be more cost effective for a business to offer discounts for immediate payment?
Developing sales into new markets.	
The exporter may be able to raise finance more readily if their sales are being credit insured (e.g. bank borrowings, invoice finance from a bank or the credit insurer themselves).	
Online credit management tools for managing contracts online can simplify processes.	
Credit insurers may be able to provide associated benefits through their network of services, for example:	
Credit reference checks (in UK and abroad).	
Economic reports.	
Receivables finance (invoice discounting).	
Receivables management (outsource of a business credit control function).	
Bond insurance/ bond issuing.	

Managing the Risks

3

HINTS *and* **TIPS**

- *Consult with a broker or insurer before agreeing final terms of trade with a customer. The terms negotiated can help improve the chances of gaining insurance, for example – open account terms at 30 days, rather than 90 days credit.*

- *Use of appropriate Incoterms.*

- *Do discuss with the broker or insurer what additional services they offer, AND the types of credit insurance available. Establish the optimum 'package' for your business in terms of cover and premium.*

Debt Recovery

On some occasions, no matter how closely debtors are managed, delayed payments and bad debts may arise. When trading overseas, the propensity for bad debt can increase, where additional issues of distance and language can heighten risks of delayed or non-payment.

If businesses are providing credit terms they should have a clear view on how they will handle late payment or bad debt collection should it arise. Clearly, if the likes of invoice finance and/or credit insurance are in place this will eliminate a large part of the risk. If they are not in place, however, a business should consider whether it has the resource to handle debt collection or whether the process is outsourced to a specialist company (possibly as part of a wider outsourcing of the credit control function, and/or as part of the insurance cycle).

Some debt recovery companies operate on a no success, no fee basis.

Debt recovery services are better used earlier in the recovery cycle, they should not be left until the last minute as very often it may be too late to recover and too late to pass to a debt recovery company. During the recent UK economic recession use of debt recovery services has increased.

In recovering debt the use of debt recovery companies can provide specific advantages:

- ▼ *Through the use of multi-lingual services, where knowledge of the language and culture will increase the chances of getting paid.*

- ▼ *Through the business not having to pay potentially expensive legal fees to recover the debt.*

TRADE for GOOD

CHAPTER FOUR

THE DIFFERENT METHODS OF PAYMENT

Chapter 4 is divided into six sections with illustrations provided by way of hints, summary boxes and key learning topics

*The Essential Guide to Business and Finance
in UK and International Trade*

SECTION ONE

METHODS OF PAYMENT

Contents

4 | The Different Methods of Payment

About This Section

Once terms of trade have been agreed between buyer and seller the next steps in the payment process will be to ensure that actual payment is received:

▼ *On Time*

▼ *For The Amount Due, and*

▼ *Without Delay*

Whilst the payment process is more clearly defined in certain terms of trade, such as Letters of Credit and Documentary Credits in others such as Open Account and Cash Up-Front it is less clear. This potential lack of clarity, in turn, can lead to delays, distrust and impact trading relationships.

This section shall look at the payment methods that apply to UK and International Trade, and what steps can be taken to increase efficiencies in the payment process. To understand how international payments work, it is beneficial to first understand the types of payment in the UK market and how they operate – before moving on to payments made internationally.

The importance of the payment processes and options should not be underestimated – a high majority of UK and International Trade is settled by these different payment forms. Understanding how they operate and what can be done better will go some way to improving efficiency and eliminating distrust between buyer and seller.

Summary: payment methods and terms of trade

Separate sections are available covering Letters of Credit and Documentary Collections.

UK Trade

Terms of Payment	Payment Method	Payment Cycle (working days)	Cost Efficient
Open Account	Bacs Payment	3 days	✔
	Chaps Payment	Same day	✔
Part Payment	Faster Payment	Same day	✔
	Cheque	Variable c3-7 days	✗
	Cash	Variable	✗
Cash Up-Front	Credit/Debit Card	c3 days	✔

International Trade

Terms of Payment	Payment Method	Payment Cycle (working days)	Cost Efficient
Open Account	*International Payment*	Same day	✔
	International Direct Debit	2-7 days	✔
	Foreign Draft	Variable c7 days	✘
Part Payment	*Cheque Negotiation*	Variable c7 days	✘
	Cheque Collection	Variable up to 21 days	✘
Cash Up-Front	*Credit Card*	c3 days	✔
	Bank Account Abroad	1-3 days	✔

The Role of Banks

Banks play a vital role in the settlement process as they maintain the bank accounts and operate or participate in the clearing and payment systems which effect transfer.

By and large these clearing systems operate effectively, although banks have been subject to increased regulation to ensure that clearing timescales and payment cycles are improved, along with bank charges being more transparent to the customer. These regulations are having an increasingly beneficial effect to businesses that shall be described later.

UK Payment Methods

This section is providing details relative to UK payment methods, in order to illustrate and compare how they operate in conjunction with international payments. This will also help develop an understanding of how payment systems operate within a country.

Electronic Payments

As technology improves, there is an increased emphasis on customers using electronic payment methods and a wider distinction between what banks provide electronically and what they provide in paper format.

BACS

- *Three days payment cycle, typically used for low/medium value payments and regular payments – for example payroll, expenses and payments to suppliers.*

- BACS is also used to collect payments by **Direct Debit** (consumer payments only).

- Automated clearing system, customers can instruct payments by telephone, fax or electronic payment (payments can be made as single payments or as part of a batch of payments to reduce cost).

- Standard bank charges generally vary from 7pence-30pence, depending on payment type chosen.

Benefits for Buyer Making Payment	Benefits for Seller Receiving Payment
Very secure means of payment	Quick means of receiving payment (providing buyer does not settle by monthly payment run)
Customer has control over when to make payment - easier to schedule payment in advance	Reduced risk of fraud
Cost effective means of making payment	Increased cash flow certainty when payments collected from consumers by way of Direct Debit
Reduced risk of fraud	

CHAPS

- Same day payment – cost to instruct a CHAPS payment is higher than most other payment types

- Applicable for urgent and higher value monetary payments

- Automated real time payment system during bank opening hours (to 4pm)

- Standard bank charges £10 to £30 depending whether instructed online or manually

Benefits for Buyer Making Payment	Benefits for Seller Receiving Payment
Secure means of payment	Very quick method of receiving payment (although care that cost of making payment is not necessarily passed onto seller)
Reduced risk of fraud	
Chaps is ideal for urgent, higher value payments	Reduced risk of fraud

4 | The Different Methods of Payment

Faster Payments

- Same day payment, for payments below £100,000 (recently increased from a limit of £10,000)
- Cheaper than CHAPS, quicker than BACS
- Operates on a 24x7 basis, real-time transfer
- Also incorporates future dated payments D+1 to D+30
- The payment method of the future
- Standard bank charges: Same day payments c£3 to £5, future dated payments c£1 or less

Benefits for Buyer Making Payment	Benefits for Seller Receiving Payment
Secure means of payment, some banks only allow payments by online banking Reduced risk of fraud Same day payment is achieved at a lower cost than CHAPS	Very quick method of receiving payment Reduced risk of fraud

Note: In the UK there is currently no Business-to-Business Direct Debit, although there is a National Payments Plan that seeks to introduce such a Direct Debit.

Paper Based Payments

Cheques

- Paper based clearing system, generally 3 to 4 day clearing cycle, once cheque is presented
- Standard bank charges: Around 50p to £1 to issue cheque, and 50p to £1 to pay-in cheque

Benefits for Buyer Making Payment	Benefits for Seller Receiving Payment
Simple to write out and post a cheque Bank account is not debited until cheque is presented, potentially assists cashflow **HOWEVER** Higher risk of fraud Use of cheques could damage supplier relationships	Limited benefit -Check could be returned by the bank as unpaid -Risk of fraud in the process -Longer to receive payment Businesses should do as much as they can to avoid trade sales being settled by cheque, especially for higher value sales

Cash

- *Should only be used in specific circumstances e.g. where a business sells 'smaller-value' purchases to the general public, such as a retail outlet in a town/city.*

Business Credit/Debit Card

- *Can be used as a method of payment from consumers especially and as a means of receipt from businesses for smaller value sales*
- *2/3 day clearance cycle*
- *Applicable for smaller value sales – due to level of 'interchange fee,' at around 2-3%, expressed as a percentage of the value of the transaction*
- *A business can also use to pay expenses and small value purchases*

Benefits for Buyer Making Payment	Benefits for Seller Receiving Payment
Convenient way of making payment	**Convenient way of receiving payment, easy to collect for example over the telephone**
Can obtain up to 6 weeks cash flow (before having to pay credit card bill)	
Reconciling payment is simplified through use of automated online systems	**Opens up another means of collecting money from 'slow payers'**

HINTS and TIPS

When making payment for goods and services some companies will link their payment cycle to a monthly, or more preferably, weekly payment run. The seller should check this with the buyer before agreeing payment.

Monthly payment runs should be discouraged as this will result in delayed payment.

Additionally, the method of payment used should be agreed at the outset. The seller should press for electronic payments as they are beneficial in terms of time, cost and efficiency.

The Different Methods of Payment

4

Feature item: cheque clearing

The cheque clearing system works within a three working day cycle and businesses should receive credit after three working days:

Working Day 1: *The cheque is paid by the seller into their bank account, usually at the bank branch where they hold their account.*

Working Day 3: *The buyer's bank account is debited and seller's account credited on the morning of working day 3*.*

There may, however, be circumstances where the buyer's bank will be unable to debit the buyer's account:

- *If the buyer does not have enough money in their bank account to pay the cheque.*
- *If the buyer has placed a 'stop' on the cheque – when they don't want it paid.*
- *If the buyer has filled out the cheque incorrectly.*

Businesses should pay cheques into their bank account straightaway, to reduce the risk of non-payment or theft.

International payments

Electronic Payments

International payments

Also known as international transfers or wire transfers

- *Different payment types apply*
  1. *Urgent Transfers: Often same day transfer of funds from buyer to seller, for payments to Europe and the USA*
  2. *Standard Transfers: Usually takes 2-3 working days to transfer funds from buyer to seller*
  3. *Low Value Transfers: Applicable for smaller monetary sums, up to 7 working days to transfer funds*
- *These timescales apply from when the bank receives the payment instruction*
- *Different payment systems apply for making international payments which shall be described below in a special feature on the international payment process*
- *Bank charges can vary from around £2.50 for a low value payment to £40 for instructing an international payment*

Benefits for Buyer Making Payment	Benefits for Seller Receiving Payment
Secure means of payment, especially when instructed through online banking *Reduced risk of fraud* *The different types of international payments create flexibility in terms of speed and cost*	***Quick method of receiving payment*** ***Reduced risk of fraud***

International payments are the most popular means of settling international trade transactions

International direct debit (SEPA direct debit in Europe)

- *In Europe this is known as SEPA Direct Debit (Single European Payment Area)*
- *Whilst direct debits are used a lot within countries they are rarely used across borders, because of limited rules covering how they operate and limited settlement systems. SEPA Direct Debit will change this – especially the Direct Debit covering business-to-business transactions (see further reference in the feature item below).*

Benefits for Buyer Making Payment	Benefits for Seller Receiving Payment
Defined and consistent means of settling payment	***Will assist cash flow and certainty of payment, collecting funds on the due date***

Paper Based Payments

Foreign drafts

- *Bank draft drawn by the buyer's bank payable at a bank abroad in the seller's (exporter's country).*
- *The buyer's bank will usually return the issued draft to the buyer, who then sends it to the seller.*
- *Stronger guarantee of payment than a cheque, however not a complete guarantee of payment.*
- *Bank charges usually vary from £5 to £15.*

Benefits for Buyer Making Payment	Benefits for Seller Receiving Payment
Costs are usually less than for an international payment	**Higher chance of receiving cleared funds than with a cheque**
	Lower clearance costs
	HOWEVER
	It will result in the seller taking longer to receive payment

 Foreign drafts are *not* a popular way of settling international trade

Currency cheque (collection and negotiation)

- Buyer will send a cheque to the seller, drawn on the buyer's bank abroad
- Upon receiving the cheque from the seller, the seller's bank will have to present the cheque back to the buyer's bank abroad, by either:
    1. Negotiating the cheque – crediting the buyer, with recourse in the event of non-payment (the buyer's bank will do this for its better credit rated customers – but in doing so may mark a credit limit). Settlement in this case can be within 2-4 business days.
    2. Collecting the cheque – mailing the cheque on a 'Clean Collection' basis. The seller is credited after final payment is received from the buyer's bank. Settlement in this case takes a lot longer, at around 21 working days. Higher bank charges apply.
- A bill of exchange – with no accompanying documents – is also settled by means of a Clean Collection.

Benefits for Buyer Making Payment	Benefits for Seller Receiving Payment
Issuance process is straightforward	**Limited, if any, benefit**
Bank account not debited until cheque is presented (assisting cash flow)	**-Payment will be received later**
HOWEVER	**-Cheque could be returned unpaid**
High risk of fraud	**-Higher bank charges**
Use of cheques is likely to damage supplier relationship	**-Profitability will be impacted**

Businesses that receive cheques in settlement of international trade, need to consider the financial impact of having to clear the cheque and time taken to credit their bank account. It will impact on profit margins and what was a profitable contract could be affected by the impact of clearance costs and delayed credit

Business credit card

- *Can apply for smaller value purchases, but more often used for expenses if employees are travelling abroad on business.*
- *Clearance cycle may take a few days longer than when used within country*
- ***Not** frequently used in international trade.*

Bank account abroad (local account)

- *Can apply when there is a higher volume of trade settlements in a given country – either as a buyer or seller of goods and services.*
- *A local bank account will be required if a local branch or subsidiary is opened. In some countries an account can be opened for a UK company – in others local regulations on what are termed 'non-resident' accounts may not make this possible, or may make it difficult and time consuming to proceed.*
- *As a way of overcoming these issues, in Europe some banks are able to provide a 'Pay Through Account' that enables the buyer overseas to make a local payment to a 'virtual account' in the name of the seller. Upon receipt of the funds the money is directed to the UK bank account.*

Flowchart for 'Pay Through Account

Buyer abroad instructs their bank to make a local payment → Local payment made to an account "in-country", which the UK bank or their partner bank maintains → UK Bank or their Partner Bank make payment to the seller's UK bank account

4 | The Different Methods of Payment

Benefits for Buyer Making Payment	Benefits for Seller Receiving Payment
Cheaper method of transfer – payment only has to be made locally (as a domestic, not international payment)	*Allows the seller to compete better with local companies, by allowing the buyer to transfer the money locally* *Usually a quicker method of receiving funds*

Feature item: *the international payment process*

The international payment process will differ depending on which region of the world the payment is being made to. Two primary payment processes apply for:

1. *Euro payments to Europe*
2. *Payments to the Rest of the World*

Payments to the Rest of the World

Payments to the Rest of the World follow the traditional means of international payment.

Step 1

Buyer instructs their bank (the UK bank) to make an international transfer, providing the bank with details of the seller's bank account.

Step 2

The UK bank sends the payment through the SWIFT system (see below), either directly to the seller's bank account abroad OR through a correspondent bank in the country that then sends the payment onto the seller's bank.

Note: In terms of speed and charges it is far better for the payment to be sent direct to the seller's bank. If the customer has a high volume of payments they should encourage their bank to send in the most direct manner possible.

Step 3

The seller's bank credits the customer. Under this process payments can be made same day to certain parts of the world, for example, for US Dollar payments to the USA. This would arise when an urgent payment is made; in the case of a standard payment transfer normally takes 2 to 3 working days.

Banks may also offer a low value payment option at a lower transfer price (almost like a BACS payment abroad). These are instructed as part of a batch of payments that a UK bank will transfer usually through a local bank abroad.

Section 1 - Methods of Payment

Some of the key terms and systems used in international payments are

SWIFT: Society for Worldwide Interbank Financial Telecommunications. It is the method by which banks transmit secure payment messages. The primary message type is known as an MT103 message, which provides full payment details. Through specific payment fields it essentially reflects a lot of the information that a buyer will complete when instructing their bank to make payment:

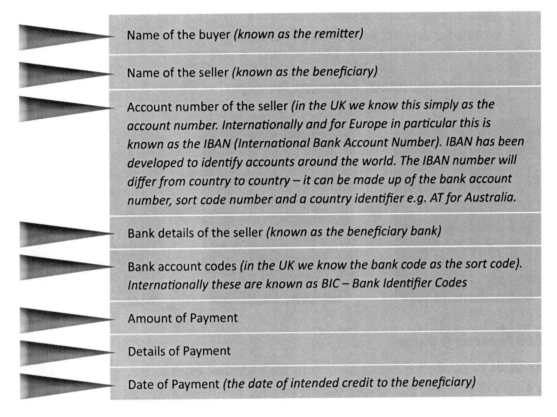

Name of the buyer *(known as the remitter)*

Name of the seller *(known as the beneficiary)*

Account number of the seller *(in the UK we know this simply as the account number. Internationally and for Europe in particular this is known as the IBAN (International Bank Account Number). IBAN has been developed to identify accounts around the world. The IBAN number will differ from country to country – it can be made up of the bank account number, sort code number and a country identifier e.g. AT for Australia.*

Bank details of the seller *(known as the beneficiary bank)*

Bank account codes *(in the UK we know the bank code as the sort code). Internationally these are known as BIC – Bank Identifier Codes*

Amount of Payment

Details of Payment

Date of Payment *(the date of intended credit to the beneficiary)*

Bank systems and indeed the SWIFT system itself are increasingly reliant on the IBAN and BIC codes being quoted. This ensures processing efficiency, reduced processing costs and increased speed of payment. A buyer should always ensure that the seller provides an IBAN and BIC code.

The SWIFT system is also used for other types of international settlements between banks, such as Issuing Letters of Credit and Bonds & Guarantees.

Settlement Between Banks

▼ **Nostro account**

▼ **Vostro account**

International payments between banks are settled by means of Nostro and Vostro accounts.

4 | The Different Methods of Payment

1. A **Nostro account** is a bank account that, for example, a UK bank maintains with a **bank abroad in the local currency (e.g. a US Dollar account with a Bank in the USA)**. It is the account that will be used to settle international transfers made on behalf of the buyer to the seller, in the local currency – where for example the UK company is the importer.

2. A **Vostro account** is a bank account that an **overseas bank will maintain with a bank in the UK, in sterling (a US bank maintains an account in the UK with a UK bank)**. Such an account would be used to settle payments in sterling from a US bank, making payment on behalf of the US buyer to a UK seller (exporter).

Summary: International Payment Process

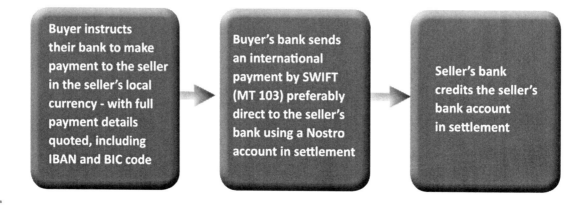

Buyer instructs their bank to make payment to the seller in the seller's local currency - with full payment details quoted, including IBAN and BIC code

Buyer's bank sends an international payment by SWIFT (MT 103) preferably direct to the seller's bank using a Nostro account in settlement

Seller's bank credits the seller's bank account in settlement

Euro Payments To Europe

Payments to Europe are moving away from the traditional international payment process to a system of payments that remove country barriers, now linked more to a domestic payment system similar to what we know in the UK, namely:

- *High value payments (CHAPS in the UK, CHAPS Euro Target in Europe)*
- *2/3 day value payments (BACS in the UK, SEPA Direct Credit and SEPA Direct Debit in Europe)*

The **Single European Payment Area (SEPA)** is a European Commission and European Payments Council initiative to 'eliminate' national boundaries and create a single set of standards for euro payments across the EU. It is aligning the cost of cross border transfers in Europe with that of domestic transfers, resulting in cost reductions for businesses. SEPA is underpinned by the Payment Services Directive, which is described later.

Section 1 - Methods of Payment

Euro payments can be made same day value - same day receipt between buyer and seller. Key to efficient Euro payments are

1. *The quoting of IBAN and BIC codes.*
2. *Payment systems that still use SWIFT (in the same manner as described above).*
3. *Use of specific settlement systems Target and EBA, designed to process Euro payments quickly and efficiently.*

Target 2 — The Target system is used for high value and urgent European payments. It provides real-time payment processing with settlement through the Central Banks in Europe.

EBA — The Euro Banking Association (EBA) is a Clearing system in Europe managed by banks, with over 200 member banks.
Used for the majority of international payments in Europe.

Efficient Payment Processing

Increasingly banks and businesses are seeking to 'straight through process' whereby payments are processed as efficiently as possible, with limited manual intervention.

Benefits of 'Straight Through Processing'	How 'Straight Through Processing' Is Achieved
Reduced processing costs for businesses and banks	*Quoting IBAN and BIC details*
Reduced payment charges	*Use of electronic banking and not paper application forms*
Payments are received quicker	*Maintain templates of correct information*
Less risk of error	
Reduced risk of fraud	

Straight-through processing is key to avoiding delays in international transfers. Whilst delays could still arise for payments to more outlying parts of the world, for a lot of countries this should not arise, **providing the correct bank account details are quoted.**

Bank payment systems (e.g. SWIFT) and international settlement systems are increasingly sophisticated with real-time exchange of payment messages. Payments from the UK to the USA and Europe can be made same day value and one day in the case of payments from the UK to the rest of the world.

4 | The Different Methods of Payment

Feature item: SEPA direct debit (SDD) scheme

About The Scheme

- The scheme will only operate in Euros (UK sterling direct debit schemes are unaffected).
- All banks in the SEPA zone have to be able to receive direct debit claims.
- The SEPA zone comprises 31 countries (the 27 in the European Union plus Norway, Iceland, Liechtenstein and Switzerland).
- Creditors (sellers) need to be sponsored in order to claim money from a debtor. They will receive a unique "Creditor Identifier."
- Two schemes operate:
  - A core scheme (more for Business to Consumer B2C).
  - An optional Business to Business scheme (B2B).
- One off and regular transactions can be made.
- Mandates can be paper or electronic, and contain a standard set of information fields.

Features of the Two Schemes

Feature	Core Scheme	B2B Scheme
Guarantee/Refund	The debtor (buyer) is entitled to a refund during a period of eight weeks after being debited.	The debtor is only entitled to a refund if the debit was deemed to be unauthorised, for example, no mandate is in place.
Advance Notification	The first, or a one-off collection must be received at the latest five bank business days before the due date.	Collections must be received at the latest one bank business day before the due date.
Returns Settlement	The latest date for settlement of the return of a collection is five bank business days after the settlement date of a collection.	The latest date for settlement of the return of a collection is two bank business days after the settlement date of a collection.
Debiting	For each collection presented, the debtor bank must debit the debtor's account if the account allows Direct Debits.	Debtor bank is obliged to obtain confirmation from the debtor before debiting the debtors account for first and one-off debits
Cancelling	Scheme rules do not require customers to inform debtor banks when cancelling a mandate	Business customers must inform the debtor bank of all cancelled mandates

Section 1 - Methods of Payment

Benefits of SEPA Direct Debits

For The Seller

- Businesses will be able to reduce the time they spend on accounts receivables work.
- Optimises the working capital cycle by speeding up settlement times and reduces sales days outstanding (Day+1 on the B2B scheme).
- Reduces the costs associated with collecting receipts due to the business.
- Increases control over the collection of receivables.

For The Buyer (Debtor)

- Efficient and on time supplier payments.
- No risk of late payment charges.
- More cost effective method than were the buyer to pay the supplier by another method of payment.

The Key Role of Electronic Banking (Online Banking)

Most businesses, employees and students will be familiar with online banking, to view bank account details and in a lot of cases to make payments.

For businesses, there are a lot of benefits that online banking provides – including real-time access to bank accounts. Ideally online banking should be used for both UK and International payments – to maximize its use a business, should ensure that payment templates are maintained online, to avoid rekeying of information. Ideally a business should consider 'uploading' information from its accounting platform (e.g. Sage).

Summary

Benefits of Online Banking

- *Internet enabled.*
- *A fast and secure means of making payment – much more efficient than completing paper application forms.*
- *More cost-effective, including lower bank charges.*
- *Reduced risk of error by customer or bank.*
- *Improves control of bank accounts and finance.*
- *Payment information can be uploaded from the accounting system to the online banking platform.*
- *Balance and account information can also be downloaded from online banking to the accounting system.*

---

4 | The Different Methods of Payment

Payment Regulations Which Assists Business

Payment Services Directive (PSD)

The aim of PSD is to provide the regulatory framework for a single payments market in the European Union, as well as:

1. *Enhancing competition by creating more of a level playing field amongst banks.*
2. *Providing transparency to the consumer and business.*

It regulates banks and payment providers covering most payment types covered in this section. It applies more for smaller businesses with an annual turnover below €2 million (classed as a 'micro enterprise'). Some banks will ensure that its principles apply for all types of business.

From the perspective of businesses PSD provides the following benefits:

- *Use of IBAN and BIC codes is mandatory.*
- *Banks must provide businesses with all the information they need to make a payment, including clear information about rates and charges.*
- *Banks must offer a consistent level of service, such as making sure all payments are completed within a pre-determined timeframe.*
- *Protecting customers across Europe when payments aren't executed correctly.*

Wire Transfer Regulations

Applicable to international payments these require the bank instructing the payment (the buyer's bank) to ensure that the payment details the name and address of the remitter (e.g. the buyer). This is to ensure transparency, making it easier for law enforcement to track funds transferred electronically by terrorists and criminals.

The Future of Payments

The future of payments promises much change to meet demands relative to:

- *Transparency of banking charges and information.*
- *Prevent fraud and money laundering activity.*
- *To help businesses more in UK and International trade.*
- *Electronic and technological developments – removing expensive manual processes.*

The following categories are examples of new initiatives. Once introduced, this and other sections will be updated accordingly.

Faster Payments	*Further increases in the Faster Payments limit in the UK, from the current £100,000*	**2011 onwards**
European Regulation	*More increased transparency on bank charges, margins and customer information. PSD 2012*	**2012**
UK National Payments Plan	*A lot of the delivery dates are currently subject to consideration*	
A) The Future of Cheques	*A planned withdrawal of cheques as a payment method*	**2018**
B) Contactless Card	*Increased use of pre-paid card options*	
C) Business to Business Direct Debit	*Introduction of a Direct Debit scheme whereby a business can initiate a Direct Debit claim against another business*	
D) Electronic Invoices	*Increased and improved use of electronic invoicing to claim trade debts*	

The Different Methods of Payment

4

SECTION TWO

DOCUMENTARY COLLECTIONS
AND BILLS OF EXCHANGE

Contents

The Different Methods of Payment

4

About This Section

This section shall look at the role that Documentary Collections and Bills of Exchange play in UK and International Trade – sometimes referred to 'Cash against Documents' or 'Cash on Delivery'.

Central to the operation of a documentary collection are

▼ *Bills of Exchange (the payment instrument)*

▼ *Bills of Lading (the document of title)*

In addition to the buyer and seller banks are crucial to the operation of documentary collections, both from a process perspective, but also as a means of reducing the risk of non-payment and in some cases in generating finance.

Documentary collections merit serious consideration as a means of settlement in international trade; this section will review how and when they can be used to support import and export trade and associated movements of cash in the business.

Bills of exchange can also be used in their own right as a form of settlement. Used alone they are not as secure a method of settlement and the protection of document control is lost. Consequently they may be used by:

A) *Larger businesses for specific large trade deals e.g. machinery purchase, or*

B) *Where the counterparties know each other well.*

C) *Where financing can be granted on the strength of the party issuing the Bill of Exchange, often with a period of credit built in.*

Key Learning Topics

Note: All areas of this section will be important with the following areas denoted by way of indicating primary content.

	For Businesses	For Employees	For Students
How a Documentary Collection Actually Operates	✓	✓	✓
When to Use and When NOT to Use	✓	✓	
Discounting Bills of Exchange when Credit Terms apply		✓	✓
Maintaining control through Bills of Exchange and Bills of Lading		✓	✓
Best practice in dealing with Documentary Collections	✓	✓	✓

4 | The Different Methods of Payment

What Is a Documentary Collection?

 A method used in international trade to provide security of payment for the exporter

At the same time, ensuring that the importer receives the goods as ordered

Documents of title (e.g. Bills of Lading) are sent through the banking system

These are not released to the importer until they have either:

a) Paid a sight Bill of Exchange, or

b) Accepted a Term Bill of Exchange

Bills of Exchange and Bills of Lading play a key part in the successful operation of a Documentary Collection

Bills of Exchange

A Bill of Exchange is an unconditional order issued by one party (the drawer), to another (the drawee), to pay a certain sum of money, either immediately (sight bill) or on a fixed future date (term bill) – for payment of goods and services.

Drawer: Exporter

Drawee: Importer

Unconditional in the sense that it is absolute, without condition.

In the United Kingdom Bills of Exchange are governed by the Bills of Exchange Act 1882.

A Bill of Exchange should contain the following:

- *The term Bill of Exchange inserted on the Bill.*
- *An unconditional order to pay a fixed sum of money.*
- *The name of the party who is paying.*
- *A statement of the 'time of payment.'*
- *A statement of the place where payment is to be made.*
- *A name of the party to whom payment is to be made.*
- *A statement of the date and of the place where the bill is issued.*
- *The signature of the person who issues the bill.*

The Function of the Bill of Exchange in UK and International Trade

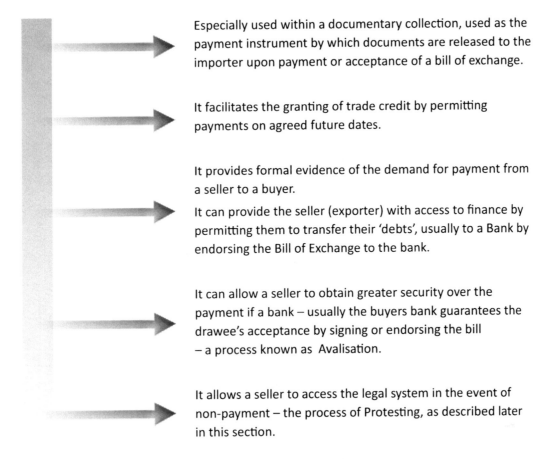

Especially used within a documentary collection, used as the payment instrument by which documents are released to the importer upon payment or acceptance of a bill of exchange.

It facilitates the granting of trade credit by permitting payments on agreed future dates.

It provides formal evidence of the demand for payment from a seller to a buyer.

It can provide the seller (exporter) with access to finance by permitting them to transfer their 'debts', usually to a Bank by endorsing the Bill of Exchange to the bank.

It can allow a seller to obtain greater security over the payment if a bank – usually the buyers bank guarantees the drawee's acceptance by signing or endorsing the bill – a process known as Avalisation.

It allows a seller to access the legal system in the event of non-payment – the process of Protesting, as described later in this section.

Bills of Lading

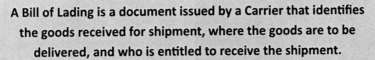

A Bill of Lading is a document issued by a Carrier that identifies the goods received for shipment, where the goods are to be delivered, and who is entitled to receive the shipment.

**It is a contract for carriage,
AND a document of title to the goods.**

The document of title is the key element with respect to Documentary Collections. The importer cannot take possession of the goods, unless they have the Bill of Lading in their possession.

The Different Methods of Payment

4

Types of Documentary Collections

Documents against Payment (D/P)	Documents against Acceptance (D/A)
Documents under a Documentary Collection are released against payment of a Sight Bill of Exchange, payable immediately by the importer. The importer cannot receive the documents until they have paid the Bill of Exchange	***Documents under a Documentary Collection are released against acceptance of a Term Bill of Exchange, payable at a future date by the importer. The exporter is allowing a period of credit to the importer***

Parties to a Documentary Collection

Seller (Exporter)

Also known as the Drawer. The seller presents documentation to their bank with a completed collection schedule

The Remitting Bank

Usually the Exporter's bank, receives documentation and forwards it to the buyer's bank along with instructions for payment

Collecting Bank

Usually the Importer's bank. Receives the documents and releases them to the importer in exchange for payment/ acceptance of a Bill of Exchange

Buyer (Importer)

Also known as the Drawee. Receives documents upon payment/acceptance of a Bill of Exchange

How A Documentary Collection Works

Step *1*

The buyer and seller (importer and exporter) agree on the terms of sale, including payment to be made on a documentary collection basis – either payable at sight or term with a period of credit.

Agreement should also be reached on who pays each bank charge: it could, for example, be the case that each pays the charges of the bank in their own country.

Step *2*

The exporter arranges for shipment, and their receipt of shipping/transport documents in order for them to progress.

Step *3*

The exporter completes a documentary collection schedule from their bank, along with a bill of exchange, drawn payable at sight or term. This is sent to their bank (known as the Remitting Bank). The schedule will provide:

- *Details of the importer's bank.*
- *It will contain the documents in addition to the bill of exchange.*
- *Instructions will be provided to release documents against payment or acceptance of the Bill of Exchange.*

Step *4*

Upon receipt the remitting bank will check the documentary collection schedule to ensure it contains the documents specified in the schedule, along with the bill of exchange.

Step *5*

The remitting bank will send the collection schedule (usually) directly to the importer's bank specified, known as the collecting bank. These are sent by secure post as they contain documents of title.

Step *6*

Upon receipt the collecting bank will check the collection schedule contains the documents specified. It will immediately contact the buyer:

- *When making contact it will send the buyer the bill of exchange for payment, or acceptance.*
- *It will also send copies (**not** originals) of the documents, either by photocopy or imaged/ online copies.*
- *Receipt of the copy documents allows the buyer to check that certain aspects of the goods are in accordance with the terms of the contract.*

4 | The Different Methods of Payment

Step 7

If the bill of exchange is paid or accepted, the buyer has to send it back to the collecting bank – in the case of Accepted Bills the collecting bank will retain the bill until maturity and present it again to the buyer, a couple of days before final payment.

If the buyer refuses to pay or accept the bill the collecting bank - **if instructed to do so on the collection schedule** – will PROTEST the bill. Protest should take place on the day of dishonour or as soon as possible thereafter.

Protest **is a procedure where a notary public (legal representative) re-presents the bill to the buyer. If it is again dishonoured the reason** *why is detailed.*

This will provide the basis on which the exporter can take future legal action.

Note: In some countries the act of protesting is similar to an act of bankruptcy, and one that a buyer will not want to face. For this reason a seller should advise the buyer *beforehand* **that they have requested protest – this will at least make the buyer aware of the consequences of non-payment.**

Noting: **this process is less used. It involves the notary public 'noting' the reason for dishonour. In this way notice of dishonour is secured, prior to formal protesting which is more severe for the buyer. Noting may be a more acceptable form of challenging non-payment or non-acceptance to allow the buyer time to make payment, before protest takes place.**

Step 8

Upon receipt of the paid or accepted bill – and if there is enough funds in the buyer's account – the collecting bank will send the documents to the buyer in order that they can take possession of the goods, primarily through the Bill of Lading.

Step 9

The collecting bank sends the funds to the remitting bank, which in turn credits their customer, the exporter.

Summary: Documentary Collection Flowchart

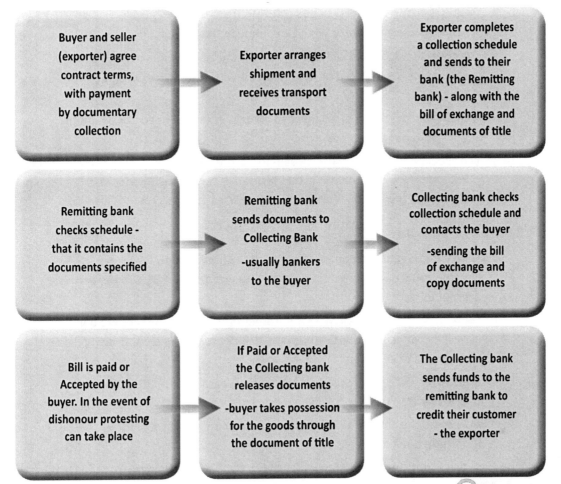

Buyer and seller (exporter) agree contract terms, with payment by documentary collection

→

Exporter arranges shipment and receives transport documents

→

Exporter completes a collection schedule and sends to their bank (the Remitting bank) - along with the bill of exchange and documents of title

Remitting bank checks schedule - that it contains the documents specified

→

Remitting bank sends documents to Collecting Bank -usually bankers to the buyer

→

Collecting bank checks collection schedule and contacts the buyer -sending the bill of exchange and copy documents

Bill is paid or Accepted by the buyer. In the event of dishonour protesting can take place

→

If Paid or Accepted the Collecting bank releases documents -buyer takes possession for the goods through the document of title

→

The Collecting bank sends funds to the remitting bank to credit their customer - the exporter

Best Practice in Dealing with Documentary Collections

Completing The Collection Schedule

- Obtain a collection schedule from the bank to have ready, prior to agreeing the sales contract. This can be in the form of the Collection schedule being on a Word document – in order that regular data is held on the template, and the detail is in typed format, rather than handwritten.

- Ensure the complete address of the buyer, and their bankers is detailed, along with an instruction from the exporter to their bank (the collecting bank), to send the Collection direct to the buyer's bank – this will assist efficient settlement and reduce bank charges.

cont'd over page

4 | The Different Methods of Payment

- Clearly specify if the bill is to be protested. The collection schedule is likely to have a box to complete in this respect.

- The collection schedule will have a box to detail clarifying who pays what bank charges – this should be in accordance with what has been agreed with the buyer.

- If applicable the name of an agent to contact in case of need can be quoted e.g. in the event of non-payment.

- The collection schedule *must* contain the Bill of Lading and should contain other important documents such as Insurance Certificate, Packing List, Certificate of Inspection, Certificate of Origin, as appropriate.

Dealings With The Bank

- Wherever possible communications with the bank should take place electronically (e-mail or online banking), to ensure any delays in the process are minimised.

- For buyers or sellers with regular documentary collections there are benefits in having a direct relationship with the bank's processing area, to avoid delay in the event of enquiries.

- Both buyer and seller (exporter) should have agreements with their banks that they will:

  a) Process the collection schedule same day on receipt from the Remitting bank.

  b) Send copy documentation – along with the Bill of Exchange – in order that can view the copy documents such as the Bill of Lading, Insurance Certificate, Packing List and Certificate of Inspection.

- If a business has high volumes of Documentary Collections they may wish to negotiate charges with the bank.

Ensuring There Is Sufficient Time To Complete The Transaction

Most importantly of all both buyer and seller must ensure that there is sufficient time to complete the transaction – whereby the goods are received at the same time as the buyer has the documents of title. This will avoid unnecessary charges – such as Demurrage (see below), and remove the risk of the goods becoming obsolete, such as in the case of fresh produce.

Demurrage is a charge applied when the goods are not removed from the Port (terminal) within a stipulated time. The longer the period of time the more charges will build up.

Considerations When Using A Documentary Collection

In addition to looking at considerations, this section will also look at circumstances in which Collections can be used. Firstly there are circumstances in which documentary collections may **not** be as suitable:

- *In the case of shipments of fresh produce – if the goods are not received on time the produce could become obsolete.*

- *For transportation by air, road or rail there will be no Bill of Lading and as a consequence no document of title to control the goods. When this arises the seller (exporter) must ensure that the buyer does not obtain the goods UNTIL the Bill of Exchange has been paid or accepted.*

When transporting by air the seller can also consider consigning the Air Waybill to the buyer's bank. This prevents release of the goods until after payment or acceptance of the Bill – whereby the buyer's bank issues an Air Release (Delivery Note) to the carrier.

From a buyer's perspective they should only agree to a documentary collection if:

1. *There is trust that the seller will ship the goods in accordance with the agreement (sales contract).*

2. *The agreement should specify all documentation required of the seller.*

It must also be borne in mind that banks do not have the responsibility to authenticate individual documents; they only have the responsibility to check that documents received appear on their face, to be specified in the collection schedule.

When Should A Documentary Collection Be Used

- *When the buyer and seller know each other to be reliable.*

- *There is no doubt ability the buyer's willingness or ability to pay.*

- *The political and economic condition of the buyer's country is stable – and that they do not have any foreign exchange controls preventing payments.*

- *In some cases it will be a condition of the importer's country that settlement should be by Documentary Collection or Letter of Credit.*

- *When the goods being shipped are easily re-sellable - in the event of non-payment the seller will still be left with the goods to sell.*

4 | The Different Methods of Payment

In practice documentary collections can be used for exports within certain European countries where there is no trading history between the parties. More commonly they can apply for exports outside Europe, either after a period of trading more securely on Letter of Credit, or as a means of avoiding the more expensive costs associated with Letters of Credit.

Uniform Rules for Collection

The Uniform Rules for Collection (URC) were developed by the International Chambers of Commerce. URC 522 has been in force since January 1996 covering:

▼ *How collections should be handled,*

▼ *The principal obligations of parties to a documentary collection and*

▼ *What procedures the banks follow.*

Key articles include:

Article 2: *Banks must verify that the documents received appear to be as listed in the collection order (schedule). Banks have no further obligations to examine the documents.*

Article 9: *The presenting bank (the collecting bank) must make presentation for payment without delay.*

Article 17: *The collection schedule should give specific instructions regarding protest in the event of non-payment, or non-acceptance.*

Article 18: *If a 'case of need' is nominated, the collection order should clearly indicate their powers, otherwise the banks will not accept any instructions from the 'case of need.'*

Obtaining Finance Under A Documentary Collection

It may be possible for an exporter to obtain finance under a Documentary Collection in circumstances where the exporter provides credit terms by way of a bill of exchange (Documents against Acceptance).

This concept is discussed further in several other sections but to re-enforce the process in involves:

In most cases the exporter's bank will NOT be prepared to discount against the credit of the buyer UNLESS they are a large corporate business. The bank will require the Bill of Exchange to be avalised (guaranteed) by the importer's bank.

The importer's credit risk is therefore substituted with the risk of their bank; on the basis that the importer's bank will be a better credit risk.

Discount is usually without recourse to the exporter.

Summary: Advantages and Disadvantages of a Documentary Collection

Advantages for the Seller (Exporter)	Disadvantages for the Seller (Exporter)
Simplicity, there are no documentary compliance rules as with a Letter of Credit.	*The exporter assumes the risk of the buyer refusing payment*
The sale transaction is settled through the bank – thus enabling simultaneous payment and transfer of title.	*If this arises the exporter will have to reship the goods or sell them in the open market.*
The exporter retains title to the goods, until payment or acceptance of the Bill of Exchange.	*The exporter assumes the credit risk of the importer's country.*
The Bill of Exchange provides a legal acknowledgement that a debt exists	*If this is an Accepted Bill of Exchange the buyer will have already received the goods (under Documents against Acceptance)*
It can provide the exporter with access to financing.	*Demurrage charges may be incurred or produce may become obsolete if the Collection is not paid or accepted on time.*
It can provide access to legal systems in the event of non-payment – through protesting.	*If documents are not transported under a Bill of Lading control through documents to title becomes more difficult.*
Faster method of payment than open account terms.	

cont'd over page

The Different Methods of Payment

4

Advantages for the Buyer (Importer)	Disadvantages for the Buyer (Importer)
The importer is not obliged to pay for goods prior to shipment.	**Refusal to pay or accept a Bill of Exchange may seriously damage the buyer's reputation.**
The Bill of Exchange facilitates the granting of trade credit.	**Legal action might be taken against the buyer if they refuse to pay or accept a Bill of Exchange.**
It avoids the needs to make an advance payment; payment for goods can be made when shipping documents have been received.	**The importer faces the risk of paying for goods that are of sub-standard quality, or not in accordance with the specified order.**
For documents released against acceptance the buyer can sell the goods, and then make payment to the seller.	
The importer can inspect the copy documents (but not the goods) prior to paying or accepting a Bill of Exchange.	
An importer does not require credit limits from their banks as with other forms of trade settlement, such as a Letter of Credit or Guarantee.	

Variations on Documentary Collections

Direct Collections

Some banks provide a service whereby Collection Schedules can be sent direct to the buyer's bank abroad by the Exporter – the Exporter's bank in this case will provide the Exporter with collection schedules on 'bank headed paper.'

This arrangement can apply to speed up the transaction and avoid the risk of the goods arriving at their destination before the documents. When sending the Collection direct to the buyer's bank a copy will also be sent to the Exporter's bank in order that they are aware of the transaction. When settlement is received from the bank abroad the exporter's bank will credit the exporter in the normal manner.

The service should only be offered to experienced exporters and when the bank is happy with the credit standing and trustworthiness of their customer.

Clean Collections

A Clean Collection involves simply a Bill of Exchange and no documents.

From the perspective of the exporter it still provides them with an instrument that evidences debt, they have no control of documents – consequently its benefits are limited.

Clean collections can be used for small value, almost follow-up exports of spare parts, AFTER the primary export has been settled by documentary collection.

Clean collections can also involve a **Promissory Note** – a written signed, unconditional promise to pay by the buyer to the seller. Like Bills of Exchange, Promissory Notes are negotiable instruments.

European Bills

Some countries will have their own systems used 'in-country' that have similarities to Bills of Exchange. On some occasions the Bills involved are issued by buyers to an overseas exporter:

- *In France Bills of Exchange known as 'LCR's are paper based future dated instruments. Whilst similar to a post dated cheque they have stronger controls, in that settlement is through the Banque de France – with non-payment being effective to a 'blacklisting' of the company concerned.*

- *In Italy RIBA operates an electronic bill receipt.*

Section Review

Having read the Documentary Collection Section you should be clear on the following:

▼ *When a Documentary Collection could apply.*

▼ *It does not guarantee payment but does provide a middle ground between Open Account and Letter of Credit.*

▼ *Means of controlling shipment through Bills of Exchange and Bills of Lading.*

▼ *The process of discounting Bills of Exchange to obtain finance.*

▼ *The impact and implications of Protesting non-payment or non-acceptance of a Bill of Exchange.*

The Different Methods of Payment

4

Topic refresher

Advantages of Documentary Collections

Importer *(Buyer)*

▼ *Can build in a period of credit through a Bill of Exchange payable at Term.*

▼ *Knows the goods are on their way.*

▼ *Improved method of payment than cash up-front.*

▼ *Does not use bank credit facilities as is the case with Letters of Credit.*

Exporter *(Seller)*

▼ *Maintains control over the goods until a Bill of Exchange has been paid at Sight or Accepted at Term.*

▼ *A Bill of Exchange can in some countries be a strong instrument to take legal action on.*

▼ *Improved terms of trade to open account.*

Mitigating the Disadvantages

Importer *(Buyer)*

▼ *Can ask for an Inspection Certificate to evidence quality and quantity.*

▼ *Liaise with bank to ensure you get sight of copy documents as soon as possible.*

Exporter *(Seller)*

▼ *May be possible to discount an Accepted Bill of Exchange to improve cash flow.*

▼ *Ensure credit checks are undertaken on the buyer.*

▼ *Ensure documents in Documentary Collections control title to the goods e.g. Bill of Lading.*

TOP LEARNING POINTS

1. *Works best when a Bill of Lading is used to control title to the goods.*

2. *Care when using with perishable goods as delays in the importer taking possession of the goods may result in produce going to waste.*

3. *Always consult/negotiate with the buyer before Protesting an unpaid or unaccepted bill, as Protest could be considered an 'Act of Bankruptcy' in some countries.*

4. *Credit terms are a matter of negotiation between buyer and seller.*

5. *Discounting bills of exchange are a means of improving cash flow*

Key Business Efficiency Measures

▼ *Ensure document control is used in order that documentary collection is used to its optimum.*

▼ *Use bank templates (electronic) rather than having to handwrite forms.*

▼ *Consider finance by discounting bills of exchange, if credit terms are provided by means of an Accepted Bill of Exchange.*

▼ *A business must understand when a Documentary Collection works well AND when it is not so appropriate e.g. Air, Road freight, perishable goods.*

4 | The Different Methods of Payment

SECTION THREE

LETTERS OF CREDIT

Contents

The Different Methods of Payment

4

About This Section

This section shall take a detailed look at Letters of Credit, what they are and the role they have to play in international trade, focusing in particular on the role of Documentary Letters of Credit.

For many years Letters of Credit have played a key role in facilitating trade, reaching all parts of the world. A lot of the traditions associated with Letters of Credit still apply today and when coupled with enhancements to banking services and electronic commerce, this provides for an important method of settlement, without which international trade would not function successfully.

It is vital for students, employees and businesses to understand the process of how Letters of Credit operate, and how associated financing, security of payment and best practice in working capital can be achieved. This section will provide the basis to support this understanding.

Key Learning Topics

Note: All areas of this section will be important with the following areas denoted by way of indicating primary content.

	For Businesses	For Employees	For Students
Circumstances in which Letters of Credit can be used	✓	✓	✓
Discrepant Documents		✓	
Non-payment by the Issuing Bank or Country		✓	✓
Risks governing Letters of Credit		✓	✓
How a Letter of Credit works	✓	✓	✓
Documents in a Letter of Credit		✓	
Types of Letters of Credit	✓	✓	✓

The Different Methods of Payment

4

What Is a Documentary Letter of Credit?

A payment undertaking given by a bank (known as the issuing bank).

Provided on behalf of the buyer (importer).

To pay the seller (exporter) *the quoted amount of money.*

Payment is made on presentation of compliant documents (usually after shipment is made):

-As specified in the Letter of Credit.

-These documents should represent those used in the supply of goods.

Documents must:

-Be presented within specified time limits.

-Conform to the terms and conditions set out in the Letter of Credit.

-Be presented at a specified place.

Most Letters of Credit issued today are **irrevocable**, whereby the Issuing Bank can only amend or cancel if agreed by ALL parties to the Letters of Credit. **Revocable** Credits should be avoided – as they can be cancelled or amended by the Importer or Issuing Bank, without prior notice to the exporter. Revocable Credits would tend to apply where there is ultimate trust between buyer and seller, for example, between family members in business in different parts of the world.

The Parties to a Documentary Letter of Credit

From the perspective of the UK business being the Exporter.

Buyer *(Importer)*

The buyer will approach their bank to issue a Letter of Credit - terms of the Letter of Credit should already be agreed with the seller

Buyer's Bank
(The Issuing Bank)

The bank issuing the Letter of Credit to a bank in the UK (usually the bank of the seller)

Seller's Bank
(Exporter's Bank)

Known as the Advising Bank, the bank will forward the Letter of Credit to the seller (exporter)

The Seller *(Exporter)*

Receives the Letter of Credit

-must present documents in accordance with the terms of the Letter of Credit to get paid

How a Documentary Letter of Credit Works

Step 1

The buyer and seller (importer and exporter) agree that the sale of goods will be settled by Letter of Credit – precise terms and conditions should be agreed, including:

- *Documents to be presented under the Letter of Credit.*
- *Terms of sales, including description of goods supplied, shipping and insurance terms.*
- *Payment terms, at Sight or Term (period of credit).*
- *Timescales for presentation of documents.*
- *Who pays what charges for the Letter of Credit?*
- *A UK exporter should explicitly request that the Letter of Credit be sent to their bank in the UK for Advising and Negotiating the Letter of Credit. This may reduce the level of bank charges – through avoiding use of multiple banks – and ensure a high standard of customer service from the bank that maintains the bank account of the business.*

Step 2

The buyer applies to their bank – the issuing bank – requesting that a Letter of Credit be issued, in accordance with the terms agreed with the exporter.

As the issuing bank is effectively guaranteeing payment on behalf of the buyer, they will need to establish a credit facility with the bank (as part of the company's lending facility).

Step 3

The issuing bank sends the Letter of Credit electronically to a bank in the seller's country - ideally this will be the seller's bank. The receiving bank here is known as the Advising Bank.

Step 4

The Advising Bank advises the Letter of Credit to the seller (exporter), known as the beneficiary under the Letter of Credit.

Step 5

Upon receipt of the Letter of Credit the exporter must check it carefully and in particular check for any additions or omissions from what was originally agreed.

Note: At this stage the business should reaffirm that it can:

- *Produce the goods within timescales.*
- *Ship them.*
- *Produce the documents required, all by the expiry date.*

If the exporter knows they cannot meet requirements at this stage they should immediately contact their customer and request an amendment to the Letter of Credit.

4 | The Different Methods of Payment

Step 6

- *The exporter arranges with the freight forwarder for the goods to be shipped – producing the necessary documentation.*
- *The exporter arranges for the documents to be produced and sent to the bank in accordance with the Letter of Credit.*

Note: The Letter of Credit may specify a negotiating bank or it may indicate 'available with any bank' – this being the bank that will check and negotiate the documents. The exporter should ideally work with their own bank, with which they have an existing bank relationship. In essence it is usually preferable for the Advising and Negotiating bank to be the same bank.

Step 7

The Negotiating bank will check the documents and ensure that they conform to the Letter of Credit. The documents are then sent to the Issuing bank.

Step 8

Upon receipt of the documents the Issuing bank will check them. If the documents are in order they will release funds to the Negotiating bank, so that in turn they can credit the exporter. Release is based on a Bill of Exchange either payable at:

- *Sight (immediately), or*
- *Term (with a period of credit e.g. 90 days).*

Step 9

The Issuing bank releases the documents to the buyer, in order that the buyer can take possession of the goods, for example through the bill of lading.

A key principle is that banks only deal in documents, and not in goods. The decision to pay under a Letter of Credit is entirely based on whether the documents presented to the bank by the exporter are in accordance with the terms of the Letter of Credit. Providing the documents conform the bank will pay.

Banks will adopt a Doctrine of Strict Compliance- the documents must conform to the Letter of Credit.

Summary: Letter of Credit Flowchart

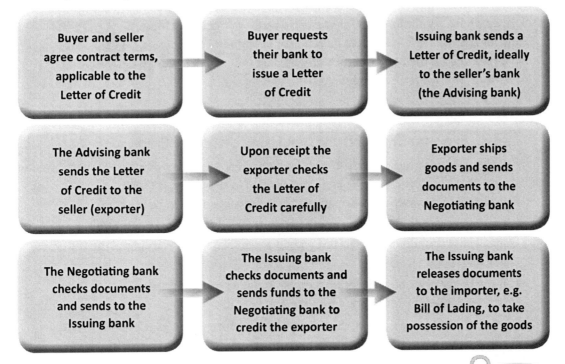

The Different Methods of Payment

An Importer Completing a Documentary Letter of Credit

Always liaise with the bank, which will provide support on completing the Letter of Credit.

When instructing the Letter of Credit give the bank clear and precise instructions – avoid unnecessary requirements. Information (content) should include:

- Who pays what charges
- The correct monetary amount
- The delivery terms (Incoterms)
- The exporter's name and address
- Ensure both company's names and addresses are exactly as stated in the sales contract, and documentation
- The goods description should be kept as brief as possible e.g. enough information for identification, and to evidence quality control. The description must be consistent with the sales contract
- Ensure the expiry date allows time for shipment and presentation of documents to the bank

4

Note: If possible the Letter of Credit should be completed on the bank's Electronic Banking platform and sent electronically to the bank. This will allow for standard information to be retained in template format and avoid rekeying for the bank – in turn speeding up the issuance process and reducing propensity for error through manual keying of data.

HINTS *and* **TIPS**

What an Exporter Should Do When Using Letters of Credit

HINTS *and* **TIPS**

- When preparing quotes for prospective customers, exporters should note that banks only pay the amount specified in the Letter of Credit – costs for shipping, insurance and other documents need to be covered.

- Ensure close contact with the buyer before they issue the Letter of Credit. Ideally buyer and seller (exporter) should agree the precise wording of the Letter of Credit before it is issued.

- If the Letter of Credit calls for documents supplied by third parties, ensure there is reasonable time for this to complete.

- After dispatch of the goods, check all the documents, both against the terms of the Credit AND against each other for consistency.

On Receipt of the Letter of Credit

- Upon receiving the Letter of Credit check that all terms and conditions can be complied with, within the quoted timescales:

  The expiry date of the Credit

  The latest shipment date

  The maximum time allowed between dispatch of the goods, and presentation of documents

- Check the Letter of Credit to ensure it corresponds with what was agreed with the buyer

- If there are any issues the buyer must be informed and their bank must amend the Credit accordingly.

Rules Governing Letters of Credit – Uniform Customs and Practice for Documentary Credits

The Uniform Customs and Practice (UCP) for Documentary Credits are a set of rules on the issuance and use of Letters of Credit. UCP is used by banks and should be adhered to by buyers and sellers in international trade.

UCP rules have been developed and standardised by the ICC (International Chamber of Commerce). The current version for Documentary Credits is UCP 600 that formally commenced in July 2007.

A Letter of Credit should be issued subject to UCP 600; the credit will then be interpreted as being in accordance with the entire set of 39 articles. Any exception to the rules must be made by express modification or exclusion.

In recognition of the importance of UCP 600 to the operation of Letters of Credit, this section contains further detail highlighting the content headings for UCP 600, along with some distinctive points. The Appendix is provided for guidance only, it is not definitive. When dealing with Letters of Credit UK businesses should turn to their sources of information and advice such as banks and freight forwarding companies.

Circumstances in Which Letters of Credit Can Be Used

Letters of Credit are commonly used to reduce credit risk. The credit risk of the customer is effectively substituted with that of a bank

Letters of Credit can apply to a variety of circumstances, being more associated with international trade:

- *Because of the level of documentation required and higher bank charges, they would normally apply for **higher value sales contracts** – at least £10,000+ and often for higher sums.*

- ***Some countries** apply a policy of selling goods to foreign buyers against Letters of Credit (although this practice is less applicable than has been the case historically).*

- ***In the Far East** in particular Letters of Credit can provide a means for obtaining bank finance, covering the period from when the Letter of Credit is issued and received from the UK bank.*

- *Where the exporter has little or **no trading history** with the buyer and wants to increase certainty of payment through a Letter of Credit.*

- *The importer may be able to **improve cash flow** by using a Letter of Credit to negotiate credit terms with the buyer. From the buyer's perspective, they still have the security of payment and may be able to negotiate finance against the issued Letter of Credit, with their own bank.*

- ***Credit insurers** may specify the need for exporters to trade on Letter of Credit terms as a condition of insurance to certain countries.*

4 | The Different Methods of Payment

Documents in a Letter of Credit

Financial Documents

- *Bill of Exchange (Drafts)*

Commercial Documents

- *Invoice*
- *Packing List*

Transport/Shipping Documents

- *e.g. Bill of Lading*

Insurance Documents

- *Insurance policy or certificate*

Official Documents

- *Certificate of Inspection*
- *Consular Invoice*
- *Certificate of Origin*

Other documents can be called for such as evidence that the vessel is seaworthy.

Risks When Using Letters of Credit

Whilst Letters of Credit do help to reduce the risk in international trade, there are still some aspects that could result in either non-payment for the exporter, or the risk of the importer not receiving the goods of the required quality. Risks can arise through:

- ▼ *Discrepant documents*
- ▼ *Goods not being of the required quality*
- ▼ *Non-payment by the Issuing Bank or Country*

Discrepant Documents

If the documents presented by the exporter are not in accordance with the Letter of Credit, **payment will not be made**. A bank has a maximum of 5 banking days after the day of presentation of documents to determine if the presentation is compliant.

Unfortunately, it is common practice for documents to be discrepant with the following items, representing some of the more common reasons for discrepancies:

- *The Letter of Credit expired prior to presentation of documents.*
- *The Bill of Lading evidences shipment prior to or after the date range stated in the Letter of Credit (e.g. the shipping date is later than that allowed in the Letter of Credit).*
- *Charges are included on the invoice that are not authorised in the Letter of Credit.*
- *The description of the goods is inconsistent or not as stated in the Letter of Credit.*
- *Bills of Lading not stipulated as in the Letter of Credit e.g. freight prepaid is quoted when it was not stipulated.*
- *A document required by the Letter of Credit is not included in the documents presented.*
- *Invoice is not signed, or does not specify shipment terms as quoted in the Letter of Credit.*
- *Insurance coverage is insufficient or does not include the risks specified by the Letter of Credit.*

A business should do all it can to avoid the major discrepancies:

- *Ensure the credit amount is sufficient to cover the shipment costs.*
- *Ensure documents will be available and can be presented before the expiry date of the Letter of Credit.*
- *Work closely with the Freight Forwarder providing them with as much time as possible to complete necessary documentation. Consult with the Freight Forwarder prior to agreeing the terms of the Letter of Credit in order that they too can agree with what is submitted.*
- *Ensure the latest shipment date (if there is one) can be met.*
- *The exporter should require at least a 14 day period in which to present documents after the shipping date. If the Letter of Credit is silent on the presentation period, the time allocated is 21 days, which may be more suitable.*

If documents do get refused by the bank, it does not always follow that a business will not be paid. Mitigating options include:

1. *To correct the documents, if possible.*
2. *To instruct the Advising (Negotiating) bank to request the Issuing Bank for permission to pay despite the discrepancies*

    -at the same time it may be necessary to contact the buyer (importer), to explain the discrepancy and see if they will accept this, and accordingly request that they contact the Issuing Bank to advise them of their acceptance.

4 | The Different Methods of Payment

3. *To send documents to the Issuing bank on a collection basis, although this then becomes less secure.*

4. *Provide the bank with an indemnity if they pay, despite the discrepancies.*

If an exporter foresees early problems with a Letter of Credit they should as early as possible request an amendment from the buyer. The amendment process can apply as follows:

- *The seller requests an amendment to the Letter of Credit – it should request the amendment with the buyer first.*

- *If the buyer and Issuing bank agree to the changes, the Issuing bank will change the Letter of Credit, notifying the Advising bank of the amendment.*

- *The Advising bank will notify the seller of the amendment.*

Goods Not Being of the Required Quality/Quantity

If an importer has concerns or wants to ensure that the goods are of the required quality and quantity, they should seek to ensure that the documents providing such evidence are contained in the Letter of Credit, in particular an independent Inspection Certificate.

Non-Payment by the Issuing Bank or Country

When advising a Letter of Credit the advising bank assumes no other liability. If also it is the negotiating bank then it also assumes responsibility for checking the documents presented are in accordance with the Letter of Credit. It has no responsibility to the exporter, should either:

- *The Issuing bank be unable to pay (due to credit difficulties with the bank concerned).*

- *The Country be unable or unwilling to pay, for example payments are blocked out of the Country for financial reasons, or because of an act of war.*

These risks can be covered by the exporter asking the Advising Bank (again, ideally their main bankers) to add their **Confirmation** on the Letter of Credit. If the Advising bank agrees to do so it will charge a fee based on their perception of the Issuing bank risk and Country risk (in many respects this is similar to a credit decision).

Confirmation can be requested by the exporter if they have concerns about the political or economic stability of the buyer's country, or the strength and reputation of the issuing bank. Access to financial press may assist an informed decision in this respect.

Confirmation must be by a well known local bank to the exporter, ideally their main bankers. There is limited, if indeed any benefit, having the Letter of Credit confirmed by the UK office of the Issuing Bank abroad.

Trans-Shipment/Partial Shipments

For large value contracts, or long voyages - such as the UK to Australia – trans-shipment or partial shipment may arise. Trans-shipment being when a cargo switches vessels at some point in its journey. In these circumstances it is ALWAYS best to indicate on the Letter of Credit whether:

- *Trans-shipments are allowed OR not allowed.*
- *Partial shipments are allowed OR not allowed.*

Summary: Advantages and Disadvantages of a Letter of Credit

Advantages	Disadvantages
Exporter	
Guaranteed payment upon presentation of the documents specified in the terms of the Letter of Credit	*Banks charges will be higher especially if the UK bank adds their Confirmation to the Letter of Credit. Additional charges will apply in the event of discrepant documents or amendment to the Letter of Credit*
The ability to structure the delivery schedule according to the exporter's interest	*The exporter will require to undertake more administrative work, throughout the company in order to ensure they comply with the terms of the Letter of Credit*
The opportunity to obtain financing for production or purchase of goods, and for the period post shipment	
The buyer cannot refuse to pay due to a complaint about the goods	*Some importers may not be able to open Letters of Credit due to the lack of credit facilities with the bank, which may as a consequence inhibit export growth*
Importer	
The possibility of structuring the payment plan according to the importer's intention	*Unless Confirmation is added by the UK bank the Exporter will be running the risk of the Issuing Bank being unable to pay, or the Country blocking payment*
Certainty that the payment will be made only upon presentation of the documents confirming shipment of the goods	*If an independent inspection certificate does not apply then the importer has limited protection against the quantity and quality of goods (even with a Certificate quality may be hard to determine)*
The use of a Letter of Credit allows the importer to avoid or reduce pre-payment, and can allow a period of credit to be built in	
The exporter must fulfil all terms of the contract as indicated in the Letter of Credit, in order to receive payment	*It will be necessary for an Importer to have a credit facility with their bank*
	Bank charges will be higher
Having opened a Letter of Credit the importer proves the ability to pay, and may be able to negotiate more favourable credit terms	*Set-up processes are likely to be more time consuming than with other forms of payment*

The Different Methods of Payment

4

Letter of Credit Checklist

Applicable for Importers and Exporters

Checklist		
1	**The Letter of Credit must state it is irrevocable**	✓
2	**Issued under UCP 600.**	✓
3	**Is the exporter comfortable with the credit risk of the Issuing Bank and Country/Political Risk – if there are concerns contact the UK bank and consider asking them to Confirm the Letter of Credit, check the cost first?**	✓
4	**Is it clear who is paying what bank costs – it may be more common practice for the importer to pay the Issuing Bank costs and the exporter to pay the Advising/Negotiating bank costs?**	✓
5	**Is it clear which Incoterms will apply?**	✓
6	**Does the shipment date and expiry date provide enough time to prepare documents and ensure payment?**	✓
7	**Are all names, addresses and locations reflected and spelt correctly?**	✓
8	**Is the description of the goods correct?**	✓
9	**Are there any particular requirements specified in the Credit e.g. pre-shipment, trans-shipment?**	✓
10	**And finally, does the Credit meet the requirements of the Sales contract?**	✓

Other Main Types of Letters of Credit

Transferable Letters of Credit

Governed by Article 38-39 of UCP 600

- This type of credit allows the exporter to transfer **all, or part** of their rights under the **original** Letter of Credit to a second beneficiary.

Usually the ultimate supplier of the goods

- *The Letter of Credit must clearly state that it is Transferable.*
- *Transferable Letters of Credit are associated when the seller (exporter) is a middleman, not the actual supplier of the goods – they obtain the goods from a third source, but do not have the resources to finance the purchase of the goods.*
- *As an "intermediary" a business can generate revenue for co-ordinating the trade transaction between the importer and exporter – BUT only if the intermediary can provide a unique skills set and* **add value** *to the transaction, in order to prevent the end importer and exporter dealing direct with each other.*
- *Value in this sense could include contacts, trust or consultancy skills which do not exist elsewhere.*
- *The Credit can be transferred only on the terms and conditions of the original Credit except for the:*
  - *Letter of Credit amount*
  - *Unit price of the goods*
  - *Expiry date of the Letter of Credit*
  - *Last date for presentation of documents*
  - *Period of shipment*

Revolving Letters of Credit

Features:

- *Used for regular shipment of goods between the same exporter and importer. The same Letter of Credit is used to cover numerous shipment schedules without the need for new Letters of Credit, or amendments to existing Letters of Credit.*
- *The Credit must state that it is a Revolving Letter of Credit.*
- *The Revolving Credit restricts the amount available for each shipment, and controls the frequency of shipments and amounts available.*
- *When a shipment has been made and documents have been presented and paid, the Credit becomes automatically re-available in its original form e.g. it is restored to its full amount.*

Back-to-Back Letters of Credit

- *Under back-to-back Letters of Credit (L/C), the first L/C services as collateral (security) for the second L/C.*
- *Used by 'intermediaries' and middlemen – they receive a Letter of Credit in their favour from the buyer. Against this, their own bank can establish a Letter of Credit in favour of the supplier.*
- *A lot of banks will avoid back-to-back Credits, due to their inherent risk.*

4 | The Different Methods of Payment

Standby letters of credit

Definitions

1. A secondary payment mechanism – a backup in case the buyer fails to pay in accordance with the terms of the contract.

2. An obligation by the issuing bank to a designated third party (the beneficiary - seller), that is **contingent** on the failure of the buyer to perform under the terms of a contract with the seller (failure to make payment).

3. In simple terms, the buyer wants to trade on open account terms, and the seller will only let them if they receive a guarantee that can be called upon in the event that the buyer does not make payment.

Points to Note

- *They are generally less complicated than documentary letters of credit, and involve far less documentation requirements.*

- *If the buyer fails to make payment, the guarantee is called upon and the bank issuing the guarantee will make payment on behalf of the buyer. Consequently the bank will seek recourse to their customer.*

- *To assist the bank in taking recourse they may request their customer to complete a counter guarantee which acknowledges the bank's right to seek recourse. If a lot of standby's are issued, the bank may seek an 'umbrella' counter guarantee, or the application form for each Credit may contain wording covering the counter guarantee*

- *The bank is likely to require security or cash collateral from their customer before issuing a guarantee – unless their customer has a strong credit rating.*

- *In general banks will not investigate the underlying facts of the transaction, e.g. they will not investigate whether or not there was a default or contract breach. In practice this favours the seller (the receiver of the guarantee).*

- *The Standby Letter of Credit is separate from and independent of the underlying contract.*

- *The bank only reviews conditions that are evidenced by a document. The bank's commitment is contingent upon the presentation of the stipulated documents, in accordance with the terms and conditions of the Standby Letter of Credit.*

- ***A payment under a Standby Letter of Credit arises out of documents evidencing that the applicant has failed to fulfil its contractual obligations.*** *In a lot of cases this is simply by means of the seller producing an unpaid invoice.*

Standby Letter of Credit Process Flow

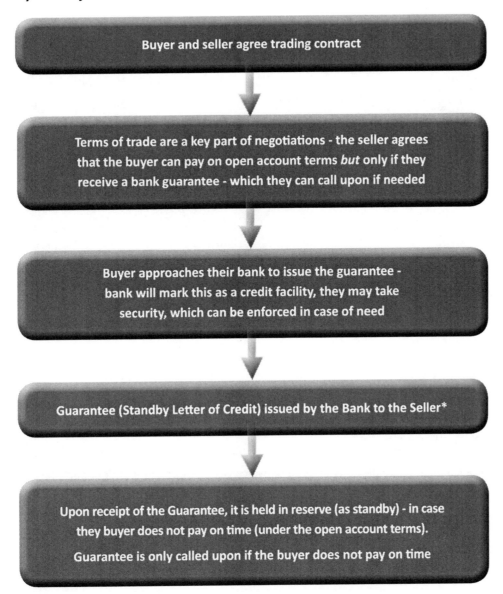

Buyer and seller agree trading contract

Terms of trade are a key part of negotiations - the seller agrees that the buyer can pay on open account terms *but* only if they receive a bank guarantee - which they can call upon if needed

Buyer approaches their bank to issue the guarantee - bank will mark this as a credit facility, they may take security, which can be enforced in case of need

Guarantee (Standby Letter of Credit) issued by the Bank to the Seller*

Upon receipt of the Guarantee, it is held in reserve (as standby) - in case they buyer does not pay on time (under the open account terms).

Guarantee is only called upon if the buyer does not pay on time

*Guarantee is usually sent direct by the Bank to the seller UNLESS the seller has concerns about the creditworthiness of the issuing bank or country/political risk. In such a case they can ask for the Standby Letter of Credit to be issued **through** a bank in their own country. Should this occur:

1. *The seller now has a guarantee added by a bank in his own country*
2. *Costs will increase as the bank in their own country will charge a fee for adding a guarantee – based on their perception of the issuing bank risk and country/political risk*

4 | The Different Methods of Payment

Differences between a Standby Letter of Credit and Documentary Letter of Credit

Standby Letter of Credit	Documentary Letter of Credit
Payment arises out of documents evidencing that the applicant has failed to fulfil its contractual obligations	**Payment under a Letter of Credit arises out of documents evidencing that the beneficiary has performed their contractual obligations**
Documents lack intrinsic value	**Documents under a Letter of Credit offer considerable control over the shipped goods**
As the Standby covers non-performance of the applicant, payment under the Standby Letter of Credit is not expected to arise	**This is a prime payment instrument**

Potential Risks to Consider

1. *Lack of expertise by the applicant to negotiate favourable terms under a Standby Letter of Credit may result in terms favouring the beneficiary.*

As the documents lack intrinsic value the applicant can try to call for additional documents to support a claim, for example copy of unpaid invoice issued by an independent party (arbitrator)

Appendix: UCP 600, for Documentary Credits

Table of Contents

Section 3 – Letters of Credit

Supplement to UCP 600 for Electronic Presentation is described shortly

Some key principles of UCP 600

- *Intention is that UCP 600 is easier to read, follow and apply*
- *Clearer rules, less room for banks to interpret to their liking*
- *UCP 600 does not only benefit the beneficiary*
- *Reduction in discrepancy rates*

Some Important Articles

Note: Wording below is, in some cases, in summary format, and not a direct quote from UCP 600.

Article 4a

The Letter of Credit is independent of the underlying contract.

Article 5

Banks deal with documents only, they are not concerned with the goods. If the documents submitted by the exporter appear to be in order then the bank is obliged to pay.

Article 10

A credit cannot now be amended or cancelled without the agreement of the issuing bank, confirming bank (if any) and the beneficiary (exporter).

Article 14

Documents no longer need to be "consistent," they need only be "not conflicting."

Article 14b

Banks have to accept or refuse documents within a defined period of five banking days.

Article 14j

Addresses of beneficiary and applicant no longer need to be as mentioned in the documentary credit, provided they are in the same country.

Article 17

At least one original of each document stipulated in the Credit must be presented for the Letter of Credit requirements to be fulfilled. This article also defines what constitutes an original document.

Transport

- *For Road, Rail and Inland Warranty, the transport document can indicate the date of receipt for shipment, dispatch or carriage (Article 24).*
- *For Courier and Post, a courier receipt may indicate a date of pickup, and a post receipt or certificate of posting can indicate a date of receipt for transport (Article 25).*

- *Transhipment – the prohibition of transhipment is inappropriate. Under Articles 19-24, transport documents may indicate that goods may, or will, be transhipped provided the entire carriage is covered by one and the same document, even if the Charter prohibits transhipment.*

Insurance

- *If "all risks" is stipulated, banks will accept any "all risks" notation or clauses in insurance documents (Article 28h).*

Special Feature: eUCP

To help avoid such delays electronic documentation can speed up the document exchange and document checking process. **The aim of this feature is not to go into great detail, but provide some direction and reference. Some of the articles are referred to, with a feature on background and benefits of eUCP referencing the market leading Cotecna E-Dox solution.**

In any economic environment efficient movement of goods, without delay, is crucial to a business – and none more so in times of economic slowdown, where every delay is a cost which a business cannot afford. Electronic documentation plays a vital role in helping to avoid potential delays.

Articles for Reference *(Sample Only)*

Article e1: *Scope of the eUCP*

Article e2: *Relationship of the eUCP to the UCP*

A Credit must indicate the applicable version of the eUCP. The Credit is also subject to the UCP. Where the eUCP applies its provisions shall prevail to the extent that they would produce a result different from the application of the UCP.

Article e3: *Definitions*

- *Documents shall include an electronic record*
- *Place for presentation of electronic records means an electronic address*
- *Electronic records means data created, generated, sent, communicated, received or stored by electronic means*

Article e4: *Format*

An eUCP must specify the formats in which electronic records are to be presented. If the format of the electronic record is not so specified, it may be presented in any format.

Article e5: *Presentation*

An electronic record that could not be authenticated is deemed not to have been presented.

The Different Methods of Payment

4

Article e6: *Examination*

Article e7: *Notice of Refusal*

Article e8: *Originals and Copies*

Article e9: *Date of Issuance*

Unless an electronic record contains a specific date of issuance, the date on which it appears to have been sent by the issuer is deemed to be the date of issuance.

Article e10: *Transport*

Article e11: *Corruption of an Electronic Record After Presentation*

Article e12: *Additional Disclaimer of Liability for Presentation of Electronic Records*

Background and Benefits of eUCP: The E-Dox Solution

With the E-Dox system, documents can now be checked and authenticated at each stage of the supply chain.

As a result:

- *There is a reduced risk of documents being lost or stolen.*
- *As the documents are in electronic format they are much easier to handle, and can be stored like any other electronic document (avoiding paper archiving).*

The E-Dox operates by means of a E-Dox is based on a state of the art security solution that was designed in-house by Cotecna IT security experts and uses the most advanced encryption technology (steganography). Even the slightest modification is detected by the authentication tool and the document is rejected. The E-Dox authenticity check is simple and immediate: it is performed through a dedicated and free on-line access. (**http://edox.cotecna.com/**).

Section Review

Having read the Letter of Credit section you should be clear on the following:

- ▼ *When a Letter of Credit can be used*
- ▼ *How a Letter of Credit operates*
- ▼ *The risks when using Letters of Credit and how to mitigate against them*
- ▼ *The different types of Letters of Credit*
- ▼ *The different parties to a Letter of Credit and their responsibility*
- ▼ *The advantages and disadvantages of using a Letter of Credit*

Section 3 - Letters of Credit

Topic refresher

Advantages of Letters of Credit

Importer *(Buyer)*

▼ *May be able to structure payment plan, introduce credit terms*

▼ *Can introduce documents which evidence quality control*

▼ *Payment is only made upon presentation of documents stipulated in the Letter of Credit*

Exporter *(Seller)*

▼ *Guaranteed payment upon presentation of correct documents*

▼ *Ability to structure delivery schedule according to the exporter's interest*

▼ *Opportunity to obtain finance for production (or purchase of goods) e.g. discount a Term Letter of Credit*

Mitigating the Disadvantages

Importer *(Buyer)*

▼ *Ensure documents evidence quality /quantity e.g. inspection certificate*

▼ *A good credit rating will improve the prospects of the bank issuing a Letter of Credit, and terms applicable*

▼ *Agree all wording beforehand with exporter (avoid amendments)*

Exporter *(Seller)*

▼ *Be clear on bank charges: only pay UK bank charges*

▼ *Try to get the Letter of Credit routed through your own bank – you can then work closely with them*

▼ *Work with Freight Forwarder to ensure documents are provided on time*

▼ *Ensure everyone in the company knows their responsibilities to make this work*

TOP LEARNING POINTS

1. *Prepare before using Letters of Credit*
   -Agree precise wording and terms with customer/supplier
   -Discuss/agree with Freight Forwarder

2. *Ensure it is clear who pays what charges*

3. *It is possible to obtain Credit Terms and/or Trade Finance through a Letter of Credit*
   -such as discounting a Credit payable at term or through an Import Loan

4. *Upon receipt the exporter must carefully Check ALL terms and wording in the Letter of Credit*

5. *Ensure documents are presented correctly AND on time*

4 | The Different Methods of Payment

Key Business Efficiency Measures

▼ *Project plan to make sure Letter of Credit is actioned correctly AND in good time*

▼ *Work with external parties, such as Banks and Freight Forwarders*

▼ *If needed consider finance opportunity to support working capital cycle*

▼ *Consider Confirmation by UK bank, but very much depending on Issuing Bank and Country*

▼ *Check all documents are in accordance with the terms of the Letter of Credit*

SECTION FOUR

TRADE FINANCE

Contents

The Different Methods of Payment

4

About This Section

Having looked at the different methods of trade settlements this section shall look specifically at the topic of Trade Finance.

The term Trade Finance can mean different things to different people – it is often over-used, and can be used in circumstances that complicate its true meaning. This section shall look at Trade Finance from the basic principle of *'How can a business generate the finance (capital) necessary to undertake UK and International Trade.'*

Undertake in this sense shall mean:

1. *Providing the means that creates the sales opportunity, such as offering credit terms, or providing confidence to the buyer that the seller is able to perform under the contract.*

2. *Providing the means by which the actual process of trade can take place between buyer and seller.*

Rather than focus on the actual term, Trade Finance, of far greater importance will be the individual financing products which comprise short, medium and long term finance - these are the tangible services available to companies. *The section will re-enforce a key principle of Trade Finance, namely it provides a business with a form of finance from within the trading transaction.*

To understand the specific methods of finance in greater detail it will be necessary to refer to other sections for detail around some of the products, notably those products highlighted under short term finance. In the case of medium and long-term finance, this section shall concentrate on Project Finance, Structured Trade and Commodity Finance and ECGD (Export Credits Guarantee Department).

Key Points to Note

As with other forms of bank lending, a key factor underpinning the availability of Trade Finance is the cost of capital, the capital a bank must set aside for providing the finance. Basel III is currently reviewing the capital rating applicable which shall determine whether favourable status can apply for the products illustrated. Particular aspects that will impact treatment of trade finance are

▽ *Exposure At Default- the amount of exposure (risk) for each transaction*

▽ *Loss Given Default- the credit loss incurred if the bank's customer defaults*

The Different Methods of Payment

4

What Is Trade Finance Seeking To Achieve?

Exporter

➤ Provides a seller (exporter) with payment earlier in the sales cycle.

➤ Provides a means by which the exporter can gain a competitive edge, by offering credit terms to the prospective buyer.

➤ Helps to reduce, or in some cases helps to eliminate, some of the risks in international trade – such as credit risk (the risk of not getting paid), or currency risk.

➤ Reduces some administrative processes from sales collection, such as chasing debtors.

➤ Allows the seller to link finance (credit) to a specific sales contract; as a result, this may be more cost effective than relying on other forms of finance to support sales, such as a bank overdraft.

Importer

➤ When provided through the export side of the transaction this may prove more cost effective than receiving finance locally through the importer's own bank.

➤ Allows the buyer to link finance to a specific purchase contract – as a result this may be more cost effective than relying on other forms of finance to support purchases, such as a bank loan or overdraft.

➤ This may provide the importer, in turn, with an opportunity to offer periods of credit to their customers, or it may provide time to 'customise' the product – without having the pressure of having to obtain a quick sale to support cash flow.

Circumstances in Which Trade Finance Can Arise

Trade Finance can cover a business need, when other, more traditional forms of finance are not appropriate, or indeed not available

Trade Finance may be particularly applicable when:

- *Credit periods are provided as part of a sales contract.*

- *Goods being supplied are part of the manufacturing process.*

- *A project requires start-up costs, prior to delivery e.g. cost of premises, materials for a construction project and/or employment costs for a consultancy project.*

- *Funding the working capital gap from the time of payment to the supplier, to receipt of payment from the buyer.*

Periods and Costs Associated with Trade Finance

The period of finance can be broken down into the following:

Short Term	Medium Term	Long Term
Generally less than a year *Especially applicable to raw materials, consumer goods, lighter capital goods and some service sector contracts*	*Periods of up to 5 years* *Project based activity e.g. construction projects and lighter capital goods*	*Periods of over 5 years* *Applicable for extensive project based activity involving flagship infrastructure projects*

For a bank the cost of providing Trade Finance is based on several factors:

1. **The customer credit risk.** *In many respects this will be no different to other forms of finance and a bank may accordingly apply the same lending margin.*

2. **The cost of providing the underlying product.** *The charge here will depend on the complexity and length of time it takes to provide and manage the product. For the more complex instruments such as Letters of Credit charges will be higher. There may also be arrangement fees for providing the finance product – as can apply with other forms of lending.*

3. **The bank and country risk** *– factors influencing pricing are discussed shortly.*

4. **The length of the finance being provided** *– in some cases a general rule may apply whereby the longer the length of the finance, the greater the risk of default. Finance costs are accordingly likely to be higher. Some banks may also be reluctant to lend for too long a period e.g. in excess of 180 days, or in excess of a year.*

The Different Methods of Payment

4

The Bank Perspective in Providing Trade Finance

> From a *Customer perspective* Trade Finance may be important in ensuring that the seller can compete for sales, and that they can finance them.
>
> From a *bank perspective* Trade Finance will be treated in a similar manner to other forms of lending – in short it must represent prudent (sensible) lending, that a bank can manage.

To assist understanding of why some forms of Trade Finance are more readily available (popular) than others, it is worth considering why banks and other providers **prefer** to use what we shall term as the more **mainstream** finance products, as opposed to niche products that are less widely available.

- *They want to provide products that are understood by the customer and bank staff alike. The higher the level of complexity the less well understood the products will be, which opens them up to misunderstanding and error.*

- *Banks will want to provide finance against risks they understand and can control. For example it is **preferable** lending money against invoices for finished goods that have been delivered to the buyer, **rather** than lending against contracts where the goods are work in progress, and delivery has yet to be made to the buyer.*

- *The costs of managing more complex finance products may not justify the controls which the bank have to put in place, especially for lower value contracts with a lower rate of return for the bank.*

Types of Trade Finance Available

For the purposes of this section, all the different terms of Trade Finance are quoted. Some in practice may represent the same outcome, it is just that different lenders and finance companies use different terms.

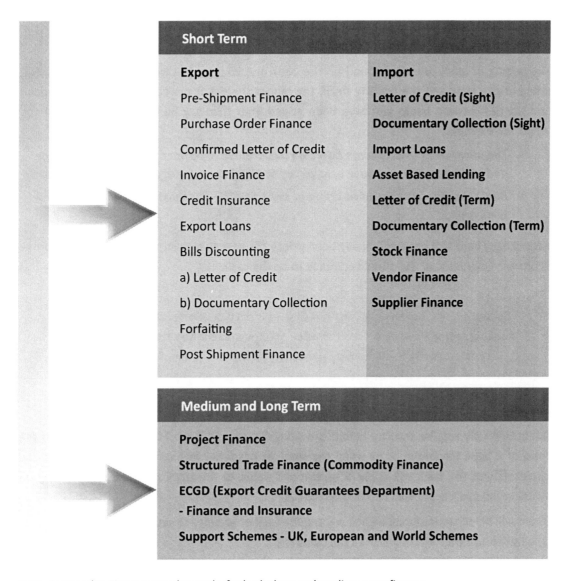

Short Term	
Export	**Import**
Pre-Shipment Finance	**Letter of Credit (Sight)**
Purchase Order Finance	**Documentary Collection (Sight)**
Confirmed Letter of Credit	**Import Loans**
Invoice Finance	**Asset Based Lending**
Credit Insurance	**Letter of Credit (Term)**
Export Loans	**Documentary Collection (Term)**
Bills Discounting	**Stock Finance**
a) Letter of Credit	**Vendor Finance**
b) Documentary Collection	**Supplier Finance**
Forfaiting	
Post Shipment Finance	

Medium and Long Term
Project Finance
Structured Trade Finance (Commodity Finance)
ECGD (Export Credit Guarantees Department) **- Finance and Insurance**
Support Schemes - UK, European and World Schemes

Note: Commodity Finance can also apply, for both short and medium term finance.

Lending Criteria and Associated Costs

- *As far as possible, banks will apply standard lending criteria to decision making, namely the financial performance of the business* **(known as customer risk).**

- *There may, however, be some circumstances when a trade transaction can be viewed in a different manner,* **allowing the finance to be provided when previously it may not be possible,** *for example, when an overseas bank has provided a guarantee of payment on a Letter of Credit or avalised Bill of Exchange* **(known as bank risk).**

The Different Methods of Payment

4

As described above, costs of providing trade finance will depend on the bank's perception of the underlying risk, be this customer or bank risk.

The pricing of bank risk will depend on the bank and country involved. The lower the credit rating of the bank and the country itself, the higher the risk is priced. Traditionally European and North American banks will have been priced finer than say banks in other parts of the world, for example:

> - *The provision of trade finance based on a guarantee of payment from Banks in Europe and North America may have been priced at 1% of the value of the transaction, or lower.*
> - *Banks in other parts would be priced at say 1.5%/2%+ depending on their country and bank rating.*

Accordingly, bank risk has traditionally been priced cheaper than customer risk and in a 'normal economic environment' this should continue to be the case.

Recent events, however, arising out of the global recession and difficulties in the banking sector, have increased the price of bank and country risk to a similar level as customer risk itself, namely a cost 2%/3%+ of the value of the transaction

Security

Banks normally require security before providing finance. In Trade Finance this can be in the form of a bank guarantee or by using the stock or customer invoice as the security. In these circumstances the bank will apply a 'repayment' value to the stock or invoice, depending on whether the stock is pre-sold and finished goods.

There will be occasions when a bank will require further security to support Trade Finance, such as a Debenture over all the assets of the company.

Short Term Trade Finance

Trade Finance for the Exporter

The type of finance available will vary during the different stages of the sales cycle – some finance will be readily available as part of a standard bank's offering and some will represent more niche finance **not** available from all banks and lenders.

Availability will be influenced by what banks and lenders feel comfortable providing, based on their ability to understand and manage the risk involved.

Section 4 - Trade Finance

The following chart highlights how finance arises during the sales cycle:

Contract Negotiation	Production of goods and services	Shipment of goods and services	Buyer receives goods and services

Pre-Shipment Finance

Purchase Order Finance

Confirmed Letters of Credit

Invoice Finance

Credit Insurance

Export Loan

Bills Discounting

a) Letters of Credit

b) Documentary Collection

Forfaiting

Post Shipment Finance

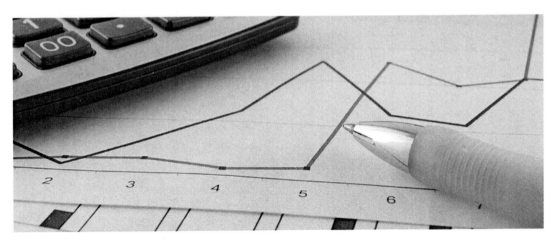

Details concerning how these methods of finance operate are highlighted in other sections of this book. In practice some of these methods of finance will be more readily available than others. The following chart illustrates availability by classifying products as either:

- *Mainstream (readily available), or*
- *Niche (only available in certain circumstances)*

The Different Methods of Payment

Mainstream Trade Finance	Niche Trade Finance
Confirmed Letter of Credit – when Confirmed by a UK bank **Invoice Finance** – comprising Confidential Invoice Discounting in particular, and Factoring **Credit Insurance** **Bills Discounting** a) Letters of Credit b) Documentary Collections Banks advance money against the buyer's – or more likely, the buyer's bank - guarantee to pay a Bill of Exchange at a future date	**Pre-Shipment Finance** – requires the bank to advance monies against a contract that is to take place. This may arise if an exporter has a confirmed order from a 'quality' buyer, backed for example by a Letter of Credit. Evidence of a long and successful trading history will support availability of finance **Post-Shipment Finance** – could be described as the process of discounting a Bill of Exchange under a Documentary Collection or Letter of Credit. When provided on a standalone basis it represents the advance of monies against the sales order of a 'quality buyer.' Evidence of a long and successful trading history will support availability of finance **Purchase Order Finance** – finance is provided against the purchase order issued to the buyer; in some respects this is a variation on invoice finance, although not as mature. Electronic exchange of the Purchase Order through banking channels such as the 'Trade Services Utility' may increase the popularity of this method of finance **Export Loans** – in some cases this is used to describe Pre-Shipment and Post Shipment Finance. In cases where it doesn't it represents a process of a bank lending against the performance risk of the exporter, in essence the bank must have confidence that the exporter will perform as stated in the contract **Forfaiting**

Summary

The availability of niche trade finance products is more likely to be applied in the following circumstances:

- *For well established exporters with a good trading history with the buyer.*
- *Where there is a Letter of Credit involved, providing structure to the trade transaction.*
- *Where there is a 'quality' (well known) buyer, usually a large company – with a Confirmed Sales Order.*
- *Where there is clear security for the bank, which they can control.*
- *Where the exports being financed are finished goods (and not in the early stages of manufacture).*

Trade Finance for the Importer

Banks and Finance providers also offer a range of trade finance services for the importer. Indeed in some instances finance may be more readily available for the importer, as a result of the greater level of control that the bank may be able to exercise – for imports, the risk for the bank is not dissimilar to other forms of lending namely the ability of their customer to repay the finance. Unlike export finance the bank does not have to rely to the same extent on the performance risk associated with their customer.

The following chart highlights how finance arises during the purchase cycle:

| Contract terms agreed with seller | Payment Period | Shipment of goods and services | Buyer receives goods and services |

Letters of Credit (Sight)
Documentary Collection (Sight)
Import Loans
Asset based lending
Vendor Finance
Supplier Finance

Letter of Credit (Term)
Documentary Collection (Term)
Stock Finance

The Different Methods of Payment

4

Mainstream Trade Finance	Niche Trade Finance
Letter of Credit (Sight) – the importer achieves a deferred payment before they have to pay out under the Letter of Credit – they do not have to pay immediately for the goods purchased.	**Stock Finance** – is available from banks and specialist lenders, but usually as a part of another larger facility, such as asset based lending or invoice finance.
Documentary Collection (Sight) – the importer will not have to pay until the Bill of Exchange is presented for payment.	**Supplier Finance** – the bank provides finance direct to the importer, based on the strength of their relationship with their customer, the exporter. In this way the exporter can support their supplier. Banks do not usually provide this type of finance as there are risks in dealing with an unknown supplier in another country, unless it is with recourse to the exporter, or the bank has a branch in the importer's country, with a knowledge of the local market and local business.
Import Loans* – banks may increasingly provide import loans as they can apply the loan to a specific purchase contract. If strong security is in place by way of a Debenture then banks may be more willing to lend, as they will have the security over the stock, the onward sales contract and other assets of the company. Additionally a bank may be more prepared to lend if the importer is able to evidence a confirmed order on the sales side.	
Asset based lending – Hire Purchase and Leasing.	
Letter of Credit (Term) - an additional period of credit is obtained from the seller if the Letter of Credit is at term, payable at a future date.	
Documentary Collection (Term) –an additional period of credit is obtained from the seller if the Bill of Exchange is drawn at term, payable at a future date.	
Vendor Finance – Finance provided by banks that allows the seller of goods and services to offer 'point-of-sale' finance to the buyer. Banks will generally have developed relationships with large suppliers of certain goods and services enabling them in turn to obtain pricing discounts through bulk purchasing. Particularly applicable for equipment finance and capital goods, office products and technology. Goods can be provided on a hire purchase or leasing basis.	

Import Loans – Features and Benefits

- Bridges the gap between making payment to suppliers and receiving money from customers (known as the working capital gap).

- Enables the importer to negotiate better terms with their suppliers, by making payment earlier.

- Available in all major currencies.

- Available on a pre-shipment or post-shipment basis.

- Loans can be provided on a stand-alone basis for open account transactions, or coupled with Letters of Credit or Documentary Collections.

- Security by way of a Debenture over the assets of a company or a 'pledge' on the sales proceeds. Transport documents may also be made out in favour of the bank.

Summary:

When Is Short Term Trade Finance More Likely To Be Available

- **For businesses with a strong trading history**

- **For mainstream trade finance products highlighted in this module**

- **When the trading counterparty are large multi-national businesses**

- **When another Bank adds their guarantee of payment to that of their customer**

- **Where an established trading instrument is in place, for example finance provided under a Letter of Credit**

The Different Methods of Payment

4

Medium and Long Term Trade Finance

Features

Medium Term Finance	Long Term Finance
Available on 2-5 year contracts	*Available for finance in excess of 5 years*
Higher value contracts	*Used to finance fixed assets, expansion of companies and construction projects on a large scale*
Associated with building or construction projects, and supply of large machinery/ capital goods	
Involves a longer production cycle	*Very high monetary sums*
Business applying for facilities will tend to be larger companies, with greater resources	*Finance may come from a number of sources, as the monetary sums are so high it is unlikely to come from one source*
Businesses will require a strong balance sheet to access finance	*Grand scale, high profile projects associated with large improvements to a country's infrastructure*
There may be limits applied to the sum advanced, in recognition of the higher monetary value of contracts. The buyer, for example, may have to make a 'down payment' in excess of 15% of the contract value	

Types

Project Finance

Structured Trade Finance
-incorporating Commodity Finance

ECGD (Export Credits Guarantees Department)
-medium term finance and medium term insurance

Development (Support) Banks

Note: Some of these methods of finance are also available on a short-term basis.

Project Finance

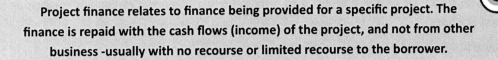

> **Project finance relates to finance being provided for a specific project. The finance is repaid with the cash flows (income) of the project, and not from other business -usually with no recourse or limited recourse to the borrower.**

Features of Project Finance

- *Usually applies for long term projects (public sector and private sector) – examples of projects include mining, transport projects, building projects, telecoms and utilities.*

- *May require large initial investments, for example in the case of a construction/ infrastructure project, such as road building.*

- *Applicable to developments in all countries, including developing countries.*

- *Many of the projects in the UK and Overseas will be government backed, and government funded.*

- *If government backed they may receive a government guarantee of payment.*

- *It is common for there to be several finance providers – with one lead finance partner syndicating the finance amongst other finance providers, in order to distribute the risk.*

- *Finance is usually secured against all the project's assets, including the sales contracts.*

- *A separate legal entity (company) can be created for each project, thereby protecting other assets owned by the business in the event of project failure. This is sometimes referred to as a special purpose entity or special purpose vehicle (SPV).*

- *Shipping finance and aircraft finance are variations of project finance*

- *Detailed legal contracts will be a feature, recognising the complexity of such contracts.*

- *Competitive tendering will arise, which is likely to include bank guarantees provided as evidence of the company's ability to tender for and perform the contract (through Bid Bonds and Performance Bonds).*

Risks in Providing Project Finance

Risks can be greater in providing finance because of the large monetary sums involved, longer repayment periods, along with the fact that the finance is repaid once the project is operational. If a major part of the project fails a lender could lose a large sum of money. The assets could also be in remote locations and be of a specialised nature, specific to the project in question.

For this reason a lender will review the project proposition in some detail, and may want to increase reliance on government and/or bank guarantees as security of payment, before providing finance.

The Different Methods of Payment

4

Structured Trade Finance

Like the term Trade Finance itself, the term Structured Trade Finance is used to describe different purposes. It can for example be used to discuss Project Finance, Commodity Finance or pre-export finance.

In general structured trade finance refers to:

▽ *Complex finance arrangements for high value contracts, usually long term.*

▽ *Large orders of specific commodities (e.g. oil, metals) or specific capital goods (e.g. machinery).*

A feature of Structured Trade Finance is that lending focus moves from the 'strength of the borrower' to the underlying transaction and the cash that is generated from it.

The bank usually lends against the value of the cash that can be realised.

-Less an amount to account for risk factors, such as damage to the goods and a lower resale value.

If the business is unable to repay the borrowing the bank will take possession of the goods and sell them to realise funds towards repaying the borrowing.

Commodity Finance

Commodity finance can be split into three main commodity groupings:

▽ *Metals and Mining*

▽ *Energy*

▽ *Soft Commodities (e.g. agricultural crops)*

It is a financing technique used by commodity producers and commodity brokers.

➤ *Finance is provided on the basis that the assets have relatively predictable levels of income, based on predictable levels of pricing.*

➤ *A business is therefore borrowing against a commodities expected worth.*

➤ *A lender is repaid through the sale of the assets.*

➤ *In the event of default, a lender has recourse to the assets (commodity).*

➤ *As commodity prices can be volatile, only certain banks and specialist lenders provide commodity finance, in some cases with high arrangement fees and higher lending margins applying.*

Export Credits Guarantee Department (ECGD)

ECGD is the UK's official Export Credit Agency. Its primary purposes are

▼ *The provision of finance to support the sale of:*

  a) UK capital goods, for example aircraft or machinery.

  b) UK services, such as project management and design.

  This support enables exporters to offer extended credit terms to the customers, and enables exporters and banks to win business in markets which otherwise would be considered as too risky.

▼ *ECGD also helps UK companies to invest in overseas projects, such as water treatment plants or power stations.*

ECGD complements, rather than competes with, the private sector by offering finance and/or insurance cover on a medium and long term basis, risks that the private sector does not cover. These terms are in excess of 2 years, with the exception of the Letter of Credit Guarantee Scheme that is described in an earlier section, <u>and the new export support schemes of which further details are provided in the website linked to this book.</u>

The objectives of ECGD include benefitting the UK economy by helping exporters of UK goods and services win business, **and** for UK firms to invest overseas. This is met through:

  ▪ *Insurance to exporters, against non-payment.*

  ▪ *Guarantees to banks to assist the financing of exports.*

  ▪ *Insurance to UK companies and banks for overseas investments.*

The largest part of ECGD's activities involve **underwriting** long term loans to support the sale of capital goods – supporting UK companies to take part in major overseas projects, such as the construction of oil and gas platforms and the upgrading of hospitals and airports. Support can be provided for contracts as low as £25,000, although some of the projects ECGD backs are in excess of £100 million.

When applying for support, applicants have to make a number of disclosures and declarations; a company must, for example, declare that none of their directors have admitted to, or been convicted of, engaging in any form of bribery or corruption.

Support Provided To the Exporter Direct

  ▪ *Export Insurance Policy*

  ▪ *Bond Insurance Policy*

  ▪ *Overseas Investment Insurance*

Support Provided To Banks Working on Behalf of the Exporter

  ▪ *Buyer Credit*

  ▪ *Supplier Credit Facility*

  ▪ *Project Finance*

4 | The Different Methods of Payment

Support Provided To the Exporter Direct

Export Insurance Policy

Protects an exporter from the following risks:

- *The insolvency or extended default of the buyer (and any guarantor of the buyer) – within six months from the due date – known as commercial risk.*
- *Political events, which prevent the settlement of contract payments, or prevents performance of the contract – known as political risk.*
- *Any event in the UK that prevents performance of the contract, for example non-renewal of an export licence.*

Insurance coverage is up to 90% with the exporter retaining the risk for the uninsured percentage.

The insurance policy can be issued in two formats:

1. *A pre-shipment policy, which is the more popular. This will include the risk before shipment.*
2. *An after (post) shipment policy – also referred to as 'Costs Incurred' and 'Amounts Owing Cover.'*

Bond Insurance Policy

This policy provides protection in the event of:

a) *An on-demand bond being called unfairly, or*
b) *Fair calls made as a result of political events (fair within the terms of the bond).*

It is usually only available when ECGD provides other support for a contract – such as the Export Insurance Policy, or Supplier/Buyer Credit Guarantees (see below).

The most common types of bonds/guarantees covered are

- *Advanced Payment Guarantees*
- *Performance Bonds*
- *Counter-Guarantees and Counter Indemnities*

Cover is **not** applicable for Tender Bonds.

As with other insurance policies the exporter will require to show that they have done all they can to fulfil their obligations.

Overseas Investment Insurance

Provides cover for investments made in developing countries. Cover can be provided for an exporter investing in an asset overseas – for example building a new factory, or to a bank providing a loan for the purchase of an overseas asset.

Events covered comprise political risks (not commercial) risks, including:

- *Assets being confiscated or nationalised.*
- *Cover against war, strikes or regulatory changes.*
- *Breach of contract, where the overseas government has caused the breach.*

Benefits of these Policies

- *ECGD provide a single source of insurance against a wide range of risks. Whilst some of these may be encountered they are outside of the control of the exporter.*
- *They provide the ability to trade with Countries/Regions that the exporter may have considered, previously, to be too risky.*
- *The exporter has the ability to compete for contracts that require export credit support.*

Support Provided To Banks Working on Behalf of Exporter

Buyer Credit

With a Buyer Credit facility a bank enters into a loan agreement with an overseas borrower, in order to finance the purchase of goods or services from an exporter. This enables the exporter to receive payment at delivery or at the different stages of the payment cycle.

In order to support the loan ECGD provide a guarantee to the bank, covering the borrower's risk of non-payment.

Buyer credits can be used for large transactions and long contract periods with several delivery and payment cycles.

Insurance is also provided to the exporter in the event the contract is terminated prior to delivery.

Supplier Credit Facility

Arises where a buyer is required to offer credit terms of at least two years for an export contract. A supplier credit facility allows the exporter to sell on these credit terms – passing the payment risk onto the bank that in turn is guaranteed by ECGD.

The seller receives the full credit value at presentation of the documents, for example, bills of exchange including proof of shipment – on occasions without recourse. Minimum contract value is £25,000 with 85% credit advanced, and semi-annual instalments.

Banks participate in the scheme through a Master Guarantee Agreement.

ECGD may require say the bill of exchange to be unconditionally* guaranteed by a third party, for example a bank. Where the buyer is a public buyer, guarantees may also be needed from the relevant Government.

Unconditionally, in this sense, means not affected by any commercial dispute between the buyer and seller. The guarantee must be unconditional for finance to be provided without recourse.

4 The Different Methods of Payment

Supplier credit is often combined with supplementary cover, by way of an Export Insurance Policy in favour of the seller, covering the pre-delivery risk period and up to the refinancing of the bill of exchange (known as the pre-credit period).

Project Finance

Where an exporter is involved in a major project overseas, ECGD may support financing arrangements, under which the banks providing finance rely primarily upon the revenues of the project for repayment.

As with a Buyer, Credit ECGD's support takes the form of a guarantee to the lending bank, in respect of the loan they have made to the company. This support will usually only be suitable for major projects with a value in excess of £50 million pounds.

Benefits of these Policies

- *Provides exporters with the ability to offer customers credit terms with deferred payments, whilst continuing to receive cash payments under ECGD supported bank facilities.*
- *Exporters have a wide choice of UK based banks, which are experienced in providing ECGD banked facilities.*
- *Competitive financing terms for exporters/customers backed by the support of ECGD (effectively a UK Government guarantee).*

ECGD Terms of Business

Premium Payable

The exporter who benefits from these facilities pays a premium to ECGD, irrespective of whether the ECGD support is provided direct to the exporter or their bank. The level of premium paid will depend on:

- **The value of the contract.**
- **The length of the credit terms.**
- **The perceived credit-worthiness of the overseas buyer, including the country rating.**

Key Conditions

Although ECGD's primary purpose is to support British exporters it also has to comply with broader Government policy and objectives.

In order to obtain ECGD support exporters will have to:

- *Provide detailed information about any overseas agents used.*
- *Complete declarations and undertakings relative to anti-bribery and corruption.*
- *Complete an Environmental Impact Questionnaire.*
- *Provide a detailed breakdown on the mix of 'national content' involved in the project (contract).*

Development (Support) Banks

Development (Support) Banks have been established with the primary purpose of supporting projects vital for economic and social benefit within regions. Globally there are Development Banks operating in different regions of the world. This section shall look at three of these banks.

The World Bank Group

▽ *The International Development Association (IDA) participates in lending to developing countries on 'soft' (competitive) terms.*

▽ *IFC (International Finance Corporation) promotes projects for development of private industry, by participating as shareholder or lender in joint ventures or projects vital to the country.*

▽ *MIGA (Multinational Investment Guarantee Agency) guarantees the political risks for investments and projects in developing countries.*

▽ *The World Bank sets five key factors necessary for economic growth:*

  ▪ *Build capacity*

  ▪ *Infrastructure creation*

  ▪ *Development of Financial Systems*

  ▪ *Combating corruption*

  ▪ *Research, Consultancy and Training.*

European Bank for Reconstruction and Development (EBRD)

▽ *International financial institution supports projects in 29 countries from central Europe to Central Asia (including many former Soviet republics).*

▽ *Invests mainly in private sector clients whose needs cannot be fully met by the market.*

▽ *Provides project finance both new ventures and investments in existing companies.*

▽ *Also works with publicly owned companies to support privatisation, and improvement of services.*

▽ *Owned by 61 countries.*

▽ *Recent initiatives include Sustainable Energy to scale up energy efficiency.*

▽ *Through the Trade Facilitation Programme EBRD provides credit facilities in the form of guarantees in favour of banks, covering the political and commercial risk of the local bank or buyer in the region.*

4 | The Different Methods of Payment

European Investment Bank (EIB)

▽ **EIB is the European Union's long term financial institution**

▽ **Its key purposes include:**

1. *To finance capital investments in the member states.*

2. *To support the EU's external partnerships and development policies.*

3. *Finance loans for small and medium sized enterprises (SME's).*

▽ **Under these schemes domestic banks apply for EIB funded loans for specific purposes, in order for the banks to offer discounted facilities to their customers.**

▽ **For larger businesses finance facilities include venture capital or individual loans Guarantees are also provided for debt.**

SECTION FIVE

BONDS AND GUARANTEES

Contents

4 | The Different Methods of Payment

About This Section

Bonds and Guarantees are an increasing feature of international trade, as importers and exporters seek to reduce risks relative to non-payment AND non-performance. This increase is taking place across a number of business sectors and in businesses of all sizes. They can also, in certain circumstances, apply to domestic UK trade.

In recognition of the increase, this section shall provide details with respect to the different types of bonds and guarantees that support trade. For the primary types of guarantees further detail is provided, along with a summary of benefits.

The difference between Bank Guarantees, Surety Bonds and Standby Letters of Credit will be highlighted, along with discussion on risks, and legal pointers when dealing with these instruments.

Key Learning Topics

Note: All areas of this section will be important, with the following areas denoted by way of indicating primary content.

	For Businesses	For Employees	For Students
Why Guarantees May Be Required	✓	✓	✓
How Guarantees Can Be Used to Support Business Growth	✓	✓	
Implications of Demand Guarantees		✓	✓
Effective Use of Guarantees (e.g. Wording, Applicable Law, Avoid Unfair Calling)		✓	✓
How Guarantees Can Be Used to Support Cashflow	✓	✓	

Key Words:

Bonds and Guarantees: The two terms are synonymous. Issued by a bank or financial institution, ensuring that the liabilities of their customers are met. If their customer fails to meet their obligations, the bank guarantee is called upon.

Beneficiary: The beneficiary is the recipient of the guarantee, often the buyer (customer/importer), who wants to cover against supplier risk.

The Different Methods of Payment

Key Words cont'd

Principal: Often the supplier (seller/exporter) who has undertaken to perform a contract. They approach their bank to issue the guarantee.

Bank or Financial Institution: The issuer of the guarantee. For the purposes of this chapter reference to bank shall also be deemed to include other financial institutions such as insurance companies and trade finance companies – unless otherwise stated.

The Role of Bonds and Guarantees in Facilitating Trade

If a business is concerned about the risk of undertaking trade, Guarantees (also known as Bonds) are worth considering. They serve a number of purposes, but principally protect customers against supplier risk by providing guarantees of compensation. They are commonly used for longer-term contracts and infrastructure/build projects.

Guarantees issued by a financial institution, such as the supplier's bank, undertake to compensate the customer to a trading contract, should the supplier default and/or not meet their obligations. An example would be performance guarantees in construction projects.

The use of guarantees has increased in recent years as customers look to cover supplier risk. The customer (beneficiary) is protected against the default, insolvency or non-performance of the supplier (principal), up to the limit of the guarantee.

Standby Letters of Credit are another form of guarantee which can be used to cover a specific purpose, or act as an alternative to bank guarantees. These will be described later in this section.

Guarantees: Overview of Benefits

▼ *Provides reassurance to enable trade with suppliers whose contract performance is not guaranteed*

▼ *Improves the probability of securing delivery of imported goods*

▼ *Offering a guarantee during negotiation can help exporters secure contracts they would otherwise lose*

▼ *Limitation of risk related to breach of contractual obligations*

The Types of Guarantees

Tender Guarantee or Bid Bond

PRINCIPAL
Supplier who is tendering for a contract

Issued by Bank at Tender

BENEFICIARY
Customer receiving goods and services

Section 5 - Bonds and Guarantees

Issued to ensure that the supplier (exporter) submits realistic bids under the tender process, to protect the beneficiary (importer) for any loss that might occur if the supplier fails to sign the contract. A bid bond also assures the customer that the supplier will comply with the terms of the contract in the event that the tender is accepted. In the event that the supplier does not perform the contract, the bond is called on.

Bid bonds are usually issued for around 2-10% of the tender amount. They are often a condition for the consideration of a tender, especially in the case of government contracts –they remain valid during the period of tender, plus a grace period to allow the beneficiary to make demand.

Summary

Bond issued in favour of the beneficiary (importer)

Bid bonds secure payment of the guaranteed amount

- ■ *In the event of withdrawal of the offer before its expiry date*
- ■ *If the contract, after being awarded, is not accepted by the tendering party*
- ■ *If the bid bond after the contract has been awarded, is not replaced by a performance bond*

A bid bond provided by a reputable bank can represent a sales advantage at the tender stage

Performance Bond

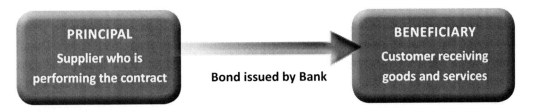

The most common form of guarantee normally required when the contract has been awarded. This safeguards the beneficiary, should the supplier fail to meet their contractual obligations. Performance bonds are issued at around 5-20% of the contract amount, sometimes higher, but may be fixed by the local law of the importer's country. Obligations under a performance bond could relate to their supply, or obligations covering function and quality during the agreed period of the guarantee.

The Bond will extend over the duration of the contract, plus a grace period to allow the beneficiary to make a demand in the event of non-performance of the obligations covered by the guarantee.

The Different Methods of Payment

4

Summary

Bond issued in favour of the beneficiary (importer)

- *Demonstrates to the contracting party (beneficiary) that the tendering party has the required financial strength to complete the contract*
- *Provides support to the contract*
- *Secures payment for the beneficiary in the event the contract is not fulfilled, for example in quality or timeliness*

Advance Payment Guarantee

PRINCIPAL		BENEFICIARY
Supplier who has received advance payment	Guarantee issued by Bank →	Receiver of the Guarantee, the Customer who has advanced funds

For a supplier it may be possible to negotiate an advance payment under an awarded contract, for example to enable initial purchase of the essential raw materials required to perform the contract. As these guarantees enable payment of cash to take place in advance of work being carried out they can provide significant cash flow benefits to the supplier.

For the beneficiary (customer) an advanced payment guarantee will secure return of the amount advanced, or part thereof, if the supplier fails to fulfil their underlying contractual obligations.

The value of the guarantee is usually the amount advanced. This can cover any amount of the contract but are usually 10-30% of the contract price. Some guarantees may provide for pro-rata reductions to the amount, on presentation of certain documents, or at specified date/s. Duration will depend on the underlying contract but these can remain valid up to the anticipated date of the final delivery, plus a grace period to allow the beneficiary to make demand in the event of non-performance of the obligations covered in the guarantee.

Summary

Guarantee issued in favour of the beneficiary (importer)

- *Provides supplier (exporter) with access to funds to proceed with completing the contract*
- *Can enhance the performance, reputation and credit standing of the supplier*
- *Provides protection for buyers who are asked to provide payment before goods or services are supplied*

Section 5 - Bonds and Guarantees

Progress Payment Guarantee

Applicable when the customer (buyer) pays in instalments before the final delivery has been made. Can apply when the buyer cannot make effective use of what the seller has provided until completion, but has had to agree to pay in connection with the progress of such work or delivery. These can be used for example in the Construction industry.

Guarantee is issued in favour of the beneficiary (importer).

Retention Monies Guarantee

Contracts may allow the buyer to retain a proportion of the contract value once the contract has nearly been completed – for example, retention of money at 10-15% of contract value. As an alternative these guarantees can be used, whereby the buyer would otherwise withhold part of the contract payment until full completion, post final installation or at start-up/working cycle of say the machinery.

These guarantees allow the buyer (beneficiary) to receive payments already made under the contract should the supplier not fulfil their obligations. Duration of the guarantee depends on the underlying contract terms and may extend for a period after completion of the contract.

Guarantee is issued in favour of the beneficiary (importer).

Warranty Guarantee

This safeguards the importer against the non-performance of the warranty by the supplier (exporter), for example, to cover a warranty on machinery and equipment.

This can act as an alternative to the buyer retaining part of the payment against the guarantee; amounts could be 10-15%, depending on the warranty commitments.

Guarantee is issued in favour of the beneficiary (importer).

Payment/Trade Debt Guarantee

This guarantee is used to cover the non-payment of a debt(s) under a transaction that extends over a period of time. This differs from a lot of the guarantees detailed above; it is issued by a bank on behalf of the buyer, **in favour of the seller (exporter)**.

Such guarantees provide financial security to the seller should the buyer fail to make payment for the goods or services supplied. They will normally remain in place up to the final scheduled date of payment, plus a further period to allow the seller to call on the guarantee in the event of non-payment.

A payment guarantee can be issued in the form of an endorsement on a draft/bill of exchange also known as an 'aval.'

4 | The Different Methods of Payment

Credit Guarantee (Facility Guarantee)

Can apply where the seller (supplier) may have a local subsidiary or affiliate unable to obtain credit/finance in its own right. The credit guarantee will support credit lines/banking facilities from local banks. These can also be provided by export credit agencies to support their country's business expand overseas.

These can also be termed as Facility Guarantees.

Guarantees in this instance are issued in favour of the party providing credit lines, such as a bank.

VAT Bonds/Duty Deferment Bonds

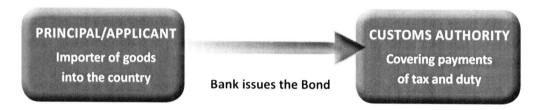

This provides a guarantee that the importer will pay all taxes and duties in connection with importing goods into a country.

In the case of the UK this is provided to HM Customs and Excise (HMRC), and allows the applicant (importer) to import goods from outside of the European Union without the immediate payment of duty/tax, which is invariably settled thereafter on a monthly basis by Direct Debit. HMRC provide paperwork for this type of guarantee, providing for protection from the risk of payment default.

Recently HMRC have introduced the Simplified Import VAT Accounting (SIVA) scheme. Importers can keep their business costs down by reducing the amount of the guarantee, whereby it only has to cover customs and excise duties and not the VAT. Not all businesses are authorised to use the SIVA scheme; acceptance will be more likely where the business has been VAT registered for at least 3 years, has a good credit history and a good VAT compliance history.

Summary

Bond issued in favour of HMRC

- *HMRC Bonds provide for payment of Duty and VAT deferred up to 45 days*
- *Guarantees usually available from banks, on a 12 month basis*
- *For an importer this frees up cash flow*
- *Use of SIVA can reduce the amount of the Bond*

Alternatives to Bank Guarantees

Surety Bonds and Insurance Companies

Surety bonds are generally issued by insurance companies who will carry out a review of audited accounts, management accounts and bank account information, prior to issuing the bond. Facilities are likely to be provided on a recourse basis, and the insurance company may require security.

A surety bond is a guarantee to pay a loss sustained as a result of a breach of contractual or legal obligations, for example non-completion of a construction project. There are usually three parties involved:

▽ *The beneficiary, who requires the surety bond to be provided*

▽ *The principal (contractor) who will be undertaking the contract obligation*

▽ *The guarantor who may be an insurance company*

The guarantor agrees to uphold the contractual promises made by the principal, if the principal fails to uphold their obligations. In return the principal will pay a premium (usually annually) in exchange for the bonding company's guarantees.

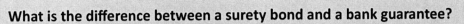

What is the difference between a surety bond and a bank guarantee?

Surety bonds are typically conditional whereas bank guarantees are on demand. *Only* the performance lies with the surety, whereas the bank has the financial risk.

Accounting wise, surety is accounted for as a liability like other insurance products, whereas credit risks in a bank are accounted for on the asset side.

Notwithstanding possible benefits described, bank guarantees may, however, still be required under the terms of a contract, eliminating the possible use of a surety bond.

In terms of benefits to a business, surety bonds may protect their lines of credits with banks, improving a company's liquidity. By using an insurance company the business will not have to use their bank lending facility for issuing guarantees, and consequently the facility can be used for other purposes.

Costs will vary depending on factors such as financial strength, the likely volume and nature of the bonds.

4 | The Different Methods of Payment

By way of example, some common types of surety bonds include:

- *Performance Bonds*
- *Duty Deferment Bonds*
- *Concession and licences*
- *Leases*
- *Construction and/or supply contracts*

Standby Letters of Credit

A Standby Letter of Credit serves a different purpose from the better known commercial (documentary letter of credit). It operates more as a secondary payment mechanism – issued by a bank on behalf of a UK importer providing a guarantee to the exporter of their ability to perform under the terms of the contract agreed between buyer and seller.

The beneficiary of the Standby Letter of Credit, the overseas exporter, is able to draw on the Credit if they provide documentary evidence, as outlined in the Credit, for example a statement of default, copies of unpaid invoices. The Credit will have an expiry date.

Through issuing the Credit the UK importer may 'avoid' having to make payment up-front gaining a period of credit that may not have been possible previously, effectively allowing the importer to operate on open account terms.

Whilst the exporter may not have received the money as early as previously they still have a bank guarantee of payment, which will be preferable to trading on account terms, providing improved certainty of receiving money on time

If the Credit is called upon the issuing bank will have recourse to their customer (the UK importer). They may also wish to take security to cover their liability. The bank will levy a fee for issuing the Credit usually at the same level as any borrowing facilities.

Standby Letters of Credit should generally be issued by a UK bank alone without the need to issue through a local bank overseas – thereby reducing cost of issuance.

Standby Letters of Credit can also be issued on a reducing clause basis, reducing the liability of the importer, if they are to make staged payments under the import contract.

HINTS *and* **TIPS**

Further details on Standby Letters of Credit are provided in a feature item in the Letter of Credit section.

Section 5 - Bonds and Guarantees

Features of Bank Guarantees

Demand Guarantees

What Is A Demand Guarantee?

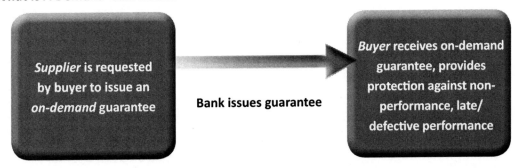

Supplier is requested by buyer to issue an *on-demand* guarantee

Bank issues guarantee

Buyer receives on-demand guarantee, provides protection against non-performance, late/defective performance

Demand Guarantees are common for a buyer (importer), who wishes to have security that a supplier will perform their obligations. Most guarantees described above will be issued on a 'demand' basis.

In these circumstances the guarantee issued by the bank would include an undertaking to pay the buyer on demand, up to the maximum sum quoted, *upon presentation* of a demand.

A Suppliers Perspective

Demand guarantees developed to replace cash deposits, which sellers (suppliers) had to provide in order to offer security for the buyer, should the seller default. From a seller's perspective this has helped to improve their cash flow and to an extent also reallocate the risks between the parties, which have been very much in favour of the buyer.

Good Practice When Issuing Guarantees

Although demand guarantees can be argued as being weighted towards the buyer, there are examples of good practice that can be used to support the supplier position.

- *Demand guarantees should require a statement that the supplier (exporter) is in breach for example:*

> **The demand for payment must be accompanied by your statement that the Principal is in breach of its contractual obligations and specify in what respect such breaches have occurred**

- *Demand guarantees should specify that the demand be accompanied by other documents supporting the claim.*

The Different Methods of Payment

4 |

- *The guarantee can be subject to the Uniform Rules for Demand Guarantees (URDG). Revised rules have come into force from 1st July 2010* which contain model forms of security and guarantee – wherever possible and if acceptable to the overseas party. Bonds will only be subject to URDG if they say they are.*

- *Demand Guarantees should include information on expiry – either in the form of an expiry date or an expiry event. Any presentation must be made on or before expiry. If issued under URDG, and if neither expiry date, nor no expiry event is quoted, the guarantee shall terminate after the lapse of three years from the date of issue.*

Standby Letters of Credit represent a possible alternative to Demand Guarantees in certain circumstances. They are similar in position in some respects with a key difference being that Standby Letters of Credit operate within the framework of more internationally accepted rules

* The changes from 1st July 2010 under the new URDG 758 include innovative treatments of payment contingency, and more precise language for determining presentation made under a guarantee or counter-guarantee, whether paper based or electronic. This is intended to curb the rate of rejection of demands, and increase the certainty of the guarantee instrument.

Direct/Indirect Guarantees
Direct Guarantee

A guarantee issued by the applicant's bank (the UK bank) directly to the beneficiary – without involving another bank overseas. From the perspective of the beneficiary abroad they will have to accept the credit risk of the UK bank

The costs (bank charges) for issuing a direct guarantee will be lower here, as only one bank is guaranteeing payment. For a UK business they should prove more popular, providing they are acceptable to the beneficiary.

Direct guarantees will apply for UK trade, and when required can also apply for trade with Europe, North America and other parts of the world, such as the Far East.

Indirect Guarantee

A guarantee issued by a local bank (usually the beneficiary's bank), upon the counter guarantee of the applicant's bank. From the point of view of the beneficiary they have the guarantee (bank risk) of a local bank

Indirect guarantees are usually issued through the SWIFT system. The costs (bank charges) will be higher as two banks are adding guarantee of payment – both parties, prior to issuance, should agree the costs and who pays such charges. In most cases the applicant for the guarantee, as the instructing party, pays all charges.

These guarantees are commonly used where government agencies or public entities are the beneficiary. In addition some countries do not accept foreign bank guarantees - in these circumstances it is usually written into the commercial contract that the guarantee is to be issued by a first class bank in for example a Middle Eastern country.

Customer Counter Guarantees

When requesting a guarantee a customer will have to indemnify their bank by way of a counter guarantee, covering items such as:

- *An indemnity issued in favour of the bank, covering the bank against all demands, claims, liabilities, costs and expenses, which may be brought against it as a result of the bank issuing the guarantee.*
- *Confirmation that the bank has no liability or responsibility if the instructions issued by the bank are not carried out.*

Applicable Law

Wherever possible, the business should insist on the guarantee being issued under English law (or Scottish law for businesses based in Scotland). The applicable law should be clearly expressed in the guarantee wording.

English and Scottish law is internationally recognised and should be acceptable to most beneficiaries of a guarantee. If there is pressure to have the guarantee governed by the law of the beneficiary's country then the UK business should contact their bank that may be able to assist and, in all likelihood, also seek legal advice.

In terms of the expiry date local law overseas does not necessarily uphold expiry dates – the liability may continue even after the expiry date has passed. In such cases the liability may be cancelled on the beneficiary's written confirmation, or confirmation from the overseas bank, that the guarantee is cancelled (if forthcoming).

Guarantee Value

Although certain types of guarantee tend to have 'average' percentage values attached to them e.g. 10% of the contract value, the value of the guarantee **should be a matter of negotiation between buyer and seller.** Negotiation should take place against other key contract discussions, such as price, terms and quality specifications.

From the perspective of the UK business, the lower the percentage the better:

- *The lower the monetary value for which they are at risk.*
- *Lower issuance charges will arise (which are usually charged at the same level as the customer's borrowing facilities at the bank).*
- *The less the customer will have to use their borrowing facilities (and the less security required). The level of facility the bank require for a guarantee will vary depending how the bank views the credit risk; some banks will mark 100% of the guarantee value and other banks, less.*

Wording on a Guarantee

Agreeing the wording on a bank guarantee is vital; the applicant should be careful to ensure that they are not over-committing themselves by agreeing with wording that increases their liability.

- *The bank can be a source of assistance on wording and should be used.*
- *In some cases the business may require legal assistance.*
- *Some overseas beneficiaries, especially government bodies may have standard wording they want quoted.*

Key clauses that require consideration include:

- *Clauses defining the scope of the guaranteed liabilities.*
- *Demand clauses.*
- *Conclusive evidence clauses.*
- *Expiry date: in addition the applicant should also state the date by which claims should be submitted (no later than the expiry date). Failure to do so may mean a valid claim could be received after the expiry date.*
- *Termination clauses.*
- *Governing law.*
- *Special instructions e.g. use of an agent.*

Unfair Calling

One of the risks of a guarantee payable on demand is that it may be unfairly called, even when the conditions of the contract have been met.

Although this is not a common occurrence, there are means of reducing the risk:

- *It is possible to take out insurance against unfair calling of a guarantee, and in some cases this could/should be a core requirement before issuance.*
- *If a guarantee is called which is considered to be unfair, try to negotiate with the customer.*
- *Try to ensure that the terms of the guarantee provide a clear mechanism for making claims.*

Section Review

Having read this section on Bonds and Guarantee you should be clear on the following:

▼ *Why a Bond or Guarantee may be needed, and how a business can use it to aid sales.*

▼ *Where Bonds and Guarantee can be used to support cash flow.*

▼ *What to do, and what not to do, when issuing Bonds and Guarantees.*

▼ *The different types of Bonds and Guarantee that apply and their purpose.*

▼ *There is an element of negotiation between buyer and seller in terms of the amount the Guarantee is issued for, the terms applicable and the benefits that issuance should have on contract terms.*

Topic refresher

Advantages of Bonds/Guarantees

Importer *(Buyer)*

▼ *A bank guarantee that the seller will perform – subject to wording in guarantee covering performance*

▼ *Terms (clauses) can be introduced into guarantees protecting their rights e.g. seller performance is evidenced by an independent quality inspection*

Exporter *(Seller)*

▼ *Can provide cash flow benefits (cash earlier in the case of an advanced payment guarantee)*

▼ *Can help to win contracts or remain competitive*

▼ *English/Scottish law is recognised internationally*

The Different Methods of Payment

4

Mitigating the Disadvantages

Importer *(Buyer)*

▽ Ensure guarantee is received from a 'first class bank' or issued through a bank in their own country

▽ Ensure wording is clear in order to evidence contract performance

▽ Be clear on the governing law under which the guarantee is issued

Exporter *(Seller)*

▽ *Issuance subject to URDG rules, provides some protection*

▽ *Be clear on expiry date and governing law*

▽ *Negotiate on the amounts that guarantees are issued for*

▽ *Reflect the benefits that a guarantee provides in the overall contract terms*

▽ *Consider insurance for unfair calling*

TOP LEARNING POINTS

1. *Ensure terms of guarantee mitigate against risks such as applicable law, unfair calling and extra bank charges*

2. *Guarantee issuance can be a matter of negotiation, for example in terms of amount, expiry date and wording of the guarantee*

3. *English/Scottish law is recognised internationally*

4. *Guarantees can be a means of supporting sales, and cash flow*

5. *There are several different types of guarantee which can apply*

Key Business Efficiency Measures

▽ *Ensure wording of guarantee reflects what your business needs*

▽ *Care on expiry dates. Issuing a guarantee will use up bank facilities and incur bank charges while the guarantee remains in place*

▽ *Know the different types of guarantee that apply and the circumstances in which they can be used*

SECTION SIX

COUNTERTRADE

Contents

4 | The Different Methods of Payment

About This Section

This short section shall look at what Countertrade is and what it represents.

Whilst some forms of Countertrade have been associated with certain regions of the world, and certain industries, today the concepts and specifics that Countertrade represent do have a wide application, and indeed remain a feature of global trade. They apply for both smaller transactions, and especially higher value contracts.

The types of Countertrade comprise:

Barter

Offset

Counterpurchase

Buyback

Switch Trading

Definitions of Countertrade

▼ *Exchanging goods or services paid for, in whole or part, with other goods or services rather than with money.*

▼ *A reciprocal trading agreement.*

▼ *A method of exchange where not all transactions are concluded in money; goods may be included as part of the asking price.*

Countertrade is traditionally more common in trade with, or between, cash poor countries – some estimates indicate that Countertrade accounts for over 20% of global trade volumes.

Countertrade also occurs when countries lack sufficient **hard currency**, or when other types of market trade are impossible.

Examples of Countertrade in recent times have included exchange of oil for food programmes and countertrade involving military vehicles (approved by the United Nations).

By its nature Countertrade is an 'ad-hoc' activity, the practices will also vary according to local regulations and requirements.

Barter

One of the more common methods of Countertrade. Goods or services are exchanged, directly for other goods or services; **no** money is involved.

A single contract covers both flows.

During the negotiation stage of a barter deal, the buyer and seller must know the market price of the items being exchanged. Barter goods can range extensively from essential items such as food to items such as furniture.

Offset

The exporter agrees to incorporate into their final product, **specified materials and components produced within the importer's country**. For some large contracts successful bidders may be required to establish local production.

Offset has been used by governments around the world when they have purchased military goods, but is increasingly popular across business sectors.

Offset arrangements also help to offset the negative effects of large purchases on a country's balance of payments and also assist local employment.

Counterpurchase

Occurs when as a condition of securing a sales order, the exporter undertakes to purchase goods and services from the country it is selling to.

Two contracts can apply:

1. *One for the principal sales order.*
2. *Another for the counterpurchase.*

Buyback

Arises when a company builds a plant in a country – or supplies, equipment and other services – and agrees to take a certain percentage of the plant's output as partial payment for the contract.

Buyback arrangements tend to be for longer and larger contracts.

Switch Trading

Practice in which a company or country sells to ANOTHER company or country its obligation **to make a purchase in a third country**.

It can be used to correct imbalances on bilateral trade **between** countries, for example:

- *Country A has a large credit surplus with Country B (Country B owes money to Country A which it wants to repay in goods or services rather than cash).*
- *The surplus can be assisted by Country C.*
- *When Country C exports to Country A, these can be financed by the sale of goods from Country B to Country C.*
- *In this way Country B, which owes money to Country A, is repaying by means of providing goods to Country C – which in exchange for receiving these goods, provides goods of equal value to Country A - which effectively receives these goods in settlement of what they are owed.*

Section 6 - Countertrade

Advantages and Disadvantages of Countertrade

Advantages	Disadvantages
Helps facilitate and stimulate trade in circumstances in which previously it may not have been possible, for example due to risk of non-payment or an inability to pay in a hard currency	**Specific conditions must exist for a transaction to take place, if it doesn't the seller (exporter) may end up entering a transaction which is not best for their business**
Good mechanism to gain entry into new sales markets	**If a country becomes too reliant on Countertrade it may make it harder for the country to adjust to enable efficient production and sales processes – which are necessary to compete in other trading environments**
Can provide stability for long-term sales	
If a firm sale of the bartered goods is agreed at a fixed price it can be as good as a cash sale	
Can help to even out imbalances in balance of payments, and create local sales and employment for the buying country	

The Different Methods of Payment

4

CHAPTER FIVE

DOCUMENTS IN UK AND INTERNATIONAL TRADE

Contents

*The Essential Guide to Business and Finance
in UK and International Trade*

About This Section

This section shall provide focus to the role that documents play in Trade, *specifically from a business and finance perspective.* Some of the documents mentioned also apply to UK trade such as Commercial Invoices, Packing List and in some cases Insurance documents.

When considering the documentation necessary it is important to consider several aspects:

> *Documents help to ensure payment*
> *- in some cases such as with a Letter of Credit they can be the key means needed to get paid*

> *Documents are a crucial part of evidencing transportation*

> *Documents can help to ensure and evidence quality control, whilst protecting the importer and exporter, for example in the case of an insurance certificate*

> *Documents are a means of ensuring that all aspects of a business work to the same standard and the same timescales*

Certain aspects of the content in this section may already have been covered to differing degrees in other parts of this book. Where necessary, however, this will be repeated to ensure emphasis and understanding.

Reference will be also be made on how documents can apply within the trade payment terms.

Financial Documents – Bills of Exchange

A Bill of Exchange is an unconditional order issued by one party (the drawer), to another (the drawee), to pay a certain sum of money, either immediately (sight bill) or on a fixed future date (term bill) – for payment of goods and services.

Drawer: *Exporter*
Drawee: *Importer*

For further details about the operation and role of a Bill of Exchange, please refer to the section on Documentary Collections.

Transport Documents

Bills of Lading

A Bill of Lading is a document issued by a Carrier that identifies the goods received for shipment, where the goods are to be delivered, and who is entitled to receive the shipment.

It is a contract for carriage AND a document of title to the goods. The importer cannot take possession of the goods, unless they have the Bill of Lading in their possession.

When working with Bills of Lading it is always important to be clear on what the Bill of Lading will detail in the Consignee Box, as this will control ownership of the document and hence how easy or difficult it will be to obtain title to the goods:

a) If to order *xxxx* - it cannot be endorsed, and can only be used by the stated party.

b) If to order of *xxxx* – it can be endorsed.

Bill of Lading and Payment Terms

Open Account: *Whilst it will be used as part of the shipment/transportation from a financial perspective, the bill of lading may already be in the possession of the buyer, prior to payment to the seller.*

Cash Up-Front: *The seller will not need to part with the bill of lading until after they have received payment.*

Documentary Collection: *As a document of title the bill of lading should be a core part of the documents contained in the Documentary Collection schedule.*
The bill of lading as with other documents will not be released to the buyer, until payment or acceptance is made against a bill of exchange.

Letter of Credit: *Core document, details should be provided within the wording of a Letter of Credit.*

Other Transport Documents

Air Waybill

Also referred to as an air consignment note, this refers to a receipt issued for goods, and an evidence of the contract of carriage (transport). An air waybill is **not** a document of title and is non-negotiable.

The goods are usually consigned directly to the buyer, although to increase control for the seller it is possible to consign to a third party, for example a bank. Goods may be consigned in this way, where the seller has concerns about the buyer's ability or willingness to pay. It can, however, delay receipt by the buyer; to affect release, the named bank will have to issue a **Delivery Order** releasing the goods, which can take time and increase charges.

The exporter may engage a freight forwarder to handle the transportation of goods.

Road and Rail Waybills

Road: *CMR Document*

Rail: *CIM Consignment Note*

Road and Rail Waybills serve as a receipt for goods and as evidence of the contract of carriage. They are not documents of title.

Post and Courier's Receipt

The post receipt is issued by the Post Office for goods sent by parcel post. The courier's receipt is issued by a courier.

The delivery charge by courier is higher than by parcel post, although courier shipment is faster and generally offers better security against loss/theft. As the goods are consigned directly to the importer, the exporter should not dispatch the goods unless they have received cash up-front OR they are fully comfortable trading on open account terms.

Other Transport Documents and Payment Terms

Open Account: *Whilst these documents can be used as part of the transportation, they apply more as receipts, unless the seller exercises some element of control through making the air waybill in favour of a third party.*

Cash Up-Front: *The seller will be in receipt of funds prior to release of goods.*

Documentary Collection: *These documents should from part of the overall documents within the Documentary Collection schedule.*

Letter of Credit: *These documents and their applicable terms should be included as part of the wording within a Letter of Credit.*

Other Trade Documents

Commercial Invoice

There are key pieces of information that an invoice should include, especially for export contracts. Invoice details should include:

- *Amount.*
- *Payment date (clearly expressed to avoid unnecessary deductions).*
- *Bank account details of exporter (quoting full bank account details, including IBAN and BIC codes – see Payments section).*
- *Full description of the goods, including item price, net weight and country of origin*
- *Any customer reference codes.*

A business should always contact their customer to establish if there is any special wording or codes they require quoting on the invoice. This may save time and money by avoiding unnecessary delays or enquiries.

The exporter's bank should also be asked to provide payment routing details – to ensure the payment is sent in the most direct manner possible.

5 | Documents in UK and International Trade

Customs authorities may use the commercial invoice to verify the details of the consignment. With this in mind it is good practice to ensure that the invoice has a signed and clear declaration that the facts are true and correct.

As some countries have specific requirements on the layout, form and content of the invoice a business should contact their freight forwarder to clarify these requirements.

Consular Invoice

Consular invoices may be required by certain countries to facilitate customs work at the destination, as well as to facilitate the collection of taxes. Information should comprise:

- *Declaration of the value of the shipment.*
- *A full description of the goods exported, as well as any discounts or rebates being offered.*
- *The name of the vessel that carries the cargo, the port of shipment and the port of destination.*

The consul of the destination country certifies these invoices.

The consular invoice should arrive as closely as possible to the time of the goods arriving, but not after the goods arrive. Delays in receipt can be penalised by the customs of the importing country.

Certificate of Origin

A Certificate of Origin is required by many countries as evidence of the origin of the goods. In the UK they are available from most local Chambers of Commerce and are usually completed by the exporter – who will require the Chamber to stamp/certify the document.

Types of Certificate of Origin include:

- **The European Community version.**
- **The Arab-British Chamber of Commerce version required for exports to Arab league states.**

In some instances, the Certificate of Origin and other commercial documents may also need to be legalised by the UK Embassy of the country of import.

A Certificate of Origin traditionally states from what country the shipped goods originate, this does not mean the country where are goods are shipped from, but the country where the goods are actually made.

The Certificate may be important for classifying the goods in the customs regulations of the importing country, defining how much duty should be paid. It may also be important for import quota purposes and health regulations.

> The e-Cert Electronic Certificate of Origin is available whereby UK exporters can now apply online, via the Internet. The Chamber of Commerce can check, approve and stamp the Certificate electronically and return to the exporter online. The exporter can then print the Certificate at their own premises

Import/Export Licence

When importing or exporting a business should check if they require a licence (e.g. check with their freight forwarder). Controls may exist on items such as:

- military goods
- technology
- artworks
- plants and animals
- medicines
- chemicals

Licence requirements may depend on the potential use of the goods and services, and where they are being exported to, or imported from.

A business may also need a licence even if goods are being exported or imported temporarily, for example, taking a sample to an exhibition.

> An *import licence* is a document issued by a national government authorising the importation of certain goods into its country. Each licence specifies the volume of imports allowed, and the total volume allowed should not exceed the quota.
>
> An *export licence* is issued by a government to an exporter, granting permission to sell certain goods to a given country.

Packing List

A packing list indicates the number and type of goods in each pack being transported, along with individual weights and dimensions. The list enables a buyer to check that the correct number of 'units' have been received.

It provides information needed for transportation purposes and Customs authorities can more easily identify a specific pack if they wish to inspect.

Inspection Certificate

Inspection certificates can sometimes be a necessary requirement, for example, in the case of industrial equipment, meat products and perishable merchandise. It certifies the items (e.g. goods) meet the required specifications and was in **good order** and **correct quality** when it left the port of departure.

In a lot of cases it will be good practice to undertake an inspection to avoid disputes:

> ▽ *A Letter of Credit for example may call for an Independent Certificate to provide evidence on the quality and quantity of goods.*

Warehouse Receipt

A warehouse receipt is a document that provides proof of ownership of goods/commodities that are stored in a warehouse. Such receipts may be negotiable or non-negotiable – negotiable allows transfer of ownership of say the commodity without having to deliver the physical commodity.

Negotiable receipts may be available as collateral for bank and finance loans, in the case of for example commodity finance, or as an additional 'security' for the bank, in addition to existing security. Banks may be more willing to lend against commodities stored in a reliable warehouse and which have been pledged to them as security for the finance (e.g. in the case of agricultural produce).

Delivery Order

A delivery order is a document from the owner of the freight or the party, to whom the goods have been consigned, authorising their release to another party. A bank can issue a delivery order for goods made out in their favour:

> ▽ *This would arise where the seller wishes to exercise some control, prior to receipt by the buyer. Should this arise the bank should be contacted first to ensure that they agree to this.*

> ▽ *In other circumstances the bank may request that the transport documents are consigned to them in order to strengthen their security.*

Certificate of Insurance

Issued by an insurance company/broker, that is used to verify the existence of insurance coverage under specific conditions. Document details include:

> ▽ *The effective date of the policy.*

> ▽ *The type of insurance cover purchased.*

> ▽ *The Certificate of Insurance is usually a key document required under a Letter of Credit.*

CHAPTER SIX

TRADE FOR GOOD

Trade can also act as a force for good in the world. This Chapter provides three examples of where trade makes a significant difference. As the author these studies were a pleasure to write, and I hope that you, the reader, will find them equally uplifting.

Section 1 - **Fairtrade**

Section 2 - **innocent drinks and innocent foundation**

Section 3 - **SLE Ltd**

The Essential Guide to Business and Finance in UK and International Trade

SECTION ONE

FAIRTRADE

Contents

6 | Trade for Good

Introduction

International trade at its core provides benefits to a country:

- ▼ *It encourages employment and welfare of its people.*

- ▼ *It can provide a feelgood factor demonstrating what is good about the country to the eyes of the world.*

International trade can also be a means of doing good in the world, not least by helping disadvantaged countries and their people to sell their goods and services overseas.

Fairtrade is an inspiring example of what international trade can achieve. It is an example we can all aspire to, and relate to, as individuals and in our working lives.

A fairer system of trade is required against a background of conventional trade failing to deliver sustainable livelihoods and development opportunities to people in the poorest countries of the world. A world left to market forces has led to a distortion in market prices for goods and services through increased concentration and purchasing power. The price does *not* reflect the productivity of the producers with lower market power and lack of market access.

What Fairtrade Represents

Fairtrade is about better prices, decent working conditions, local sustainability and fair terms of trade for farmers and workers in the developing world. It represents a trading partnership between consumers and producers in Asia, Africa, Latin America and the Caribbean. It is aimed at sustainable development for excluded and disadvantaged producers who have been marginalized by conventional trading systems.

Producers are at the heart of the movement – they sit on boards and are part of the standard setting and calculation of the minimum price described below. The focus is on direct relations between producers and organisations that directly buy the product, avoiding intermediaries that can misuse their power.

Fairtrade is a strategy for alleviating poverty and providing for sustainable development. Its purpose is to create opportunities for producers who have been economically disadvantaged or marginalized by the conventional trading system – it promotes trading partnerships based on dialogue, transparency and respect that contributes to sustainable development by offering better trading conditions to producers and workers.

6 | Trade for Good

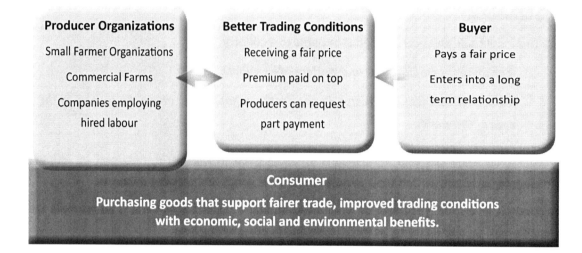

Producer Organizations

Small Farmer Organizations

Commercial Farms

Companies employing
hired labour

Better Trading Conditions

Receiving a fair price

Premium paid on top

Producers can request
part payment

Buyer

Pays a fair price

Enters into a long
term relationship

Consumer
Purchasing goods that support fairer trade, improved trading conditions
with economic, social and environmental benefits.

Fairtrade is about:

- *Providing better trading conditions for producer organizations and their workers.*

- *Ensuring producers receive a **fair price for their goods**. The Fairtrade minimum price is the price that a buyer of Fairtrade products has to pay to a Producer Organization for their product. It is not a fixed price, but should be seen as the lowest possible starting point for negotiations between producer and purchaser.*

  - *It is set at a level that ensures that Producer Organisations receive a price that covers the cost of production for their product.*
  - *It also acts as a safety net for farmers at times when world markets fall below a sustainable level.*

When the market price is higher than the Fairtrade minimum prices, the buyer must pay the market price.

Producers and traders can also negotiate a higher price, for example, on the basis of quality.

- *Fairtrade standards aim to ensure that all the relevant ingredients of products carrying the FAIRTRADE Mark have been purchased from organisations that meet the producer standards, and that those ingredients have been traded in accordance with the trading standards. The standards result in:*

  Farmers receiving a fair and stable price for their products.

  Extra income for farmers and estate workers, to improve their lives.

  A greater respect for the environment.

  A closer link between consumers and producers.

  Small farmers having a stronger position in world markets.

- The Standards also allow producers to request **partial pre-payment of the contract**. This is important for small-scale farmer organizations, as it ensures they have the cash flow to pay farmers at the time they deliver their crop. Businesses are also requested to enter into long term trading relationships so that producers can predict their income and plan for the future.

- **The Fairtrade premium** contributes to the empowerment of producers. It is a sum of money paid on top of the agreed Fairtrade price – for investment in social, environmental or economic development projects, such as healthcare, education or investing in processing equipment.

As part of the Fairtrade Standards, elected workers must form a Joint Body with the management of the farm and in the case of farmers, a democratically elected premium committee. The members of the producer group decide how they want to spend the Fairtrade premium and the Joint Body or premium committee manages the projects. The management members use their skills and experience to guide the Joint Body in project management, finance, accounts, and administration, while the overall decision-making power rests with the elected members.

Fairtrade standards exist for:

Food Products		Non-Food Products
Bananas	Cocoa	Cotton
Coffee	Dried fruit	Flowers and plants
Fresh fruit & vegetables	Honey	Gold
Juices	Nuts/Oil Seeds and pulses	Sports balls
Rice	Herbs and spices	Timber
Sugar	Tea	
Wine		

In each category there is a list of certified producer organisations maintained by an FLO register (Fairtrade Labelling Organizations International).

6 | Trade for Good

Producer Organizations and Standards

Fairtrade standards cover two types of producer organizations:

▼ *Small farmer's organizations and commercial farms.*

▼ *Other companies that permanently employ hired labour.*

Producers must meet specific standards, covering social, economic and the environmental conditions - producers work to protect the natural environment and make environmental protection a part of farm management. Producers are also encouraged to minimise the use of energy, especially energy from non-renewable sources.

The Benefits of Fairtrade

Economic Benefits

Buyers pay a stable minimum price to cover costs of production

Buyers pay a premium to producers to improve local communities

Partial pre-payment of contracts

Contracts that allow for long term planning Increased access to export markets

Social Benefits

Farmers and commercial firms must be set-up in a transparent way - bringing social rights

They must not discriminate against any social group

Training opportunities for workers

Conditions of employment exceed legal minimum requirements

Environmental Benefits

Safe use of agrochemicals Proper and safe management of waste

Maintenance of soil fertility and water resources

Prohibits use of genetically modified organisms

Organizations must develop plans to mitigate environmental impacts

The Fairtrade Foundation

The Fairtrade Foundation is the independent non-profit organisation that licenses use of the FAIRTRADE Mark on products in the UK, in line with agreed Fairtrade standards.

The Foundation is the UK member of Fairtrade Labelling Organizations International:

▼ *Uniting 21 initiatives across Europe, Japan, North America, Mexico and Australia/New Zealand.*

▼ *As well as networks of producer organisations from Asia, Africa, Latin America and the Caribbean.*

Vision: A world in which justice and sustainable development are at the heart of trade structures and practice – so that everyone through their work can maintain a decent and dignified livelihood, and develop their full potential.

The History of Fairtrade

Late 1980s
Fairtrade Labelling was created in the Netherlands in the late 1980s.

1988
The Max Havelaar Foundations launched the first Fairtrade consumer guarantee label in 1988- for coffee sourced from Mexico.

1992
In the UK the Fairtrade Foundation was established in 1992 by founder members CAFOD, Christian Aid, Oxfam, Traidcraft and the World Development Movement - the first products to carry the FAIRTRADE Mark were launched in 1994 - coffee, tea and chocolate.

2002
The FAIRTRADE Mark was adopted by FLO International in 2002

2009
- *23 countries have adopted the FAIRTRADE Mark covering more than 6,000 products.*
- *Globally consumers spent €2.9bn on Fairtrade certified products – a 22% increase on the previous year.*
- *This benefits over 7.5 million people in 59 developing countries (farmers, workers and their families).*

UK
Globally Fairtrade is promoted and supported by a wide range of development agencies, campaigning organizations, faith groups, social enterprises and consumer organizations. In the UK there are more than 400 Fairtrade Towns – towns where a commitment to Fairtrade has been made by the council, shops and businesses – together with 50 Fairtrade universities and a Fairtrade Schools scheme.

Fairtrade Fortnight
Key to the success of Fairtrade in the UK is a Fairtrade fortnight, an annual event uniting businesses, campaigners, producers and shoppers by which fair and ethical trading values are celebrated. Awareness raising and the promotion of Fairtrade products to the public are the main objectives of the Fairtrade events, such as Fetes, Fairs and Fashion shows, are supported by local authorities, government, charities, schools and colleges and the local population.
In 2010 between 22nd February and 7th March the campaign focus was on the Big Swap, for two weeks the nation was asked to swap its usual goods for Fairtrade goods. As part of the campaign 11,000 events took place.

6 | Trade for Good

Fairtrade in the United Kingdom

In recent years, trusted brands have converted some of their best-known products to Fairtrade.

- Cadbury Dairy Milk
- Tesco's Finest tea label
- Sainsbury's & Waitrose bananas
- Sainsbury's own brand tea and coffee
- Starbucks
- Tate & Lyle's entire retail sugar range
- Nestle four finger Kit Kat

Green & Blacks are to convert their entire chocolate and beverage range to Fairtrade by 2011.

Ben & Jerry's ice cream is to be progressively converted to Fairtrade in the UK and Europe by the end of 2011.

Availability of Fairtrade

Major Supermarkets

Independent Shops

Cafes

Restaurants

Catering Suppliers

Wholesalers

Online Shopping Channels

Shops that are part of BAFTS - British Association Fair Trade Shops

Details of national stockists can be found at **www.fairtrade.org.uk**

The Fairtrade Foundation has licensed over 3,000 Fairtrade certified products for sale through retail and catering outlets in the UK.

What Can We Do To Support the Concept of Fair Trade?

There are a number of things that businesses and individuals can do to support Fairtrade.

- *As individuals our purchasing habits can comprise Fairtrade products.*
- *Becoming a Fairtrade school is something that young people and adults can do together.*
- *Businesses can change their buying habits to purchase Fairtrade products. Employees can also encourage their businesses to purchase Fairtrade.*
- *Encourage friends and family to buy Fairtrade products.*
- *Use Fairtrade products in the work place.*

Contact Points

If you would like to find out more about Fairtrade and what you can do to support the concept of fair trade for all there are several points of contact:

www.fairtrade.org.uk   **Tel. +44 (0)20 7405 5942**

www.fairtrade.org.uk/schools

www.fairtrade.org.uk/universities

www.fairtrade.org.uk/faiths

Case Study: **Yeni Navan, MICHIZA**

Introduction: Yeni Navan (meaning eternal sunrise) began in 1985 as a small organization linking coffee producers from various ethnic groups in the regions around Oaxaca, Mexico. The name MICHIZA is an abbreviation of five indigenous groups:

-**Mixtecos, Chinantecos, Chatinos, Cuicatecos** and **Zapotecos**

Location: Oaxaca is located on the southern coast of Mexico. It is the fifth largest state with an area of 36,820 square miles. It is also one of the most mountainous states in Mexico. The climate is moderate all year. The name of the state comes from the Nahutl (the language of the Aztecs).

The Development of Yeni Navan

- *Initially coffee was only sold on the local market.*
- *In 1989 the organisation obtained legal status under the name Yeni Navan and they received authorisation to export.*
- *By 1991 they were capable of exporting independently.*
- *Today there are exports to 12 countries. There are 936 members; approximately 95% of members are now organically certified.*

6 **Trade for Good**

What They Provide

- *Technical support it provided to members to improve their capacity in organic agriculture and overall coffee quality and yields.*

- *It is responsible for marketing and direct export of their members' coffee making.*

- *MICHIZA aims to enhance the quality of life for all of its partners and their families through sustainable agricultural practices and the construction of a fairer and more equitable market.*

Fairtrade Impacts

- *Fairtrade's higher prices increase gross household income.*

- *Reduces household debts and enhances their economic options, increasing the possibility of better provision and education for the children.*

- *Affords peasant farmers' partial protection from some of the worst aspects of commodity crises, and in many cases provides the opportunity to engage in more sustainable agricultural practices.*

- *The extra capital can generate important economic ripple effects within communities, providing additional employment, even for non-participating families.*

SECTION TWO

innocent drinks

Trading Ethically, Morally and Successfully:

The Story of innocent drinks

The story of innocent drinks, whilst one of success, is matched equally by providing products that are healthy and building a support structure around the countries it imports from. In 12 years the business has grown to a turnover of more than £100 million and its drinks are sold in over 11,000 outlets across 13 countries in Europe

Through the support that innocent drinks provide for the innocent foundation, the company is also putting something considerable back into the developing countries it sources fruit from, and more importantly the wider world community.

From small acorns

Once upon a time there were three young friends from college, who came up with many ideas – the one they struck upon was an idea of making a totally natural drink from fruit that tasted amazing and was good for people of all ages.

In the summer of 1998 the young friends bought £500 worth of fruit, turned it into smoothies and took them to a jazz festival to try out the idea. They put up a big sign saying:

> *"Do you think we should give up our day jobs*
> *to make these smoothies?"*

➤ *and put out a bin saying YES*

➤ *and a bin saying NO*

➤ *asking people to try out one of their drinks and then to put their empty bottle in the appropriate bin*

➤ *at the end of the weekend, the YES bin was full, so they went to work the next day and resigned.*

The first innocent smoothies went on sale in April 1999, in 'Out To Lunch' the local sandwich shop. At the end of the day half of the 24 bottles had been sold.

Since then things have gone from strength to strength, but not without some challenges. In the early stages, trying to raise finance was difficult and it took many, many pitches to banks and equity investors, before they finally received an equity investment. The three founders however never gave up and applied a key business principle: *success is not determined by age or intelligence or race or gender, it is determined by whether you are determined, whether you keep going or not.*

Since 1999, innocent has extended its range of drinks to nine smoothie recipes, one of which changes each season. There are two thickies (yoghurt based fruit drink), an NFC orange juice, four smoothies for children and a range of veg pots (healthy ready meals).

The company have also published two smoothie recipe books called, 'Little book of drinks,' and, 'innocent smoothie recipe book,' as well as a simple guide called, 'Stay Healthy Be Lazy.'

Innocent have expanded from just three people to over 250 in offices across Europe, including London, Paris, Dublin, Amsterdam, Copenhagen and Salzburg. Where a local presence has been set up overseas, innocent have used a blend of employees from their offices in Fruit Towers, London and local know how – the combination has worked well with both sides bringing important experience to the new country.

Throughout, innocent have maintained an overall principle **'Make food good'** – food that tastes delicious is genuinely healthy and made in a way which is sustainable.

The International supply chain

Innocent buy fruit from all over the world. The supply chain is based in Holland (importing and blending) and England (packing), with distributors throughout the UK and Europe.

Innocent have a work programme to ensure that fruit is bought from farms that look after their workers and the environment; this includes the use of both the companies own minimum standards and international certifications such as the Rainforest Alliance. The company has also recently commenced projects to support research into sustainable agriculture and to buy fruit from smallholder farmers in Africa.

Business and environmental ethics

At innocent the culture is to undertake business in a more enlightened way, they take responsibility for the impact of their business on society and the environment. It's part of a quest to become a truly sustainable business, having a positive effect on the world around us all.

The innocent foundation

The innocent foundation is a grant giving organization that work with non-government organizations (NGOs) to deliver their vision of building sustainable futures for the world's poorest people.

They currently have 15 partner organizations working on projects primarily in countries where innocent source the fruit. There is an agricultural focus, as it is essential for communities to get the most out of the natural resources available to ensure a sustainable and improved future. They keep everyone in touch with their current partners on their website: **innocentfoundation.org.**

Each year innocent drinks give at least 10% of its profits to charity, mainly to the foundation.

The focus for the foundation is currently on sustainable farming for secure futures. The strategy has three key elements:

- ▼ *Focus the investment*
- ▼ *Work in partnership*
- ▼ *Be wise with the money*

Focus the investment

There are several ways in which the foundation select and prioritise the projects they work on:

- ▩ *Use the **UN Human Development Index** to understand which countries are the world's poorest.*
- ▩ *Focus on those countries where there is the greatest need and from where innocent drinks sources its fruits.*
- ▩ *Invest in projects with long term, sustainable aims.*
- ▩ *Work with European based NGOs in order to maintain a constant dialogue with the partners and ensure that systems are in place for monitoring and distributing investment on the ground.*

6 | Trade for Good

Work in partnership

- *Set clear, mutually agreed goals at the start.*
- *Maintain a constant dialogue with the partners, with six monthly reports provided prior to release of staged payments.*
- *Work on projects with timeframes of up to three years where possible.*
- *The foundation try to offer more than simply financial input, innocent employees for example have visited a project in India to help them work on their marketing and website and visited Malawi to help a fledgling juice company get off the ground.*

Be wise with the money

- *The Trustees never commit to any project if there are not enough funds to see it through to its completion – usually three years worth of cash.*
- *The funds are kept in high interest accounts until they are needed.*
- *The foundation aims to build a capital base for the future.*

More about the Innocent Foundation

The foundation was set up in 2004 as a registered charity. Since 2004 £1.3 million has been committed to 37 projects, helping NGO partners to raise a further £5.8 million through leverage to support 500,000 people.

You can also join the innocent family online via the innocent website to stay in touch – in return you will receive emails and the chance to win drinks, as well as receiving invites to events and the odd present.

SECTION THREE

SLE LTD

When the smallest thing matters:

The Story of SLE

Sometimes business is business, but sometimes a business through its products and services can make a real difference to people's lives. An example of this is SLE Ltd based in Croydon, who are the only UK Company that designs life support ventilators exclusively for the neonatal market (the newborn period after birth).

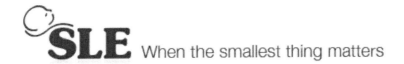

A Company Dedicated To Saving Lives

SLE's products have been at the forefront of technology for over 30 years. The company's guiding principle has always been to support clinical and nursing staff in their everyday work. A baby's lungs are the last organs to develop so problems with underdeveloped lungs are a feature of a high percentage of premature babies. Caring for these babies demands very high precision products that work.

➤ *In the 1980's SLE were the pioneers of neonatal Patient Trigger Ventilation decreasing the work of breathing in newborn babies.*

➤ *In the 1990's SLE introduced combined HFO (High Frequency Oscillation), which is the delivery of air to the baby at fast frequencies - both inspiration (air breathed in) and expiration (breathed out) are active, reducing the likelihood of gas trapping.*

➤ *In the last decade SLE have launched new products including the SLE 5000 ventilator, which is the gold standard infant/paediatric ventilator. Today many thousands of SLE Infant Ventilators are now in use and have provided respiratory support and assistance to millions of infants in all corners of the globe.*

SLE have a team of highly qualified technical staff providing both technical and clinical training and also prompt service support – with a 24/7 service to customers, 365 days a year.

In the early part of this century SLE, already having a 70% share of the UK market, continued to expand abroad. To achieve this they have invested heavily in finding and training specialist distributors throughout the world – demonstrating a real commitment to making distributor relationships work. Export turnover has increased from £2.1m in 2003 to £7.9M in 2008 with successful orders in over 70 countries.

In recognition of their achievements SLE have won the Queens Award For Enterprise: International Trade in 2009, and the Best Business for International Trade in the South London Business Awards in 2010.

6 | Trade for Good

THE QUEEN'S AWARDS
FOR ENTERPRISE:
INTERNATIONAL TRADE
2009

**2010 South London
Business Awards**

The company remains as committed as ever to ensuring that the new products developed meet the needs of the clinicians who use the ventilators. New products under development will broaden out the range being offered and add further modes of ventilation and enhancements to analysis and support facilities.

For further information about SLE Ltd please visit their website at **www.sle.co.uk**

Section 3 - SLE Ltd

CHAPTER SEVEN

SUCCESSFUL BUSINESSES

In addition to this being an education book, I am keen
to provide the reader with some examples of successful
businesses. The examples provided are interesting reading
material in their own right, they cover different business
sectors and business sizes; my thanks goes out to these
businesses for agreeing to contribute to this book.

Contents

*The Essential Guide to Business and Finance
in UK and International Trade*

A Breath of Air:

Air Engineering Controls Ltd

Air Engineering Controls (AE) is a story of a small local business that has grown steadily through innovation, attention to detail and most importantly providing their customers with what they need.

Many aspiring businesses will be able to identify with AE. Here is the story to date.

AE: The Business

AIR ENGINEERING CONTROLS LTD

AE design and supply both standard **pneumatic products** and customised **electro-pneumatic control systems**. In simple terms this means they supply equipment that will control the flow, pressure & direction of compressed air, vacuum, water & various gases. The products can be high tech and require a strong approach to innovation, but most of all a commitment to quality and customer service. They provide an end-to-end service, from 3-D design concept and prototyping through to product launch. Pneumatic comes from the Greek word "Pneu" meaning "breath of air", relating to anything controlled by or using air. A wide range of products are produced across a range of industries including:

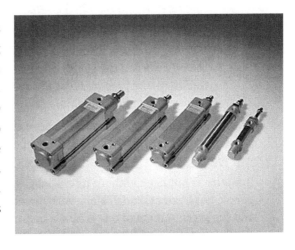

▽ *Medical*
▽ *Commercial Vehicles*
▽ *Instrumentation*
▽ *Process*
▽ *Automation*

7 | Successful Businesses

AE: *The History 1997- To Date*

The business began in 1997 when Gary Dean Joined a company Air Engineering Systems Ltd, to establish a pneumatic controls division. Having previously worked in the industry for larger companies Gary saw an opportunity to create a business focussed on delivering products in a manner which met with what the customer specifically required; in essence it is a customer first led approach, rather than a supplier led approach, which can lead to a business developing what they want to the exclusion of customer needs.

Within 3 years the business concept was proved to such an extent that a standalone company was formed and Air Engineering Controls Ltd (AE) came into being. During the course of the last 10 years additional skilled staff have been recruited and the company now employ 23 people, including an Operations Director, Sales Director, Marketing Director and Project Managers.

The approach throughout has been people led.

Business growth has seen several milestones and several economic cycles;

- *One of Gary's previous employees Mead Fluid Dynamics who were originally a supplier closed their operation in Sussex. Whilst initially a setback this turned into an opportunity with AE filling the gap that Mead had left.*

- *In 2004 AE won their first six figure contract exporting control systems to Holland, providing fuel control on petrol tankers.*

- *Further contracts were won with a key development in 2009 being awarded the supply of a pneumatic chassis to the medical industry. The product helps to save lives by providing the air/gas control for infant ventilators.*

- *Recently a large contract has been won supplying standard pneumatic products to an established catalogue distribution company.*

Growth has not been without its challenges – recruitment and staffing of the correct people has been essential, along with maintaining close relationships with customers and suppliers. A team of one is now a team of 23 and growing, annual sales turnover is now approaching £3.2m. In addition to the company's premises in Forest Row, East Sussex, a new factory and design facility has been opened nearby to support the increased stock and manufacturing requirements. AE continue to be at the forefront of new designs and new technology, designing products to meet their customers' needs

For more information about the products and services of AEC please contact **www.aireng.co.uk** or telephone 01342 826488.

Air Engineering Controls Ltd

Moving People:

The Story of Alexander Dennis Ltd

Introduction

The story of Alexander Dennis Ltd is one of good business practice, comprising innovation and a professional business approach, whilst being environmentally conscious.

The story has its roots over 100 years ago. A brand and a business formed then, still exists today, developing and overtaking the times whilst still retaining its historic roots. The company remains leader in its field of bus and coach vehicle manufacture.

This wholly British company has survived whilst many competitors have been taken over by foreign competitors or ceased to exist altogether by:

1. *Being highly innovative throughout its history.*
2. *By remaining close to its customers, almost always selling products direct to the end user, knowing their needs and aspirations first hand.*
3. *Most importantly of all, through the contribution of its employees.*

From a financial perspective and as part of the contract tendering process, Alexander Dennis use Bid Bonds and Performance Bonds. These bonds are part of a rigorous checking process necessary to win overseas contracts on acceptable terms.

Moving People

Every minute of every day, in numerous towns, villages and countries around the world, Alexander Dennis buses carry 25,000 passengers – with over 3.5 million per day in London alone. Each journey is different ranging from the extremes of tropical heat and humidity of the Far East, to the dry heat of the Arizona desert and the depths of the Northern Winter.

7 | Successful Businesses

The Formation and Growth of Alexander Dennis Ltd

Alexander Dennis was formed from several well-known UK brands:

- ▽ *Walter Alexander Coachbuilders*
- ▽ *Dennis Chassis*
- ▽ *Plaxton*

The story of the Dennis business started in 1895 when John Dennis left his native Devon, firstly working in a firm of ironmongers in Guildford and in his spare time built a bicycle that he sold at a profit. In 1895 he set up his own business 'The Universal Athletic Stores' originally manufacturing and selling bicycles – then in 1898 the first motorised vehicle was produced. Joined by his brother the business developed in the early stages of car development at the start of the 21st century.

Dennis Brothers was formed as a private company in 1901, and in 1904 Dennis built its first commercial vehicle. In the same year the first Dennis bus took to the street.

Dennis produced its first fire engine in 1908 and since then has expanded to more than 75 countries in the world.

Today Alexander Dennis is the largest bus builder in the UK and one of the largest in the world. It is also at the forefront of new hybrid electric vehicles in the UK.

The Enviro 400 hybrid bus (picture above), which is built at Guildford and at the headquarters in Falkirk, can reduce fuel consumption and CO_2 production by up to 40%.

Alexander Dennis is currently the only bus manufacturer in the world with a range of single deck, two-axle and three-axle double deck hybrid buses.

Overseas Markets

For many years now Alexander Dennis has been a global business with sales covering a wide range of countries in each of the continents of the world. Alexander Dennis (Far East) for example are responsible for the sales, support and assembly of double decker buses for Asia and Australasia, where the buses form the backbone of some of the world's largest passenger transport operations. In Hong Kong alone the buses carry 4 million passengers every day.

Alexander Dennis Ltd

Fire Testing Technology Ltd

FTT established in 1989 were the first company in the world to specialise in the manufacture, supply and maintenance of reaction to fire testing instrumentation.

Today FTT retains its distinction as the only exclusive manufacturer of fire testing apparatus and software, with a range that has expanded to more than 35 different types of instrument. They are internationally recognised as the world's leading supplier of fire testing instrumentation and have supplied the majority of leading fire research groups and testing laboratories.

Through a worldwide network of agents, FTT provide support to clients, for example test houses, universities and product manufacturers.

For further information about their products and services please contact FTT at
Sales@fire-testing.com   Website www.fire-testing.com.

7 | Successful Businesses

Using Information Wisely:

The Story of pH Group

Introduction

pH Group, an Experian company, puts the science into B2B customer and prospect marketing, creating powerful tools for customer insight and risk prediction.

Optimising prospect and customer databases and adding new dimensions of data create an ongoing, recurrent, dynamic lead generation machine, which hunts and breeds.

pH is an expert at analysing data from all necessary angles. The information buried in business data – whether its customers' employment history, patterns of export activity, corporate generosity or the spread of geographical demand – is a precious asset for a business and key decision-makers.

When overlaid with multiple other variables and matched to historical trends and relationships, it can be utilised to launch a product successfully, cut sales costs, optimise distribution channels and maximise business performance. By consulting with clients, a bespoke service is tailored to individual client needs and can range from simply providing access to data by selecting profiled prospects to delivering superior analytics for modelling specific behavioural scenarios.

Services include:

- ▼ **Data optimisation & processing**
- ▼ **Customer segmentation**
- ▼ **Propensity & opportunity modelling**
- ▼ **Risk prediction**
- ▼ **Data management services**
- ▼ **Web based access & prospect management tools**

With full operations in both London and Paris, pH has worked with major blue-chip clients since being formed.

pH became part of the Experian Group in July 2007.

pH Group

From The Beginning

pH Group was established in 1987, with the objective of helping clients in the B2B space better understand their customer base and identify new business opportunities.

The innovative pH offering was, and continues to be, focused on data, but the key differentiator is the experts who deliver the analysis and client service, which has resulted in continuous client relationships spanning up to two decades.

Riding Recession

Over the years, pH Group have worked through two recessions of the early 1990's and the more recent global downturn. The business has evolved from concentrating efforts on a small pool of larger clients, diversifying to garner extensive insight across a host of sectors including Financial Services, Utilities, Automotive, Insurance, Public Sector, Telcos, IT and Industrial Services.

Success has also been achieved in expanding the scope of B2B service provision to reach Europe, North America and Latin America.

As a result of the mixed client base in terms of sector and geography, pH are well positioned to weather past, present and future economic storms.

Maintaining Growth: Today and For the Future

The core focus, over 20 years later, remains on creating true business advantage with the unique blend of data integrity testing, analytics, and risk prediction. Their approach and expertise is clearly well appreciated in the B2B marketplace with average annual growth at 25% since 1987.

In order to remain an industry leader, pH have evolved to meet the changes of the last two decades by maintaining:

- *A humanised, people-centric approach to the analysis of data – with a seventy-strong team of consultants, analysts, database developers and client directors.*
- *Providing a sophisticated bespoke service to meet complex client requirements.*

The purchase by Experian, 3 years ago, has helped pH develop over and above their own organic growth by enabling them to become part of the vast experience and capabilities that a larger organisation is able to offer, in terms of sales resources and brand visibility, among other attributes. In essence pH can offer the best of both worlds, as part of a larger organisation they are able to offer a wider range of services whilst at the same time maintaining the same approach that the small company always offered.

For further information about pH Group and their products and services please contact:
+44 (0)20 7598 0310   info@phgroup.com
Experian pH, Royalty Studios, 105-109 Lancaster Road, London, W11 1QF

7 | Successful Businesses

CHAPTER EIGHT

KEY TRADE INTERMEDIARIES

This book provides a selection of key contacts and key trade intermediaries, without which UK and International Trade would not function. Details are provided in order that the reader can understand the vital role that these companies and organisations undertake.

Contents

The Essential Guide to Business and Finance in UK and International Trade

Expert advice and value for money from Bluefin

Bluefin

Having the right level of insurance cover is key for businesses of all shapes and sizes, even more so for those involved with UK and International trade. Specialist insurance advice is vital to ensuring that a business is able to cover both its immediate, but also longer term insurance needs.

As a leading insurance broker, with over 50 offices throughout the country, Bluefin Insurance Services Limited are experienced at delivering innovative insurance solutions for businesses and can negotiate the most appropriate terms on behalf of their clients.

Bluefin are able to advise on a wide range of trade insurance needs, including:

Cargo Insurance (Goods in Transit)

▼ *Insurance of loss of or damage to goods whilst in transit within the UK, import or export.*

Trade Credit Insurance

Protecting the company against the risk of bad debt, covering:

▼ *Customer insolvency*

▼ *Protracted default*

▼ *Political risk*

Credit Intelligence

Credit referencing services on both existing and potential customers.

Bluefin can also assist in the arrangement of trade finance, including:

▦ *Invoice discounting*

▦ *Factoring*

▦ *Import Finance*

▦ *Forfeiting*

▦ *Silent confirmation of letters of credit*

The Role of The British Chambers of Commerce and Local Chambers of Commerce

British Chambers of Commerce

The British Chambers of Commerce (BCC) is the national body for a network of Accredited Chambers of Commerce across the UK.

Chambers of Commerce serves not only their members who are made up of local businesses of all sizes, they also sit at the heart of the local business community:

▼ *Representing the needs of local business in forums and national issues*

▼ *Providing information and guidance to its members on local and national issues*

▼ *Offering networking opportunities whereby local businesses can exchange ideas, and seek out new customers and suppliers*

▼ *Providing training to its members on a range of subjects from taxation to use of new technology*

▼ *Provision of Export Documentation, in particular the eCert – Electronic Certificates of Origin*

Key areas of focus for Chambers of Commerce are International Trade, Skills Development and Business Services.

Examples of What Chambers of Commerce Provide

Note: these Services may vary from Chamber to Chamber

▼ *Certificates of Origin*	▼ *Legal Advice*
▼ *Local Business Advice Surgery*	▼ *Public Sector Contracts*
▼ *International Trade Seminars and Missions*	▼ *HR Advice*
▼ *Office Services*	▼ *Business Partner Opportunities*
▼ *Training Courses*	▼ *Identifying Grants and Loans*
Member to Member Discounts	▼ *Networking Events*

Key Trade Intermediaries

Inspecting, Testing and Certifying Goods: The Key Role of Cotecna

COTECNA

Irrespective of the terms of trade there will be risks around ensuring goods purchased are of the correct specification and quality. This applies to both domestic and in particular international trade; for both buyer and seller there are considerable benefits in ensuring that these risks are reduced as far as possible. Risks which have indeed increased in recent years as a result of a reduction in Letter of Credit terms taking away some of the controls which exist around certainty of payment against conforming shipping documentation.

As a leading inspection, testing and certification group, Cotecna perform a key role in international trade:

- ▼ *Monitoring physical goods at any, or indeed all stages of the supply chain (production, storage, processing, transit).*
- ▼ *Providing "physical inspection" of the goods.*
- ▼ *Certifying goods and services, through a range of certification services, such as laboratory testing and marine surveys.*
- ▼ *Providing local control and handling of title, or other documentation relating to the goods.*
- ▼ *Offering Marine (Cargo) Insurance if required. Cotecna can provide comprehensive cover, including theft and misappropriation, issued by top rated underwriters.*

These services also provide a strong means of supporting trade finance - further details are highlighted in the Trade Finance section.

About Cotecna

Cotecna has a worldwide network close to 100 offices and workforce of over 4,000 employees and affiliates, focused around two main areas of business:

a) *Institutional Services. Cotecna are mandated by governments to carry out inspection services on imported containers and goods – with the main objective being to ensure the correct declarations and payment of import taxes.*

b) *Commercial Services.*

Key Trade Intermediaries

8

Commodities	Consumer Goods
Agricultural products, minerals, metals and petroleum: providing:	**Specialising in garments, textiles, toys and other consumer goods, providing:**
■ *Vessel hatch and hold inspection. Water tightness*	*Raw material quality control*
■ *Loading and discharge supervision*	*Online production quality control*
■ *Supervision of weighing / Tally control*	*Pre-shipment inspections (final random inspection, loading supervision)*
■ *Draft survey and tank gauging*	*Factory audit or vendor assessment*
■ *Contractual sampling, samples preparation and sealing*	*Manufacturing process audit*
■ *Testing and analysis*	*Social accountability audit*
■ *Traceability/identity preservation*	*Product conformity testing*
■ *Miscellaneous*	

Approach to Business

As a family run business, Cotecna offer a unique personal approach. They have also implemented a Business Ethics & Compliance program throughout its network of offices, in relation to the following areas, all of which are subject to an annual independent examination by the company's external financial auditors:

▽ *Integrity* ▽ *Conflicts of Interest* ▽ *Confidentiality*

▽ *Anti-bribery* ▽ *Fair marketing*

The business also recognises its responsibility for social, community and environmental support; Cotecna is involved with local communities specific to some of the African countries in which they operate, identifying how they can best help the underprivileged. 80% of all charitable contributions are made in the areas of greatest humanitarian need: clean water supply, health and education. Recent donations and contributions have included building and renovating schools, supplying school uniforms and books, building water boreholes, helping communities in the aftermath of natural disasters, providing food and the refurbishment of specialized hospital rooms, particularly in the following countries; Burkina Faso, Congo, Ghana, Niger, Nigeria, Tanzania.

Supporting and training Customs staff is also a feature of the commitment to improving trade services abroad.

Key Trade Intermediaries

Enterprise Europe Network

Providing free online tool to help south east businesses find European partners

enterprise
europe
network

Business Support on Your Doorstep

One of the core services provided by the Enterprise Europe Network is helping businesses find the right European partner for them. Innovative companies may need to find a technology partner to help bring their products to market. Commercial companies may be looking for an agent, distributer or supplier to help them make that first crucial step to internationalization, or other companies may be looking for sources of European funding for research and development projects – a top priority for the European Union.

Enterprise Europe South EastUK have launched a new 'Partner Finder' online tool on their website. This is an embeddable tool for the secure display and dissemination of ALL types of collaboration opportunities across 44 countries and 550 partners, belonging to the Enterprise Europe Network, including: technology requests, technology offers, business collaboration partnerships (including suppliers, distributers and agents) and FP7, within a single searchable interface. 'Partner Finder' will allow effective dissemination of ALL profile types to client businesses, giving them the choice of RSS subscription, email alerting or direct web searching. The Tool uses a simple 'keyword' search - for example, if you are interested in 'Aerospace,' your search will call up commercial, innovation and research partnering opportunities. This is a valuable, effective way for you to view all types of collaboration opportunities, which are relevant to you and that can help you take that next step to trading with Europe.

For more information about this exciting new online tool and our other free services that can help you trade with the rest of Europe or expand your existing trade, please visit **www.enterpriseeurope-se.eu,** call **0844 7252244** or email **info@enterpriseeurope-se.eu**

Key Trade Intermediaries

8

ICC: International Chamber of Commerce

ICC is the voice of world business, championing the global economy as a force for economic growth, job creation and prosperity. It is the world's only truly global business organization with direct access to national governments throughout the world through its national committees.

It has a global network of national committees and groups in more than 90 countries, with an international headquarters in Paris.

Member companies and business organizations have the opportunity to shape the ICC stance on any given business issue by participating in the work of ICC.

Origins

The ICC was formed in 1919 with an overriding aim that remains unchanged: to serve world business by promoting trade and investment, open markets for goods and services and the free flow of capital.

Today the ICC is a global business organisation with thousands of member companies and associations in around 120 countries. Members include many of the world's most influential companies, as well as many smaller companies, business associations, and local chambers of commerce.

Key Functions

The following represents a sample of the key role that the ICC performs:

1. **Setting Rules and Standards**

   - *ICC's Incoterms rules are standard international trade definitions used every day in thousands of contracts. In addition ICC model contracts make life easier for small companies that cannot afford big legal departments.*

   - *ICC's Uniform Customs and Practice for Documentary Credits (UCP 600) are universally used rules for Letter of Credit transactions.*

   - *ICC codes on advertising and marketing are frequently reflected in national legislation and the codes of professional associations.*

Key Trade Intermediaries

2. Promoting Growth and Prosperity

- ICC is the main business partner of the United Nations and its agencies.

- It provides world business recommendations to the World Trade Organization, and numerous other international fora such as the G-20.

- ICC speaks for world business whenever governments make decisions that crucially affect corporate strategies and the bottom line.

- ICC provides business input to the United Nations, the World Trade Organization, and many other governmental bodies, both international and regional.

3. Spreading Business Expertise

- Together with the United Nations Conference on Trade and Development (UNCTAD) ICC helps some of the world's poorest countries attract foreign direct investment.

- In partnership with UNCTAD, ICC has set up an Investment Advisory Council for Least Developed Countries.

4. Combating Commercial Crime

- In the early 1980's, ICC set up a London-based services to combat international commercial crime, comprising the:
  - ▼ International Maritime Bureau
  - ▼ Counterfeiting Intelligence Bureau
  - ▼ Financial Investigation Bureau

8 | Key Trade Intermediaries

The World Chambers Federation (WCF)

WCF operates as the world business organisation's department for chamber of commerce affairs. WCF also administers the ATA Carnet system for temporary duty free imports.

For further information on the work of the ICC in the United Kingdom please contact **info@iccorg.co.uk**. There is also an online bookshop from which all ICC publications can be purchased (**www.iccbookshop.com**)

Institute of Credit Management

In the modern world of business the provision of credit terms is often a customer expectation and on some occasions, a necessity in order for a business to compete. Whilst this book and in particular the section on Credit Terms has looked at some of the factors involved in credit management, it is important for businesses to consider the services provided by the Institute of Credit Management (ICM).

*The Institute of Credit Management (ICM) is Europe's largest credit management organisation. The trusted leader in expertise for all credit matters, it represents the profession across trade, consumer, and export credit, and all credit-related services. Formed over 70 years ago, it is the only such organisation accredited by Ofqual and it offers a comprehensive range of services and bespoke solutions for the credit professional (**www.icm.org.uk**) as well as services and advice for the wider business community (**www.creditmanagement.org.uk**).*

ICM covers a range of business activities including:

- ▽ **Cash collections**
- ▽ **Credit reporting within a business**
- ▽ **Credit checking**
- ▽ **Credit insurance**
- ▽ **Debt recovery**
- ▽ **Insolvency**

The services offered by the ICM include:

- *Professional membership grades* ▨ *Recruitment agency* ▨ *Conferences and seminars*
- *Professional Qualifications and unit awards* ▨ *Bookshop* ▨ *A network of local branches*
- *Consultancy* ▨ *Training* ▨ *Credit Management Helpline* ▨ *Online services through icmOS*
- *Credit Management magazine and monthly email briefings* ▨ *Member website forums*
- *Quality in Credit Management accreditation* ▨ *Member benefits and discounts*
- *Social networking community*

ICM also plays a key role in consulting with and making recommendations to the Government, European Commission, other professional bodies and trade associations.

Key Trade Intermediaries

8

ITS Training services - providing leading education and training in shipping and international trade

www.itstraining.co.uk

ITS Training specializes in education and vocational training for students either embarking on a career in international trade or those already employed in the industry looking at developing their knowledge. It offers nationally certified qualifications and works with shipping industry, professional organizations, such as the Institute of Export, to offer valid, recognised and relevant courses and qualifications. ITS is a fully approved and accredited Centre with various examinations boards and professional bodies, plus it is approved by Government to offer funding and it is regulated and inspected by OFSTED to guarantee the quality of its provision.

International trade has a number of careers available from those involved in buying and selling goods internationally to transporting goods internationally by sea, road, air, rail and waterways each of them requiring specialist knowledge and skills. International trade provides careers globally and has many opportunities available for staff with the skills and knowledge demanded by the industry.

Opportunities for a career include:

- ▽ *Marketing which requires an understanding of the different countries, culture, national laws, raw material, political stability and costs.*
- ▽ *International logistics & supply chain which require skills in geography trade routes and international conventions relative to the method of transport.*
- ▽ *Freight logistics including shipping lines, airlines, rail and road operators, as well as the freight forwarding industry offering impartial advice and services.*

Key Trade Intermediaries

SDV Ltd

With a powerful global network of 520 offices in 89 countries, SDV provides logistics management services including air, courier, ocean and road transportation, project management, customs management, warehousing and distribution. SDV specializes, and has a proven history of success, in delivering shared user solutions across the Aerospace, Healthcare, Oil & Gas, Chemical Logistics, Wines & Spirits and Cosmetics & Fragrance sectors.

At the very heart of the Group strategy is to establish SDV as a uniquely 'Solutions First' provider of global freight and supply chain logistics management. SDV move rapidly to ensure that all significant new business is developed on the basis of first understanding the needs of each individual client and then offering solutions and services specifically designed to meet them, with built-in flexibility to accommodate change. This strategy moves SDV definitively away from traditional, commoditised, low margin freight forwarding, and completes our migration into high added value services - bringing with it greater opportunities for sales and profit growth.

The Group's strength in this area is greatly reinforced by its extensive experience and high capability in every aspect of freight movement and warehousing, by unique expertise in the design and application of Information Technology systems to logistics management and by a thorough understanding of supply chain dynamics. The methodology that drives this approach is Logix®, the Division of SDV that generates supply chain logistics solutions. Employing an award winning methodology, together with teams of experienced, qualified specialists in logistics, international trade and customs, material handling, warehousing, transportation and other supply chain disciplines, Logix® identifies and removes dysfunctionalities, designs and installs new, fit for purpose practices and provides the information and expertise for continuous improvement.

All projects are controlled and monitored with the aid of a cutting edge project management methodology and advanced analytical tools. Common benefits arising out of Logix® projects include:

▼ *The identification and removal of dysfunctionality and performance deficits throughout the entire supply chain.*

▼ *Dramatic reduction in total supply chain costs and improved customer fulfilment.*

▼ *The provision of total visibility and control, with the creation of an objectively measurable environment for performance improvement.*

▼ *Total transparency of operational activity, transaction cost and quality performance through clear, relevant management reports providing a powerful tool for superior decision making.*

▼ *Information technology systems creating synergies within the supply chain to drive greater productivity.*

▼ *The release of time for core priorities, and a platform for continuous improvement.*

www.sdv.com

The Institute of Export and International Trade

www.export.org.uk

The Institute of Export was incorporated in 1935 by Licence of the Board of Trade.

The Institute now adds 'International Trade' to its name, as it has always been working with importers and exporters. We are actively engaging in the use new technologies and ideas to help businesses to understand how international trade works and to give British businesses the knowledge they need, not only to sell internationally but to do it profitably.

A vital element of our support for British businesses is education and training. Our role is to increase the export performance of the United Kingdom by setting and raising professional standards in international trade management and export practice. This we achieve principally by providing the education and training programmes.

Using new ideas to increase competence with innovations such as Search for Knowledge based programmes, Bite Sized Chunks of Knowledge and our brilliant new shipping office 'boot-camp' – for those in a hurry to get up to speed! These courses sit alongside the traditional Dangerous Goods, Financial Risks and Introduction to Exporting/Importing courses.

Dedicated to professionalism and recognising the challenging and often complex trading conditions in international markets, The Institute is committed to the belief that real competitive advantage lies in competence and that commercial power, especially negotiating power, is underpinned by a sound basis of knowledge.

The Institute of Export is one of a small number of professional organisations in the UK to have successfully met, and continue to meet, the stringent requirements for approval as an Awarding Body by the UK Qualification & Curriculum Authority (QCA). We offer short courses and full academic courses to suit all the needs of those trading internationally. Membership costs starts by affiliation at just £60 –with discounts and benefits available to individual and business members.

Our innovative approach to communicating and promoting international trade has won an international accolade from International Association of Trade Training Organisations (IATTO) for our GURU On-Line projects which keeps traders informed in video bite sized chunks, explaining elements of both international trade and market knowledge. IOE is a founder member of IATTO many of whose members have based their qualifications on those pioneered by The Institute in the UK. The UK qualification has been accredited by this body and is recognised internationally.

Key Trade Intermediaries

8

UK Trade and Investment

http://www.ukti.gov.uk/

UKTI work with UK based businesses to ensure their success in overseas markets, and encourage the best overseas companies to look to the UK as their global partner of choice.

A wide range of support is available under two primary categories:

▽ **Developing Your International Trade Potential**

▽ **Accessing International Markets**

Developing Your International Trade Potential

UKTI offer a range of support services to UK companies getting started in international trade.

International Trade Advisers

Providing access to experienced International Trade Advisers helping both new and established exporters – based in over 40 local offices around the country. In addition every UK region has dedicated sector specialists who can provide tailored support to your business.

An International Trade Adviser will provide professional advice on a range of UKTI services, including:

▽ *export documentation*   ▽ *contacts in overseas markets*

▽ *overseas visits*   ▽ *e-commerce*

▽ *export training*   ▽ *market research*

▽ *access to grants for eligible SMEs*

Passport to Export

The highly regarded Passport to Export scheme assesses a company's readiness for international business, and helps it build international trade capacity, offering new and inexperienced exporters:

▽ *capability assessments*   ▽ *support in visiting potential markets*

▽ *action plans*   ▽ *mentoring from a local export professional*

▽ *customized and subsidised training*   ▽ *ongoing support*

Gateway for Global Growth

Entry to the Gateway for Global Growth scheme helps exporters diversify into new markets. This is a service to experienced SME exporters offering a strategic review, planning and support to help grow a company's business overseas.

In addressing solutions this could require a combination of UKTI services, and services offered by other public or private sector organizations.

Gateway offers a single route to a wide range of guidance and support from UKTI, and others to help take a company to a new level of international success.

Key Trade Intermediaries

Export Communications Review (ECR)

ECR provides companies with impartial and objective advice on language and cultural issues to help them improve their competitiveness in existing and future export markets.

The Scheme offers companies an on-site review of the way the company currently communicates with its export markets. Such a review can include advice on:

- ***the Company's website***
- ***written materials***
- ***personal meetings with customers or agents/distributors***

Export Marketing Research Scheme

EMRS gives advice on Export Marketing Research and can help a business to carry out export marketing research on all the major aspects of any export venture:

- *Market size and segmentation*
- *Regulations and legislation*
- *Customer needs usage*
- *Distribution channels*
- *Trends*
- *Competitor activity, strategy and performance*

Companies with fewer than 250 employees may be eligible for a grant of up to 50% of the agreed cost of market research projects.

Accessing International Markets

UKTI also provide services that allow UK companies to break down the barriers to trade, and access new markets for their business. This includes:

- *Information, contacts, advice, mentoring and support from UKTI staff, based both in the UK and Overseas, through their network of embassies, consulates and other offices in some 96 markets.*
- *Support for a company to participate in trade fairs and exhibitions overseas, along with opportunities to take part in sector based trade missions and seminars.*
- *Access to major buyers, governments and supply chains in overseas markets.*
- *Advice on forming international joint ventures and partnerships.*
- *Visits to new markets and alerts to the latest and best business opportunities are published across all sectors and in over 100 markets each month, ranging from private sector opportunities, multilateral aid agency to public sector leads.*
- *Key foreign office reports on emerging markets, and a wide range of established markets. These comprise Country Updates on political and economic issues.*

- *Information relating to security related risks which UK companies may face when operating overseas via an Information for Business Service.*
  Information provided includes:
  - *Political and economic*

  - *Bribery and corruption*

  - *Intellectual Property*

  - *Protective security advice*

  - *Terrorism threat*

For further information about the services provided by UKTI please contact **020 7215 8000** or visit **www.ukti.gov.uk**

Key Trade Intermediaries

CHAPTER NINE

A RETURN TO MANUFACTURING

A further theme of this book and my associated work, is to advocate and support British manufacturing - with 10% of the proceeds of this book being donated by way of support. An example of a company that embodies much of what is good about UK manufacturing is Emma Bridgewater Ltd. It has been my pleasure to work with this company and visit their factory in Stoke. The following represents a summary of their business.

Contents

*The Essential Guide to Business and Finance
in UK and International Trade*

A Return to British Manufacturing:

The Story of Emma Bridgewater Ltd

Emma Bridgewater
Feels like home

Introduction

Success in business can be measured in different ways. It is not all about growth and profitability.

The story of Emma Bridgewater Ltd measures success at different levels, in addition to a growing business these measures include:

- ▼ *The sheer enthusiasm of company employees*
- ▼ *The feeling of being part of a community*
- ▼ *An emphasis on UK manufacturing and a UK supply chain*
- ▼ *Providing a creative product*

Yes this is an inspirational business– but equally it is a story of drive, determination and innovation.

Starting Out

- ▦ *The company was born in 1985 when the founder Emma Bridgewater was looking for a birthday present for her mother. She couldn't find anything she liked or that was suitable.*
- ▦ *Undeterred Emma drew four shapes: a mug, a bowl, a jug and a dish and went to Stoke-on-Trent to find a model maker. When the shapes were sampled she started experimenting with the forgotten decorative technique of sponge painting, applying simple patterns with a cut sponge. The samples were shown to a selection of buyers and almost all placed orders and the business was on the road.*
- ▦ *At first the designs were made under contract, but within a few years the company acquired their own manufacturing facility and soon expanded into a large 19th century factory in Stoke, where they remain today.*
- ▦ *In addition to a commitment to UK manufacturing, wherever possible, materials are sourced in the UK. This is a real commitment when other companies in this industry are increasingly sourcing from overseas, to the detriment of UK jobs, which eventually leads to the loss of much needed skills in this country.*
- ▦ *As well as skills retention a key benefit of UK manufacturing is that modification to the products and processes can be made quickly. Quality control is also enhanced.*

9 | A Return to Manufacturing

Today and Beyond

Today the company is the largest pottery manufacturer based entirely in the UK, with all its products made at the factory in Stoke, using production techniques that have stood the test of time, and which deliver a hand decorated, high quality product.

The business employs 233 staff, all of whom take great pride in what they do, having the opportunity to carry out work which is as much an art as a manufacturing process.

Each piece of Emma Bridgewater pottery is made by hand by a team of 150 people, designers and decorators, fettlers and glazers, casters and polishers based at the Emma Bridgewater factory in Stoke-on-Trent. It is the largest company to produce all of its pottery by hand in Britain. Every mug, bowl, plate and jug has its own English personality and each item is individually signed by the decorator.

The Emma Bridgewater Collectors Club was set up 10 years ago in response to requests from keen members and now has over 8000 members.

The pottery can be purchased from high street stores such as John Lewis, Harrods and Selfridges, or online, or by visiting the Stoke factory shop and shops in Fulham, Marylebone, Chiswick and Edinburgh.

The Stoke Factory

The Stoke factory is an important part of the local heritage, situated on the Calden Canal, and with one of the famous Seven Sisters Bottle Kilns still remaining in part.

As well as a factory shop, there is a large collection of 'seconds,' a gift shop, cafe and studio where visitors can decorate their own design. There is also a museum and Art gallery nearby-housing a large collection of British pottery.

For further information on Emma Bridgewater Ltd please visit emmabridgewater.co.uk or the Stoke factory or one of their shops.

PEOPLE IN TRADE

People In Trade

This book I hope will be of benefit to these readers who are starting out in a career in the world of business and trade and indeed to those who are reviewing career options. In addition to providing information and facts, the book has reviewed some uplifting examples of success and how trade can operate for good. Additionally, I would like to profile two people I have been fortunate to work with.

Lesley Batchelor - Profile:

Lesley Batchelor is a qualified member of both the Chartered Institute of Marketing and The Institute of Export (IOE). She has worked for both organizations lecturing for the CIM and advising on marketing strategy and specific projects for the IOE. As a Trustee and Director of the IOE she was voted National Chairman in September 2007. She has been actively involved in strategic level decisions and consultations with Government Office, DTI and UKTI.

Lesley worked in a Blue Chip environment for over fifteen years within international and UK marketing. She worked appointing and supporting agents and distributors across the world. Companies include CIBA-GEIGY Pharmaceuticals, Fujitsu Europe, Coca-Cola and Canon with a couple of years experience in the computer industry distributing, among many other products, Novell Networking solutions. Lesley left to start her own company, CMC Marketing in 1992.

CMC Marketing is involved in devising workable and affordable marketing strategies and plans for export markets and internal programmes. It targets the SME market the average size of business ranging from 3-20 employees, although it has worked for several larger companies. CMC Marketing develops market entry and market extension plans, looking at the most appropriate methods of providing support programmes for both new and existing channels of distribution. Also working with young companies set up to exploit patented computer architecture.

Directorships:

CMC Strategy & Training Limited (Trading as CMC Marketing)
Director General Institute of Export and International Trade

Membership of Professional Bodies:

Institute of Export	MIEx Grad.
Chartered Institute of Marketing	MCIM

9 | A Return to Manufacturing

Bryan Treherne

Current: International Trade Advisor at UKTI London
Education: University of Surrey 1959 - 1963
Industry: Import and Export

Bryan Treherne is a member of the national executive of the Institute of Export and chairman of South London Export Club. This Club meets every 6 weeks in South London keeping its members up to date with the latest opportunities for trade in various parts of the world. They also run Trade Missions to places like South Africa, Ghana and the Caribbean. It also gives members an opportunity to network with other people doing International Trade.

A seasoned trader with decades of international experience, he was made an MBE in 2008 for services to export at the behest of UK Trade & Investment (UKTI), a British government department.

Each month Bryan will have something to say about Britain's place in the global economy and how firms in South London Export Club webpage **www.slec.biz** can take advantage of the wealth of international trading experience.

Bryan has devoted over 40 years to London business - whether it be working for a company, running his own business or, in his current capacity, as an International Trade Adviser with UKTI.

Bryan is quoted as saying enthusiastically: *"I really enjoy helping companies, giving the benefit of my experience and watching them thrive in the international marketplace."*

UKTI's London Team is dedicated to increasing the competitiveness of small to medium-sized enterprises through international sales development. A team of International Trade Advisers delivers support to businesses across London who are either exporting for the first time or entering new markets.

Working internationally has been a career devoted to learning new things about new countries every day whether it's to do with culture, opportunities for business, arranging Trade Missions, bringing in customers from overseas or answering the telephone to someone in Scandinavia looking for help to export to the UK.

Every day is different and time differences between countries make life complicated and sometimes mean long days.

People should think about a career in trade because it is really interesting, you meet lots of people, lots of useful contacts usually involves lots of travel which means that you need to know about different cultures and of course languages are very helpful but not essential as many people speak English. As the world becomes more global there will be more international business and therefore more opportunities for those who have studied International Trade.

People in Trade

The Importance of Understanding Trade

In order to provide the reader with further insight into the world of trade, the following three examples have kindly been provided by Sandra Strong. These are for reference and can I thank Sandra for their provision.

Further information/reports such as these can be requested through the Website accompanying this book.

Not understanding the true cost of letters of credit

Company A in the UK received an order from Company W based in Pakistan; not having previously traded with this organization, Company A decided they wanted to trade under the terms of an irrevocable letter of credit. The order value was £35,000.00. Company W, Pakistan, had no problem with this and set about opening a letter of credit (LC) through their normal bank. The LC was received by the UK company, checked briefly to ensure all details were OK and the goods were shipped.

The contract terms agreed had been "ExWorks" Company A's premises; the letter of credit asked for a bill of lading to be presented to the bank with the claim document. Once the goods had been shipped, Company A approached the freight forwarder who had been nominated by their customer requesting the Bill of Lading. After a delay of 10 days the Bill of Lading was received but did not conform to the requirements of the letter of credit. Company A had 21 days to present shipping documents to the bank for payment, so was running out of time. The forwarder failed to return the Bill of Lading in time so the documents were submitted late.

It was once the submission had been made and rejected by the bank, that Company A became aware that they were responsible for all bank charges – this had not been noted in their brief check on documents required. Payment was severely delayed until Company W in Pakistan agreed to accept the discrepant documents and the payment was made to Company A less the bank charges of £3,500.00 – which was 10% of the shipment value.

Incorrect use of the Incoterms ® rules

In an export order quotation for a customer in Brazil, a UK company supplied prices based on an "exworks" cost of the goods. The order was accepted at £97,000 ExWorks UK company premises and payment was made against a proforma invoice. The invoice was raised and paid on the 9th July 2010. The UK company then awaited shipping details; in early August the Brazilian customer notified them that they wanted the goods shipped by XXX Freight Forwarders and asked the UK company to contact XXX's UK offices to arrange collection. The UK company did this and the goods were collected on the 24th August 2010 for shipment to Brazil early September. The UK

9 | A Return to Manufacturing

Company released the goods to XXX Freight Forwarders and was advised that the forwarder was collating other goods for the Brazilian customer and the shipment would not happen until the end of September.

It was at this stage that the finance director (FD) began to worry because under UK VAT laws to zero-rate an export supply the goods must moved within 3 months of the supply having taken place. This is called the tax point. In most cases the time of supply will be the earlier of either the date:

▽ *The goods are shipped to the overseas customer or the customer takes them away, or*

▽ *When the seller receives full payment for the goods.*

As this order was paid for in early July 2010, the FD contacted the Brazilian customer to advise that if the goods did not leave the UK before the 9th October 2010 they would have to charge VAT. The Brazilian customer ignored the messages and XXX Freight Forwarders were unhelpful. The FD was left with the problem of how he was to recover 17.5% of £97,000 if he could not obtain evidence of export within the set timescales and the customer ignored his demands to pay the additional amount (£16,975.00).

Controlling customs duty payments

When buying goods from a supplier based outside the European Union (EU) you will have to ensure that the correct customs duty and VAT is paid. Normally this is calculated on arrival of the goods, by the freight company submitting the import declaration to the Customs Authorities. The customs duty rate (or percentage) is based on the type of goods being imported. The type of goods is defined for customs purposes against a commodity code number. The import duty rate varies in the EU from 0% to 30% so selecting an accurate commodity code is important.

Customs duty is, therefore, charged at this set percentage against a "customs value" built up by including:

▽ *The cost of the goods (the transaction price).*

▽ *The transit insurance premium applicable.*

▽ *The cost of international freight incurred to get the goods to the import point.*

The customs valuation rules used within the EU are based on the WTO/GATT Valuation rules which permits a number of "contract" costs to be removed from the dutiable value. This means that there are opportunities to make legal adjustments to the "cost" of goods declared for duty purposes. You have to be careful providing evidence of the way the value is broken down, but

People in Trade

sometimes, the value invoiced by the supplier includes elements that, if invoiced separately, would not be liable for import duty payment. These costs include:

- *Delivery costs incurred within the EC (airfreight).*
- *Generally available discounts on quantity.*
- *Settlement discounts given on early payments.*
- *Buying commission.*
- *Software costs (some).*
- *Work to be done after import.*
- *Other costs:*
- *Dividends.*
- *Export quota and licence payments (if you can evidence that the supplier has paid them to their country's authorities.*
- *Rights of reproduction.*

9 | A Return to Manufacturing

Glossary

Advanced Payment Guarantee	*Guarantee supplied by a seller who is receiving an advanced payment. The advanced sum will be returned if the contract (conditions) are not fulfilled*
Advising Bank	*The bank that receives a Letter of Credit from the Issuing Bank (buyer's bank) and forwards it to the beneficiary (seller)*
Air Waybill	*Transport document used in airfreight that acts as a receipt of goods and evidence of the freight agreement. It is not a document of title and not needed to claim the goods*
Amendment to a Letter of Credit	*Amendment to the original instruction of a Letter of Credit*
Angel investor	*An investor who provides capital, business expertise and contacts to a new or fast growing business - usually in exchange for an equity stake in the business*
Avalisation	*The guarantee of a bill of exchange, say by a bank guaranteeing payment*
Back-to-Back Letters of Credit	*A new Letter of Credit on which an existing Letter of Credit is used as collateral to support. Not favoured by banks because of risks in performance of the first Letter of Credit may not support the second Credit*
Balance Sheet	*Represents a snapshot of the total inflows and outflows generated by the business. It lists all the assets and liabilities of a business and all of its financial resources at a given moment in time*
Beneficiary	*The individual in whose favour a Letter of Credit is drawn. In an export transaction the UK exporter (seller) is the beneficiary*
BIC code	*A standard format of Bank Identifier Codes - being the unique identification code of a particular bank*
Bid Bond	*Bond usually issued by a Bank guaranteeing that a bidder of a contract enters into that bid in good faith and will properly execute the contract if the bid is successful*

Glossary

Bill of Exchange	*An unconditional order, issued by a business which directs the recipient (the buyer) to pay a fixed sum of money to a third party (the seller), at a future date. The future date may be either fixed or negotiable (e.g. 30 days after date of Bill of Lading). A Bill of Exchange must be in writing and signed and dated*
Bill of Lading	*Document issued by a transport company, which acknowledges receipt of specified goods for transportation to a specific place. A document of title to the goods*
Business Plan	*A formal statement of a set of business goals, the reasons why they are attainable and the plan for reaching those goals. It may also contain information about the business and its directors/employees*
Cash In Advance	*Up-front payment. The seller requires payment from the buyers, prior to sending the goods or services*
Cash flow budget (projection)	*Document projecting future trends in the cash flow of a company, detailing payments and receipts over say a month, or three month period*
Certificate of Inspection	*Document certifying that merchandise was in good condition at the time of inspection. Pre-shipment inspection is often a requirement for importation of goods into a country*
Certificate of Origin	*Written statement attesting to the country of origin of goods*
CHAPS	*A bank transfer of funds that ensures the money is transferred the same day*
Clean Bill of Lading	*Bill of Lading acknowledged by the carrier for goods received "in apparent good condition" without damages or other irregularities*
Clear Title (to the goods)	*Refers to a legal title of ownership on an asset, which is clear of any legal encumbrances (burden affecting title). Very important that there is clear title to the goods before finance is provided*

Glossary

Confidential Invoice Discounting	*A finance facility is provided but the lender (e.g. bank) takes no active involvement in collecting the client's invoices, and there is no disclosure of finance on the invoice. The facility is confidential and customers are unaware that finance is being provided against the invoice*
Confirmed Letter of Credit	*The advising bank adds its guarantee to pay the seller, in addition to that of the buyer's Issuing bank*
Consignee	*An individual, or business, to which merchandise has been consigned*
Country Risk	*The risk that a foreign government obstructs the payment of funds by the buyer, for financial, economic or political reasons*
Credit Insurance	*Insurance cover against default by debtors (customers). Cover can protect all of the debtor book or specific debtors. Some credit insurance companies also provide credit reference services*
Creditor	*Someone to whom you owe money*
Current Assets	*Consisting primarily of stock, debtors and cash*
Current Liabilities	*Consisting primarily of creditors and short-term bank borrowings (due in less than one year)*
Current Ratio	*Measures whether the assets to be converted into cash, in less than one year, exceed the debts to be paid in less than one year. Obtained by dividing current assets by current liabilities*
Debtor	*A person or firm that owes you money*
Deferred Payment Under a Letter of Credit	*The buyer accepts the documents related to the Letter of Credit and agrees to pay the issuing bank after a fixed period. Provides the buyer with a grace period for payment (a Term Letter of Credit)*
Demand Guarantees	*Undertaking which is called upon on the presentation of a written demand, not conditional on proof of default*

Glossary

Documentary Collections	*Method of payment where the exporter ships the goods to the buyer, but sends the documents through their bank, which release the documents against payment of a Sight Bill of Exchange (or acceptance of a Term Bill of Exchange)*
Document of Title	*Transport document where the carrier will release the goods against an original document e.g. Bill of Lading*
Expiry Date	*The last date under a Letter of Credit at which the seller can present documents to the bank*
Factoring	*A business sells its invoices to a factor (e.g. bank) at a discount in exchange for immediate funds. The factor will manage the debtors on behalf of the business*
Faster Payments	*A UK banking initiative to reduce payment times between customers of different banks; from three working days under the Bacs system to near real-time – up to a monetary limit of £100,000*
Finished Goods	*One of three classes of stock (the other two are raw materials and work in progress). Goods that have completed the manufacturing process, but have not yet been sold or distributed to the end user. A business is more likely to receive finance against finished goods*
Foreign Currency Option	*An option that gives the customer the RIGHT to buy or sell an amount of foreign currency at a specific price. The customer does not need to take the contract up*
Forfaiting	*An exporter (seller) sells for example a Bill of Exchange payable by the buyer, at a discount to the Bill's face value*
Forward Foreign Exchange Contract	*Agreement between a bank and a customer to exchange one currency against another e.g. $/£, at a future date. Either a fixed forward contract on a specific date, or an option forward contract between a range of dates. The customer MUST take up the forward contract*

IBAN	The International Bank Account Number, an international standard for identifying bank accounts. Originally adopted in Europe, later adopted as an international standard
Insurance Policy	Entire written contract of insurance
Invoice Discounting	A form of short-term borrowing often used to improve a company's working capital. Money is advanced to a business against its debtors (customers). The company will continue to manage their own debtors
Irrevocable Letter of Credit	Issuing bank must follow through with payment to the seller as long as the seller complies with the conditions and documents listed in the Letter of Credit
Issuing Bank	The bank issuing the Letter of Credit on behalf of the buyer (the Applicant)
LIBOR	The London Interbank Offered Rate (LIBOR) is a daily or weekly reference rate based on an interest rate at which banks are able to borrow unsecured funds from the other banks in the London interbank market
Multimodal Transport Document	Transport document evidencing shipment of goods by more than one means of transport
Negotiating Bank	The bank authorsed by the Issuing Bank to negotiate (check) documents under a Letter of Credit
Nostro account	An account held in the name of say a UK bank, with a bank in another country in their local currency; in order to make payments in the foreign currency
Noting	Can be the first stage in the Protest of a dishonoured Bill of Exchange
Online banking	Allows customers to view account balances and instruct payments over a secure Weblink (all done electronically)
Open Account	The seller sends goods or services to the buyer, before they have received payment

Glossary

Ordinary Shares	Carry full rights to participate in the business through voting in general meetings. Ordinary shareholders are entitled to payment of a dividend out of profits and ultimately repayment of capital (the sum invested), in the event of liquidation, but only after other claims have been met
Payment At Sight	Payment on demand (of the bill of exchange)
Payment At Term	Payment at a defined future date (e.g. 30 days after Acceptance of a Bill of Exchange)
Performance Bond	A bond usually issued by a Bank which protects the beneficiary (buyer) against loss in case the terms of a contract are not fulfilled
Political Risk	Risk of default due to cancellation of an import or export licence, war, and introduction of exchange control
Preference Shares	Shares that pay dividends at a specified rate and have a preference over ordinary shares in the payment of dividends and the liquidation of assets. They do not carry voting rights
Project Finance	Finance arrangements for larger projects, can be based on the revenues of the project
Revocable Letter of Credit	May be modified or even cancelled by the buyer without notice to the seller. They are therefore generally unacceptable to the seller
Revolving Letter of Credit	The issuing bank restores the Letter of Credit to its original amount once it has been used or drawn down. The Credit may limit the number of times the buyer may draw down, over a predetermined period
Spot Exchange Contract	One currency is exchanged against another immediately, usually within two working days
Standby Letter of Credit	Guarantee issued, only to be drawn in the event of the buyer (applicant) failing to make agreed payment in accordance with the terms of the guarantee

Stock Control	*Used to evaluate how much stock is used. It is also used to know what requires to be ordered. Stock control can only happen if a stock take has taken place*
SWIFT	*The Society for Worldwide Interbank Financial Telecommunications (SWIFT) operates a worldwide financial messaging network that exchanges payment and trade messages between banks and other financial institutions*
Trans-shipment	*The unloading of cargo at a port or point where it is then reloaded, sometimes into another mode of transport, for transfer to a final destination*
UCP 600	*Uniform Customs and Practices for Letters of Credit*
Unconfirmed Letter of Credit	*The Issuing bank is the only bank responsible for payment to the seller.*
Unfair Calling	*Claim by the beneficiary under a demand guarantee without having any contractual reason to do so*
URDG	*Uniform Rules for Demand Guarantees*
Venture Capital	*Type of private equity finance provided for early stage, high-potential growth companies*
Vostro account	*When a foreign bank holds an account with say a bank in the UK, to settle payments in Sterling*
Working Capital	*The amount by which current assets exceed current liabilities*

Glossary

Index

Index

Index